Guy Gibson

Guy Gibson

Dam Buster

Geoff Simpson

Pen & Sword
AVIATION

First published in Great Britain in 2013 by
Pen & Sword Aviation
an imprint of
Pen & Sword Books Ltd
47 Church Street
Barnsley
South Yorkshire
S70 2AS

ISBN 978 1 78159 055 3

A CIP catalogue record for this book is available from the British
Library

Typeset in Ehrhardt by
Mac Style, Driffield, East Yorkshire
Printed and bound in the UK by CPI Group (UK) Ltd, Croydon,
CRO 4YY

Pen & Sword Books Ltd incorporates the Imprints of Pen & Sword
Aviation, Pen & Sword Maritime, Pen & Sword Military, Wharncliffe
Local History, Pen and Sword Select, Pen & Sword Military Classics,
Leo Cooper, The Praetorian Press, Remember When, Seaforth
Publishing and Frontline Publishing.

For a complete list of Pen & Sword titles please contact
PEN & SWORD BOOKS LIMITED
47 Church Street, Barnsley, South Yorkshire, S70 2AS, England
E-mail: enquiries@pen-and-sword.co.uk
Website: www.pen-and-sword.co.uk

Contents

GUY GIBSON – DAM BUSTER   vii
Introduction   viii
Foreword   x
Acknowledgements   xii
Abbreviations   xiv

Chapter 1   Early Life   1

Chapter 2   Towards a Career   9

Chapter 3   Flying the Hampden   14

Chapter 4   Phoney War   16

Chapter 5   Destroying the Barges   25

Chapter 6   Into the Night   36

Chapter 7   Closer to London   48

Chapter 8   Back to Bombers   53

Chapter 9   Gus Walker at Syerston   64

Chapter 10   Why the Dams?   76

Chapter 11   Preparing the Way   82

Chapter 12   To the Dams   93

Chapter 13   Two Very Different Debates   108

Chapter 14   Anti-Climax   112

Chapter 15   The Final Flight   128

Chapter 16   The Film   135

Chapter 17   Mrs Gibson   139

Appendix 1   Birth Of A Legend   142
Appendix 2   Guy Gibson the man   147
Appendix 3   Harris and Gibson   152
Appendix 4   Gibson's Dog   155
Appendix 5   Notes on Some People in the Gibson Story   156
Appendix 6   The Squadrons and the Airfields   162
Appendix 7   The Crews and the Decorations   173
Appendix 8   **Some** Memorials   179
Appendix 9   Citations for Guy Gibson's Decorations   181

Bibliography   185
Index   188

GUY GIBSON – DAM BUSTER

There are no words with which I can do justice to the aircrew who fought under my command. There is no parallel in warfare to such courage and determination in the face of danger over so prolonged a period, of danger which at times was so great that scarcely one man in three could expect to survive his tour of operations.

Marshal of the Royal Air Force Sir Arthur Harris, *Bomber Offensive*, 1947

Poppies bloom in the fallow fields of Lincolnshire, sudden outbreaks of red in a verdant landscape – nature's unintended tribute to the thousands of young men who flew from this place into the dark heart of Nazi Germany, never to return.

The Second World War lingers here, in bomber country. Small memorials commemorating long-disbanded squadrons mark rural crossroads, and white headstones adorned with the Royal Air Force crest dot medieval churchyards. Lincolnshire is far from prairie flat but it enjoys a big sky. It needed to be big in the years 1942 to 1945 when, as the epicentre of RAF Bomber Command, the county was home to hundreds of Avro Lancasters.

Neil Tweedie, writing in the *The Daily Telegraph*, 27 June 2012

Introduction

That Guy Gibson, almost seventy years after his death, remains, in the public's mind, one of the great British heroes of the Second World War cannot be disputed.

There were many successful and heroic RAF pilots in the war. Very few of them, seven decades later, have any claim to be thought of as names familiar to those beyond the historians, authors and researchers who study the period. In that sense, Gibson is one of the few. To some extent this is because he was selected at the time to be a public figure as part of Britain's war effort. The attack on the dams was regarded as a spectacular success when it took place, both for the destruction it caused and for its value in lifting morale and impressing Britain's allies.

Gibson had planned and led the attack brilliantly and was the natural person to be pushed forward when a figurehead was needed.

His tragic death, aged twenty-six, added to the aura around him, as famous and youthful death usually does. Then, in the 1950s Paul Brickhill's book, followed by the film, *The Dam Busters* (or *The Dambusters* as the story has gradually become) firmly implanted the legend in many minds. A battered paperback copy of the Brickhill book, with schoolboy annotations from the 1950s, sits a few inches from me as I write.

The musical march for the film provided, somewhat reluctantly at first, by Eric Coates helped the process along, remaining an instantly recognisable piece of music. One result of the film is that most people picture Gibson, not as the man he was, but as the actor who played him.

That was the best part of sixty years ago, but the process has continued. In the 1990s a young newspaper reporter, clearly star-struck, recounted to me how she had recently interviewed some of the Dam Busters. 'To be in the same room!' was her theme.

Nor is the legend immune to modern technology. Those who understand these things may now play with *The Dambusters App*, in which the chance is offered to try, 'a 3D flying game inspired by the famous WW2 mission.' You are required to fly across Europe on your mobile phone, 'bomb the great dams of the Ruhr Valley' and return to England. What is more you only have nineteen aircraft and nineteen weapons at your disposal, just like Guy Gibson.

Here then is a clue to the cheering fact that Britain's Second World War heroes have not been forgotten and a younger generation is learning about them. The debt is still understood even if the knowledge of what was achieved sometimes manifests itself in new ways.

Gibson was an heroic figure, who was placed at the forefront of a major operation which became also a significant British propaganda coup. He earned the Victoria Cross, the greatest award of all, and his other achievements include introducing the role of master bomber (though it was not called that at the time) to Bomber Command. He was also a person with greater accomplishment than most of us are given and, like all of us, he had frailties. His allure as a subject of study is irresistible.

Geoff Simpson, 25 August 2012

Foreword

A biography of an individual as famous as Guy Gibson presents the author with a number of challenging questions. Does the biographer concentrate on the better known details of that person's career and characteristics or attempt to bring to light less familiar aspects of the individual's life? With Guy Gibson, the great raid upon the Ruhr dams is the operation for which he is justly famous, overshadowing all his other achievements.

Though just one of around 174 missions that Gibson undertook before his death in September 1944, Operation Chastise has caught the imagination of the general public like no other. Geoff Simpson has been compelled, therefore, to examine this mission in some depth but has not allowed it to dominate his treatment of the Gibson story.

Gibson himself, in his own account of his war service, devotes only part of his book, around 60 pages out of almost 300, to Operation Chastise. Much of the rest of *Enemy Coast Ahead* relates his conventional bombing operations against Germany which, cumulatively, achieved far more than Chastise.

Amongst those early operations against the enemy were the sustained attacks upon the Channel ports in 1940 which helped prevent an invasion of Britain during its most vulnerable few months. This feature of the Battle of Britain is often overlooked by historians, yet night after night Bomber Command (supported by Coastal Command and the Fleet Air Arm) struck at the ports where the Germans attempted to assemble an invasion fleet.

In what became known as the Battle of the Barges the slow, lumbering Handley Page Hampdens, Vickers Wellingtons and Bristol Blenheims bombed the enemy-held ports day and night at alarmingly low level. At night the enemy coastline was lit with the fires of the burning vessels and port installations and was laughingly referred to by the aircrews as the 'Blackpool Illuminations'.

Gibson's role in this offensive was not insignificant. On 1 July 1940, for example, he was the pilot of one of the No 83 Squadron Hampdens tasked with attacking German warships, including the battleship *Scharnhorst*, at Kiel. During the raid his aircraft delivered the first 2,000lb bomb dropped by a Hampden of Bomber Command.

Around 500 Bomber Command crew were killed during this period, approximately the same number as in Fighter Command in the Battle of Britain.

What is often not appreciated is that after completing his first operational tour with Bomber Command, Gibson himself joined Fighter Command. With 29 Squadron he flew Blenheims in day fighter and bomber escort operations as well as night-fighter patrols. It was in this role that he claimed to have accounted for four enemy bombers.

As well as dealing with the purely factual elements of an individual's life, the next question the biographer has to deal with is that of sensationalism. Guy Gibson became a national hero, a person in whom everyone can feel justifiably proud – indeed, Sir Arthur Harris once described him as 'as great a warrior as this island ever bred'. Should Gibson's exploits be trumpeted without reserve, or is it incumbent upon his biographer to reveal the flaws in his character of which many of his contemporaries were acutely conscious?

Geoff Simpson has met these challenges head-on. Gibson is famous for his exploits in the Second World War and this new book is dedicatedly a book about Gibson's war. At the same time Geoff Simpson has not shied away from the fact that early in his career Gibson was not thought highly of by some of his colleagues and that it was only when the war started, in other words when the fighting began, that he was identified by Air Marshal Sir Arthur Harris as having the potential for greater things.

As he was one of Bomber Command's most experienced flyers, the subject of Gibson's death was at the time, and still is, the subject of much controversy. Was Gibson shot down by the rear gunner of one of the RAF's own Lancaster bombers, or did he run out of fuel? Geoff Simpson has examined all the available evidence and the many proposed theories and draws his own conclusion.

A new book on Wing Commander Guy Gibson VC, DSO & Bar, DFC and Bar is sorely needed to bring together all the most recent revelations and to put into perspective Gibson's attributes and his failings. Geoff Simpson's book does precisely that, as might be expected of the author of *A Dictionary of The Battle of Britain* and *A Dictionary of Bomber Command* where facts are the only relevant currency.

Hard facts may be the basis of *Guy Gibson – Dam Buster*, but the adventures of one of Britain's greatest warriors makes for a cracking read.

Martin Mace
Editor, *Britain at War Magazine*

Acknowledgements

Many people and organisations have been generous in sharing their knowledge and expertise with me over the years on matters relevant to this book.

Michael Gibson, Guy Gibson's nephew, responded cheerfully and helpfully to yet another person interested in his uncle. The same was true of Trish Knight-Webb, Guy Gibson's cousin. Vic Strike, a more distant relative, showed, while being most helpful, both his deep respect for Gibson and how he loved his native Cornwall, as did Gibson. Squadron leader George 'Johnny' Johnson, DFM, was also tolerant of enquiries about Gibson, the like of which he has received many times before. Robert Owen willingly shared his vast knowledge of No 617 Squadron. Richard Morris, an outstanding writer on Gibson, was happy to enter into correspondence. From the vantage point of the museum at the Derwent Dam in Derbyshire, Vic Hallam provided his own perspective.

Chris Nathan, archivist at St Edward's School, never objected to questions, in sickness and in health.

Richard Hunting CBE, Group Captain Patrick Tootal, OBE, DL, Martin Mace and John Grehan were much valued sources of information and suggestions. Patrick's interest in Bomber Command stems from the contribution made by his father. Flight Lieutenant Jack Stuart Tootal was the skipper of a Halifax lll of No 462 Squadron in No 100 Group, lost with no survivors, over the Ruhr, during the night of 24/25 February 1945.

Not for the first time, Victoria Thompson demonstrated an ability to find gems in archive dust.

Gary Godel revealed yet again his remarkable knowledge of the RAF in the Second World War.

My wife, Margaret, was an enormous help throughout the process. Another family member, Susan Wacker, happily has German as her native language and the excellent English to make her findings clear to me. Gert Falbe also contributed in this regard.

The late Richard Todd, OBE and the late Richard Leech, have over the years provided the actor's view, the latter through his friendship with my brother Stephen.

There are many other people and organisations who I want to thank for information and assistance over a long period. They include:

Air Historical Branch (RAF)
Frank Armstrong
Avro Heritage Centre
Maurice Bann
Suzanne Bidlake
Phil Bonner
Gerry Burke
Alan Cooper
Sebastian Cox
Dr Jeremy Crang
Hazel Crozier
Philip Curtis
Group Captain Alex Dickson OBE, QVRM, AE
Mervyn Hallam
Dave Harrigan MBE
Flight Lieutenant Duncan Hewat
Harry Holmes
Dom Howard

Flight Lieutenant Bernard Hyde, AE
Imperial War Museums
Squadron Leader Tony Iveson DFC, AE
John Oxley Library
Stuart Millson
Howard Lee
Edward McManus
Bill Morran
No 617 Squadron
Muriel Pavlow
Tim Pierce
Douglas Radcliffe MBE
RAF Scampton Museum
Jim Shortland
Colin Smith, Vector Fine Art Prints
Flight Lieutenant Ken Trent DFC (and bar)

Abbreviations

AO C-in-C = Air Officer Commanding in Chief
BASO = Base Air Staff Officer
CGM = Conspicuous Gallantry Medal
DFC = Distinguished Flying Cross
DSO = Distinguished Service Order
LAC = Leading Aircraftman
MC = Military Cross
MO = Medical Officer
OTU = Operational Training Unit
RAAF = Royal Australian Air Force
RAF = Royal Air Force
RCAF = Royal Canadian Air Force
RNZAF = Royal New Zealand Air Force
RT = Radio Telephony
TI = Target Indicators
US = United States
U/S = Unserviceable
VC = Victoria Cross

Chapter 1

Early Life

The words, 'By Tre, Pol and Pen shall ye know all Cornishmen' or their variations, stretch back hundreds of years. Guy Penrose Gibson was born far from the county in the extreme west of England, but his middle name told the world of his Cornish ancestry. The Penrose estate stands near the village of Porthleven, home to Gibson's maternal grandparents.

When Elsie Balme produced a book called *Seagull Morning* about a thirties and forties childhood spent in Porthleven she wrote of,

'that strange grey, sprawling, rather ugly, yet infinitely appealing village of Porthleven, with its rumbustious community life; its unabashed scandalmongering; its infinite capacity for interfering in people's private affairs; and its uncanny ability to draw back to itself those who belong to it, so that if you have lived there, then you will never be completely alive again anywhere else, because some part of you will live there for ever.'

She also lamented many of the changes that had occurred by the time her book appeared in 1990.

The house that Captain Edward Carter Strike, a master mariner, and his wife Emily lived in immediately before the First World War still stands. It offered them, and offers its present occupants, a spectacular view across the town and harbour of Porthleven, from a vantage point up on Breage Cliffs.

There is a suggestion in the family that Captain Strike, having been born the son of a fisherman and risen in life, later wanted to keep his distance from the men who still sailed from the harbour. From his house Captain Strike could see them, but was well removed from their presence. The Strikes were a prosperous family and so they could afford to place themselves in such a desirable position.

The name Strike is one that stands out and it occurs with some frequency in West Cornwall, but one authority at least does not regard 'Strike' as having a particularly Cornish origin. It is said to be an early English occupation surname, given to someone whose work involved the measuring of quantities of corn. Such a person used a flat stick, known as a strike (from an old English derivation), to level the crop in its container.

One of the daughters of Captain and Mrs Strike was Leonora Mary, 'Nora', who finished her education in Belgium in 1913 and came back to Porthleven. She was attractive, outgoing and not short of male admirers. Before the end of the year she had married Alexander James Gibson, aged thirty-six, who at first did not commend himself to Nora's parents.

Alexander had been born in Russia while his father was working there. Known as 'AJ' in his family, he lived in India and was rising in the Indian Forest Service.

In those days, there were often rules, or at least guidelines, on when it was suitable for people in particular occupations to marry. Alexander came home on leave and stayed in Porthleven. Some accounts suggest that he was actively looking for a wife. If so, Nora, nineteen at the time, was a suitable candidate and the situation developed quickly. The wedding took place on 2 December 1913 and Alexander, after a honeymoon in Europe, took his bride back to his base in Lahore, capital of the Punjab.

The marriage was troubled from the start, but continued in India at Lahore and at a bungalow at Simla in the hills, which the family used during the hottest of the Indian weather. The bungalow was called 'Talland', a reminder of Cornwall. Talland Bay lies between Looe and Polperro in the south east of the county, with two beaches, one sandy, and rock pools. Today the South West Coast Path passes by.

In the early twenty-first century Simla is known as Shimla and, placed in the Himalayan foothills, is a major tourist attraction. Many visitors arrive on the 2ft 6in gauge railway, opened in 1903, which takes them up into the hills from Kalka. The journey is ninety-six kilometres long and offers spectacular views. When the Gibson family spent part of the year in Simla, it was the summer capital of British India, a status it had enjoyed since 1864.

In June 1915 the eldest child of the Gibsons was born, a boy christened Alexander Edward Charles, who would become known to his immediate family as 'Alick'. Alexander was a name that ran in the Gibson family.

Two more children followed, the first being Joan Lemon in 1916. The family account is that 'Lemon' was the name of a family friend and the naming of Joan a tribute to that friend. Joan would later change her middle name to the more feminine sounding Lemona.

Then on 12 August 1918, another Gibson son was born to Nora in Simla. It was on 11 September, exactly two months before the armistice and the end of the First World War fighting, that he was christened Guy Penrose Gibson by the Reverend H.J. Wheeler, the minister at Christ Church in Simla. The name 'Guy' was a tribute to another friend.

Wheeler officiated at an imposing church which had been consecrated in 1857, the first church in Simla and claimed to be only the second in northern India. Built of stone and brick in lime mortar, it still stands and has a chancel window designed by Lockwood Kipling, father of Rudyard. The memorials include one to Lieutenant General Sir Gerald de Courcy Morton, credited with playing a leading role in the development of the dumdum bullet.

Early life in India was very comfortable for the children with plenty of servants at hand. Attention and affection, though, often came from these servants rather than from the mother and father of the three Gibson youngsters. Meanwhile the marriage of Nora and AJ continued to be rocky.

In 1922 Nora took the children to Porthleven and a first meeting with their maternal family. In addition it was a first glimpse of the Cornish town for Guy in particular and of the harbour and seascapes that he grew to love. Then there was a return to India. AJ became chief conservator of forests and the amount of travelling he did increased.

Two years after the first visit to England, Nora and the children came back to Cornwall. The marriage to an older man, who, it is suggested, was regularly unfaithful and less interested than his wife in socialising had in reality come to an end.

So Nora, Alick, Joan and Guy came again to Cornwall. Nora moved the children around between hotels and rooms. Not starved of male company just because her husband was in India, she started an affair, which seems to have been obvious in its debauchery to the children.

Joan and Guy escaped at times to the home of their grandparents in Porthleven, where they received affection not always granted them at their various homes. Their grandmother proved to be a rather more competent mother than their actual mother. Other relatives rallied round and this produced a circle of childhood acquaintances.

Trish Knight-Webb, a cousin of Guy's, wrote in 2012:

'My own memories of Guy are very sketchy so these are mostly from my sisters who were contemporaries of his.

'Guy spent many of his holidays with my family in their rectory because my uncle and aunt were mostly absent. There was the incident of the chickens which took place, I think, when my father was a curate possibly in Castle Cary, Somerset. Guy claimed that he had persuaded some chickens to walk in a straight line.

'On another occasion Guy stood on a chair and waved a knife about chanting "here comes the chopper". This definitely took place when the two sisters had rented adjacent cottages in Penzance when home on leave. I know my sister Bunty was very scared!

'We all spent our holidays down in Porthleven, either with or near our grandparents so there were many family picnics with cousins all of whom were gathered there. Those in the forces who were on leave foregathered including my brother, Keith who also went into the RAF. He was killed in a fighter plane in 1942.'

Trish's brother, Keith Lloyd Davies, was around a year older than Guy. He was lost on 27 November 1941, flying a Hurricane of No 607 (County of Durham) Squadron. His aircraft was hit by flak off Boulogne and went into the sea. The body of Keith Davies was not recovered by either side and his name is recorded on panel 30 of the Runnymede memorial.

Two other pilots from No 607 Squadron were lost at much the same time, though their aircraft were engaged by German fighters, as well as by anti-aircraft fire. They were Sergeant R. Weir and Sergeant W.E. Hovey.

Now Guy Gibson's love affair with Cornwall and the sea took off. He would spend long periods talking to the fishermen at the harbour. Equally he was content to spend time on the harbour wall watching the sea, which could be spectacularly rough, and the arrivals and departures of craft in the harbour.

In later life he was guarded about the impact on him of his dysfunctional childhood, but his time at the harbour certainly provided happiness and escapism. The plaque in commemoration of Guy Gibson that has been placed on the clock tower building in Porthleven is very appropriate in its location.

Alick Gibson was sent to Folkestone, Kent to become a boarder at the now long gone St George's Preparatory School and, aged eight, Guy followed him. Around this time their mother and sister were living in a flat in Kensington. Joan was not sent to school.

AJ had bought a house at Saundersfoot in southwest Wales, in part to further a romantic attachment, but also, he claimed, to provide a base for his family.

The school in Folkestone was situated at 23/25 Earls Avenue, on the corner of Westbourne Gardens in the town. The Headmaster was the Reverend C.A. Darby, who had founded the establishment as Earl's Avenue School.

A fellow pupil, though he was older than Guy, was David Tomlinson, who would achieve fame as an actor – for example, as Pilot Officer 'Prune' Parsons in *The Way to the Stars* and as George Banks in *Mary Poppins* after an early spell in repertory in Folkestone. Tomlinson served in the Grenadier Guards and in the RAF during the war, partly as an instructor in Canada, reaching the rank of flight lieutenant. In 1956 he survived a crash in a Tiger Moth and a subsequent prosecution for reckless flying.

Another local clergyman, the Reverend W.H. Elliott, who was vicar of Holy Trinity Church, Folkestone, from 1918 to 1929, wrote an account of his life in which he noted that Guy attended children's services at Holy Trinity. Mr Elliott said that during the Second World War he read an article by Guy Gibson in which it was gratifying to find that the services were referred to and that Gibson said he owed much to Mr Elliott's teaching.

Folkestone is, of course, the seaside too. It was and is a much larger and more formal place than Porthleven. The ships that came in and out of the harbour were often much bigger. Perhaps Guy continued his love affair with the sea while he was at St George's, but it has to be assumed that maritime Kent did not come to have the same influence on him as nautical Cornwall.

AJ retired from his last Indian post as conservator of forests in Bihar and Orissa, close to Nepal. He undertook consultancy work in Australia, then came back to the UK, took a new job and had quarters in London. He had little contact with his children.

Alick went on from Folkestone to St Edward's School, Oxford and Guy followed him in September 1932, when he had just passed his fourteenth birthday. Thirteen was the typical age at which boys started at English public schools. Guy happened to be born in August, a month which the educational system finds a little difficult to accommodate.

St Edward's School, Oxford

St Edward's, 'Teddies' to those connected with it, has very strong military and Royal Air Force links. The school claims that more of its old boys served their country in The Great War than, pro rata, any other British independent school.

It is an interesting thought, though it can be no more than coincidence, that amongst the St Edward's men who served in the Second World War were three of the most famous, charismatic and controversial RAF pilots of the day – Guy Gibson, Douglas 'Tin Legs' Bader and Adrian Warburton, particularly associated with service in Malta. Another old boy was Sergeant Arthur Banks, awarded a posthumous George Cross in 1945. Banks was shot down over northern Italy in August 1944 while flying a Mustang of No 112 Squadron on an armed reconnaissance mission. In trying to regain Allied lines he linked up with partisans and operated with them against the enemy until December 1944, when he was captured, tortured, by both Germans and Italians and eventually murdered.

St Edward's was founded in 1863, one of a number of educational creations of Reverend Thomas Chamberlain, Senior Student (Fellow) of Christ Church, Oxford and vicar of St Thomas's Church. Chamberlain was a leading figure in the Oxford Movement which argued against what it saw as the increasing secularisation of the Church of England and harked back to historic Catholic doctrines. The regime at the school was harsh and continued to be harsh at the time that the Gibson brothers were there, though whether it was any more so than the generality of English public schools at the time is debatable. Over the years further members of the extended family followed Alick and Guy to 'Teddies'.

One great advantage that the school offered parents of the time was that it was considerably cheaper than more prominent establishments. In 2012 the school, now a considerably friendlier place at which to be educated than in the 1930s, had about 660 pupils, about one third of whom were girls, the first having enrolled in 1982.

At such schools brothers tended to go where their elder siblings have gone. Alick was in Cowell's House and so Guy went there too, finding himself across the road from the main school in a separate building, formerly a large residence for an affluent member of the Oxford community. Cowell's was named in honour of Wilfred Cowell who remains, and is likely to remain, the school's longest serving teacher. Mr Cowell arrived in 1880 and served until 1937.

There was a great advantage to this allocation. It brought Guy under the auspices of the Cowell's housemaster, A.F. ('Freddie') Yorke, who combined distinction as a schoolmaster with being a civilised man. Mr Yorke became, both in practical terms and to some extent legally, a father figure for both boys, somebody who would influence their thinking in their later lives.

One of Freddie Yorke's former charges recalls today, 'a superb housemaster who was respected by all those who knew him. A good looking man, he was a bachelor who ran his house quietly but very competently, preferring others to recognise the errors of their ways rather than ramming it down their throats. If a problem was reported to him he would take the approach that he had been aware all the time and was just "wondering when you were going to come and tell me about it"!

'He understood his boys and earned their respect by being scrupulously fair and absolutely ordinary. Never heavy handed, though corporal punishment was always at his disposal, he preferred a more logical approach – if the junior dayroom made too much noise he confiscated their only radio. He was a background man who preferred a small circle of friends from within the common room and remained especially close to the Reverend Ken Menzies, another softly spoken and shy member of staff.'

As well as being housemaster of Cowell's Freddie Yorke was second master to the warden (headmaster) for some years and the senior science and chemistry teacher at the school. When he retired he followed Menzies to Eastbourne but their friendship was swiftly ended when Menzies died soon afterwards. At this time the boys of Cowell's presented Yorke with a huge television set with which he was absolutely thrilled.

As with many schools there was an initiation ceremony to endure. At St Edward's, Alick and Guy were called upon to stand on a table and sing a song, recite poetry and probably do other tasks demanded by older boys. The proceedings finished with the newcomer's shorts descending.

Being small didn't help, as well as not being more than average at games. So one way and another Guy got off to a poor start socially. On the credit side, it is usually a help to have an older relative as a pupil in such circumstances.

Parents weren't of much assistance in this case. AJ rarely appeared and when Nora did it usually didn't take much perception to realise that she had refreshed herself very well on the way.

Overall, Guy's school life did improve with the guidance of Mr Yorke. He played hockey and rugby and represented his house at cricket. Eventually he became a house prefect, though he failed to rise to the top of the school's prefectorial system.

Guy was interested in photography and how things worked and his fascination with flying was developing. It might have been supposed that the Royal Navy would attract him more than the RAF, but that was not the case. A master kept an elderly aircraft near the school and trips were possible. That may have been a factor in Guy's burgeoning interest.

He served in the Officer Training Corps (OTC) and managed to become a lance corporal. In every aspect of school life he did enough and achieved a bit, but the glittering prizes eluded him. Academically he did not easily obtain the passes that would help him towards his future career.

Flying has glamour today. In the 1930s it was even more glamorous. Records were being set, new routes opened. New types of aircraft were in the news. The men and women who achieved these things had a celebrity and media exposure which has now moved elsewhere. Then as now in the aviation world, the pilots were naturally the elite and many boys and some girls aspired to form the next flying generation.

Flying was expensive too and so the goal for many was to learn to fly at somebody else's expense. This might be through the RAF, the Royal Air

Force Volunteer Reserve, the Auxiliary Air Force (though that was mainly for the wealthy or at least well off) and other forces' reserve organisations. There were the airlines and lots of other ways into aviation, which in those days was still a field in which small manufacturers and pilot/entrepreneurs could thrive.

For Guy, flying was the important thing. The RAF was merely one means of achieving his goal. Though the RAF had plenty of glamour, it also had its critics amongst those called upon to advise schoolboys on a choice of career. It was the junior service and, for all its achievements, sometimes seen as slightly disreputable, attracting the more raffish elements. Army types might be heard to remark that, 'Army officers marry other army officers' daughters, RAF officers marry barmaids.'

However that may be, flying offered the chance to many middle class youngsters of escaping the confines of a desk amongst a room of clerks and achieving adventure, without enormous struggle.

With a career as a test pilot in mind, Guy took a very sensible course and sought advice from Captain Joseph 'Mutt' Summers, chief test pilot at the Vickers company and one of the era's aviation personalities. He was also a man that Guy would meet again later. The advice from Summers was to follow the course that he had done and learn to fly by joining the RAF.

Chapter 2

Towards a Career

The advice of Mutt Summers was followed and Guy applied for a short service commission in the junior service. These commissions were one of the measures introduced by the future Lord Trenchard when he was seeking to establish the RAF as an independent force for the long term, immediately after the First World War and, through the 1920s, to maintain its independence.

So many of the features that came to be taken for granted as part of the service were created under the driving personality of Trenchard at that time. The apprentice school at Halton, the cadet college at Cranwell, the Oxford and Cambridge University Air Squadrons and the Auxiliary Air Force were other examples.

By the time that Guy appeared on the scene the short service commission had acquired an additional purpose in the sense of being a tool to overcome the shortage of pilots which was feared if and when war with Germany came about.

At first there was difficulty in achieving his objective. Views vary as to why. Guy was short and may have been considered too short at first. Perhaps he managed to grow a bit, hardly surprising around the time of his eighteenth birthday. His medical history was not perfect. He had been suffering from migraine attacks.

Perhaps also needing consideration is the impression he may have made at interview, though these were often cursory affairs, far removed from the rigorous assessments carried out today. Years at public school had helped, but Guy was not entirely the well-rounded character that the services look for. He had faced difficulty at school and would do so in his service life because of an unusually pronounced failure to understand the impact he was making on other people. It is possible that the officers he initially came into contact with were amongst those whose handling he misjudged. It was inevitable that his lack of a proper relationship with his parents would leave its mark and this is one way in which it may have done.

Persistence on the other hand is an excellent quality to have and Guy's persistence paid off. He was finally accepted by his chosen service and on

16 November 1936 he arrived at Yatesbury airfield near the A4, Bath Road, between Marlborough and Calne in Wiltshire and close to the Cherhill white horse. Here Gibson would undergo *ab initio* training under civilian instructors as part of No 6 Flying Training Course.

Ab initio training was short and sharp, or that was the idea. The students should have completed this stage of their development before Christmas 1936, but November and December, unsurprisingly, provided some foul weather and the course was not completed until the beginning of January.

Possibly the extra time was a benefit to Guy. He struggled with some of the classroom work, a familiar experience for him, but managed to satisfy his instructors, both on the ground and in the air. His pilot rating, on Tiger Moths, was 'average'.

If that sounds a relatively uninspiring beginning to a distinguished RAF career, it should be kept in mind that six of the thirty-four hopefuls on the course did considerably worse and were invited to find a profession other than that of pilot.

'Uxbridge' is a word engraved on many an RAF heart. There was no airfield there and it is no longer an RAF base (though the bunker from which No 11 Group of Fighter Command was controlled during the Battle of Britain is proudly cared for), but in former days it was difficult to escape. You might encounter it early in your service career or when you were demobbed. You might serve there in reality or receive a nominal posting there if you were temporarily out of action through illness or injury.

For the students who had been in Wiltshire this was their next destination. Yatesbury had been largely influenced by civilians. Uxbridge was very much the RAF and the place where king's regulations, drill and the protocols of service life would be taught, as well as uniforms fitted. The old world had gone and the new one had arrived. In contrast to their previous rural billet, Uxbridge, officially then in Middlesex, was firmly in the outer London suburbs.

It took just over a month to remove any last vestiges of civvy street from Gibson and his colleagues and bring them to the point where RAF authority considered that they could be commissioned as acting pilot officers.

The bull and routine of Middlesex having been coped with, it was back to the near West Country and the venerable RAF Netheravon, close to Amesbury in Wiltshire. Here awaited No 6 Flying Training School and further flying training, leading, if all went well, to the award of the flying badge.

An interesting experience for Gibson to deal with here was the proximity of other ranks. The majority of course members, like Gibson, had been commissioned, but there were leading aircraftmen too.

The key task was to master more advanced flying in Hawker Hind and Hawker Audax aircraft. Progress was made to what was known as the Advanced Training Squadron, where combat flying was taught.

By 24 May 1937 Gibson had completed the first part of the course and had qualified for his wings. Modern fast jet pilots have been heard to remark that the amount of training of those days wouldn't be enough to teach you to switch on now. The instruction in the 1930s was very quick, the machinery was far simpler and the number of accidents was considerable. It is difficult to say how far those different factors have a relationship.

In June, newly embarked on his advanced training, Gibson journeyed the short distance to Tidworth, where the OTC from St Edward's was in camp. He addressed the boys and made clear that flying, even more now than before, was his passion and his life. He was still not a top class pilot and it can be argued that he never quite reached the rarefied heights of the masters of that craft, but he stood before the schoolboys who were potential future officers as a shining example of what they could achieve.

As Gibson's course moved on, the juncture was reached where some regard had to be paid to future specialisation. Did the student want to become a fighter pilot or a bomber pilot? With Gibson's intention to leave the RAF at the expiry of the short service commission and progress his flying career in civil aviation, bombers were the obvious pick. He would gain experience on multi-engined aircraft and this was something he needed on his CV when he left the RAF.

Gibson came to Sutton Bridge, in the southeast corner of Lincolnshire, but also penetrating Norfolk and Cambridgeshire, on 1 August 1937. Three days later, in misty conditions, a Hawker Audax took off first thing in the morning. At the controls was Acting Pilot Officer Philip Baily, who was in C Flight with Gibson. With him, acting as observer, was Acting Pilot Officer Douglas Bagot-Gray, not a member of C Flight, but also on No 5 Course.

Perhaps some administrative convenience had placed in the same aircraft two students with surnames so close in the alphabet. Certainly they appeared one after the other in the *London Gazette* dated 8 January 1937 as third and fourth on a list prefaced, 'The undermentioned are granted short service commissions as acting pilot officers on probation with effect from and with seniority of 21 Dec 1936.'

Whether fate arrived at its conclusion in that way or some other, the flight was brief. The take off appeared unexceptional, but then apparently Baily decided to abort and come into land again. Possibly he found himself lacking confidence to continue in the weather conditions. At the inquest the theory was put forward that Baily then made a mistake in his handling of the controls, though it also had to be taken into consideration that there was a particular technique for maintaining good vision when landing an Audax.

Whatever happened in the cockpit in a very short space of time, the result was that the aircraft crashed into a field less than a quarter of a mile from the airfield and pilot and observer were both killed.

Philip Baily was buried at Netheravon, in a part of All Saints churchyard set aside for the inevitable casualties of the local flying training. Douglas Bagot-Gray's family arranged for him to rest in the churchyard of St Mary at Ewell in Surrey.

That flying was a very dangerous occupation, as well as fun, and more widely than at Sutton Bridge, is illustrated in the RAF section of *Flight* magazine, dated 19 August 1937. Fatal accidents were a frequent occurrence amongst the inexperienced of the RAF.

Flying Accidents

The Air Ministry regrets to announce the following accidents:

Pupil Pilot Edward Owen Thomas James Poyner lost his life in an accident which occurred at Brough on July 30 to an aircraft of the Blackburn Flying School. He was the pilot and sole occupant of the aircraft.

AP/O Albert Edward Ralph Ferris, of ? Flying Training School, lost his life as the result of an aircraft accident which occurred at Flolbeach on August 2. AP/O Ferris was the pilot and sole occupant of the aircraft.

AP/O Philip Herbert Baily, the pilot and AP/O Douglas Leslie Parnell Bagot-Gray, passenger, lost their lives in an accident at Sutton Bridge, Cambs., on 4 August, to an aircraft of No 6 Flying Training School, Netheravon, Wilts.

Sergt. Harry Scaife and A/C1 Ernest Albert Withey lost their lives in an accident which occurred at Andover on 9 August, to an aircraft of No. 42 (Bomber) Squadron, Andover, Hants. Sergt. Scaife was the pilot of the aircraft and A/C1 Withey a passenger.

Sergt. William Jeremiah Postlethwaite and A/Ci Robert Ernest Barber lost their lives as the result of an accident which occurred at Cottisford, Oxfordshire, on 10 August, to an aircraft of No 18 (Bomber) Squadron. Sergt. Postlethwaite was the pilot and A/Ci Barber the passenger of the aircraft.

Obviously the atmosphere on the course was ruined by what had happened, but training continued at Sutton Bridge and over The Wash until, on 14

August, the bomber specialists returned to Netheravon and more practice. Guy Gibson passed out without too much difficulty, but, yet again, he did not stand out as a high achiever. His passion was flying and he was competent at it, but not a star. He passed his ground tests, but not in a way that suggested great intellect and future high rank and he still had the unformed personality.

Richard Morris at this point used a range of words to describe Gibson, including, tenacity, charm, frankness and defensiveness. He did not do things well and seemingly without effort, felt Morris.

Now, Gibson could move on to the actual business of the RAF. There was a graduation parade on 31 August, then some leave. After that Gibson set off for Scotland. He had been posted to No 83 Squadron, flying Hawker Hind aircraft and based at Turnhouse, later to become Edinburgh airport.

Chapter 3

Flying the Hampden

On arrival at Turnhouse and No 83 Squadron Gibson, still an acting pilot officer, was allocated to A Flight and was given Pilot Officer Anthony Bridgman as a mentor. Bridgman recorded that he was not over impressed with the reports he had seen of Gibson's progress through training. Nor did he take to what appeared to be the newcomer's over enthusiastic efforts to make an impression.

Bridgman took Gibson up in a Hind to show him the area. Already the reputation for being gung ho, over enthusiastic and eager to please that Gibson would build on the squadron was taking root. The familiarisation trip helped this process. They passed a sanatorium at low level and Gibson would later claim, frequently and to the point of considerable irritation in others, that they had caused great consternation amongst the patients.

Turnhouse had a fairly relaxed regime which was heaven for a man whose passionate wish was to fly. Gibson could take to the air almost daily on weekdays and Saturday mornings. When the weather was poor he could sit around with the other pilots and talk about flying. Though for some of his fellows who were not as obsessive about the activity as Gibson was, he could go on for considerably too long about it.

Morris illustrates Gibson's desire to impress, as well as his inability to understand how others perceived him, in the story of the packet of cigarettes.

In the mess one evening Gibson asked the waiter to bring him twenty Players. When he received the packet Gibson handed all twenty cigarettes round and then ostentatiously threw the empty packet on the fire. Most men of twenty-one, especially those who had passed through the communal life of prep school, public school and RAF training would have had a good idea that in acting in that way, they were giving their peers the impression of being a 'show off', perhaps a 'line shooter' too.

Many people would have gone further and worked out that this was not the way to endear themselves and influence others. However, Gibson frequently displayed this lack of understanding of the reaction of others throughout his life.

In the spring of 1938 No 83 Squadron moved to Scampton in Lincolnshire. Now they were in what was fast becoming 'bomber country'. Most of the nearby entertainment was provided by the city of Lincoln, a rural location and with not enough life to meet Gibson's taste. When war came, though, Lincoln would be packed with bomber crews because it was there and accessible. There were plenty of pubs, including the Saracen's Head, which Gibson himself would visit. It was described as the 'Five Group Briefing Room' and it was claimed that the barmaid knew more about what was going on in Bomber Command than some senior officers. Regrettably the Saracen's Head closed in 1959 and shops and offices now adorn the site.

For coming down to earth after the pub crawl, there were sometimes refreshments outside the cathedral, provided by the Women's Voluntary Service. The cathedral, set on a hill and with twin towers, was a landmark of Lincolnshire and a boon to the bomber navigators, something that could hardly be missed.

Lincoln has not forgotten the airmen of Bomber Command and other parts of the RAF. The cathedral contains an airmen's chapel, a Bomber Command window and a Book of Remembrance which contains the names of more than 27,000 aircrew who were killed when flying from the airfields of Lincolnshire in the Second World War.

In 2006 a ledger stone was added with an inscription reading, 'Dedicated to the men and women of Bomber Command, 1939–1945, over 50,000 of whom gave their lives in defence of our liberty.' The unveiling ceremony was performed by wartime veterans of Bomber Command.

There are also plans for a Lincolnshire Bomber Command Memorial, close to Lincoln.

For Gibson and his colleagues the months ahead were filled with talk of war in the papers and preparation for war at Scampton.

Chapter 4

Phoney War

By his own account Guy Gibson's journey to war began in the less than warlike setting of Saundersfoot. Life was good, progress was being made with young ladies and he was lazing in a sailing dinghy when the telegram arrived. Gibson placed the date for this event as Thursday, 31 August 1939. He was off the sands of Monkstone Beach, a beautiful spot. The girl from the post office cycled down with the message, there was a shout about it from another boat and a boy started to swim out to the dinghy, the telegram clenched between his teeth.

The telegram was marked 'urgent'; the message could nonetheless have been inconsequential. However, it said 'Return to base immediately'. For a man who had just taken part in air exercises and was keeping in touch with the news, the message was pretty clear.

Later that day Gibson left the village as a passenger in an elderly Alvis car driven by his friend, Freddy Bilbey, newly down from Oxford, where he had been studying towards becoming a doctor. The irony struck Gibson – he was going off to war to kill. His companion would go off to the war as well, but with a brief to save life.

It was Oxford to which they drove, via a meal of steak in a pub, and one of Gibson's memories of that journey would be the queues at filling stations. There was a general assumption that the terrors and inconveniences of war would arrive as soon as the starting pistol was fired. One of the inconveniences was likely to be the rationing of petrol.

At the university city, Gibson and Bilbey went into a pub and bumped into college friends of Bilbey. All were on the way to hostilities via the Navy, Army or Air Force. Then there was a meal and Gibson was unimpressed with the apparently decadent young people who were also dining.

From Oxford, Gibson's journey continued by train. He was squeezed in with many military types heading somewhere in a hurry and civilians too. By now he had a hangover but he finally arrived at Lincoln station and then got to Scampton.

At this point Gibson had completed the kind of journey that would become so familiar to many in Bomber Command as the war wore on: packed trains that stopped often and then finally arrived in Lincolnshire. The county is not all flat, but much of it is and many veterans would retain the memories of the fields of crops stretching off into the distance, so often through the rain and then the eventual arrival at a remote airfield with sparse facilities. At least Gibson was an officer returning to one of the pre-war bomber stations and could therefore look forward to reasonable comfort in the mess.

By now it was the early hours of 1 September, the day on which Germany invaded Poland.

Unlit street lights were one of the hazards of that journey and a not entirely successful attempt had been made to black out the officers' mess and other buildings at Scampton.

Gibson received cheerful greetings from colleagues, plenty of whom had been on stand by.

In *Enemy Coast Ahead* he went on to record two days of 'flap' as the apparently inadequate preparations for war developed – the station commander with furrowed brow, frantic attention to any ailment large or small with the aircraft, all transport dispersed around the camp, tight security at the operations room, gas detectors of doubtful value being installed all over the place and, of course, the Hampdens being taken off to distant parts of the airfield to minimise the impact of any enemy attack that might occur.

A glance over the station commander's shoulder seems to have revealed Wilhelmshaven as a likely early target.

From the information which Gibson gave, this was a period, for him, of nervous tension, as it must have been for many of the other aircrew who shared this wait for 'the balloon to go up'. Others though have recounted that Gibson displayed enthusiasm that the moment for heroics was arriving. To them, he was the 'gung ho' type.

Wilhelmshaven was indeed a target that Bomber Command was planning to attack. At this point the command was under firm orders that, when hostilities arrived, only clearly defined military targets should be attacked and then only when there was no risk of causing civilian casualties.

Remarkable as it may seem in view of later events, Britain, France and Germany had all responded positively to a call from the American President Franklin D. Roosevelt, that restraint should be exercised in the deployment of their bomber forces. Harbours and shipping met the requirements of the situation.

At Scampton, the radio was on in the officers' mess for Prime Minister Neville Chamberlain's announcement at 1100 hours, that as the German government had failed to respond to a note demanding the withdrawal of troops from Polish soil, Britain and France were at war with Germany.

Chamberlain went on to express views that would have resonated with Guy Gibson and his wish to go to war. He declared that Hitler's 'action shows convincingly that there is no chance of expecting that this man will ever give up his practice of using force to gain his will. He can only be stopped by force.'

Later Chamberlain said, 'The situation in which no word given by Germany's ruler could be trusted, and no people or country could feel itself safe, has become intolerable. And now that we have resolved to finish it I know that you will play your part with calmness and courage.'

Despite much criticism of him at the time and ever since, the chief of the Air Staff, Air Chief Marshal Sir Cyril Newall had done much to prepare for the conflict. It was not adequate preparation, but it ensured that the RAF was in a position to do something positive from the outset.

At Scampton and plenty of other airfields aircraft and aircrew awaited the command to go into action. Shortly after the Prime Minister's broadcast, a Bristol Blenheim of No 139 Squadron took off from Wyton in Huntingdonshire and crossed the North Sea on a reconnaissance sortie.

Despite difficult weather conditions, German capital and other ships were glimpsed near the Schillig Roads at the approach to Wilhelmshaven. When this information was radioed, the wireless sent only a garbled message and so it was not until the Blenheim returned to Wyton that a plan of attack could be put into action. For No 83 Squadron there was a summons to hear a talk on the situation from Group Captain Emmett, the station commander.

Other squadrons were in action and suffering casualties. A Blenheim from No 107 Squadron at Wattisham was shot down in the vicinity of Wilhelmshaven. The pilot, Sergeant Albert Stanley Prince, 27 years old and married, was killed. The two other crew members, Sergeant G.F. Booth and AC1 L.J. Slattery became prisoners of war and remained so until 1945.

Sadly, little was achieved in conditions which included thunderstorms. Probably nothing much was achieved either by the dropping of propaganda leaflets over the Ruhr.

For No 83 Squadron the situation developed quickly. Gibson was in the 'A' flight office when the CO, Squadron Leader Snaith, appeared with the news that six aircraft from the squadron were required for a sortie against an unknown target. Gibson would be going.

Despite all the years of knowledge of impending war and all the preparations for that eventuality, there were many ways in which Bomber Command was still unprepared.

In *Enemy Coast Ahead* Gibson would write,

'Soon everything was fixed. The crews had all been got together, the
bombs had been put on our aeroplane, and we went to the briefing.
Actually, to call it a briefing would be absurd. We all gathered round a
table while the station commander told us where we were going. "You
are going to attack the German pocket battleships which are lying in
the Schillig Roads at the entrance to the Kiel Canal. If by any chance
there are no warships there, you may bomb the ammunition depot
at Marienhof, but on no account, and I must warn you that serious
repercussions will follow, must you bomb civilian establishments, either
houses or dockyards.

"The weather will be bad, you will have to attack very low. There have
been some reports of balloons in this area, but you will not see them;
they will be flying in the clouds. Do not stay in the area long. Return if
you think that an attack cannot be carried through according to plan."'

Instructions on formation followed. There was concern that bombs might
bounce off the armoured decks of the ships and the direction was to try to
lodge bombs in the superstructure. The best height to attack was 3,000ft,
above the expected machine gun fire and below the heavy flak.

There was an explanation provided of how to take off with a bomb load. If
Gibson's account is accurate, the pilots did not actually know if the Hampdens
would unstick from Scampton with this 2,000lb load on board. If the hedge
was approaching fast, the stick was to be yanked back and emergency boost
was to be used.

This was treated as sound advice by the pilots, though Gibson would write,
'On looking back I sometimes think how absurdly little we did know at that
time.' No 49 Squadron was also involved in the attack and so the boys from
No 83 were able to watch their comrades from across the airfield practise
bomb-laden take off techniques first.

The lighter side of Gibson's character is revealed by the fact that one of
his ground crew felt able to give him some encouraging words, including the
forecast that he would always come back.

If Gibson was a seeker after glory, he had no opportunity to achieve his aim
on this sortie. Take off was delayed, rain, low cloud and darkness frustrated
the primitive navigation aids available and Squadron Leader Snaith decided
to turn back. Gunfire could be seen ahead, but Snaith did not know how far
off course he might be or what he might be bombing.

The decision was the right one, but the situation was still very frustrating. Even more frustrating, though it could not be known at the time, would be the fact that Gibson would not get the chance to go into action again for a good many months.

So No 83's first operation of the war was an anti–climax and Gibson came back safely. He was, however, 'wounded' shortly afterwards. His affection for dogs led to him to attempt to pat one as he entered the mess. The affection was not returned: he was bitten and needed stitches so with an arm in a sling he was off flying.

There was compensation in this rather ignominious incident. Gibson was able to travel to Rugby for the wedding, on 5 September 1939, of his brother Alick, serving in the Royal Warwickshire Regiment, to Ruth Harris. Guy was best man and seems to have drunk rather a lot.

Gibson arrived back at Scampton to find that the squadron had gone to Manchester, or more precisely the airfield at Ringway. Bomber Command squadrons were being scattered for the time being as a defence against the Luftwaffe.

Gibson was back at Scampton ten days later, but clearly regarded his time in Lancashire with some pleasure. Manchester could, of course, offer more in the way of diversions than Lincoln.

There is an example here of how *Enemy Coast Ahead* was 'improved' by other hands. Gibson wrote with enthusiasm of the plentiful supply of girls, not least WAAFs who were under training at Ringway. Deleted from his original manuscript was the assertion that girls were 'laid on'. Perhaps the person improving the work felt that Gibson's precise meaning was not clear.

When socialising was not going on, much time at Ringway was spent testing the aircraft. Back at Scampton, however, tedious training continued with Gibson finding some relief in flying antics including beating up Scunthorpe.

A foretaste of the problems Bomber Command would encounter in the early years of the war came when it was decided to enlarge Scampton and, in the process, demolish Aisthorpe House nearby, which had been struck by a Hanley Page Heyford before the war. A bombing competition was organised in November 1939 to rid the RAF of the unwanted property in which Gibson was a spectator rather than a participant. He noted that the majority of the bombs fell short or bounced over the target and exploded elsewhere.

There had been a good many alerts for No 83 Squadron, but nothing concrete in the way of an offensive operation until four days before Christmas 1939, when a force was put together to search for and attack the German pocket battleship *Lutzow*, formerly *Deutschland*. Gibson, on leave and meeting his future in laws, hastened back to Scampton but did not take part in the operation.

That may have been just as well. Disaster struck. In deteriorating weather conditions and running low on fuel, they did not find their prey. It would be April 1945 before the RAF managed to sink the *Lutzow*.

On their return a number of aircraft headed for the airfield at Acklington in Northumberland. Their approach was monitored by the Chain Home (radar) station at Ottercops Moss, confusion reigned and two Hampdens of No 44 Squadron from Waddington were attacked. The culprits were Spitfires of No 602 (City of Glasgow) Squadron, airborne from Drem in East Lothian.

Seven of the men from the two aircraft were rescued from the sea, but Leading Aircraftman Terrance Gibbin, a wireless operator/air gunner, was killed. The grave of this friendly fire victim can be found in the churchyard at Kirkleatham near Redcar in Yorkshire.

A Hampden from No 49 Squadron, out of fuel, crashed one mile short of Acklington. The pilot was injured and two others of the crew killed.

An immediate court of enquiry was held and it was concluded that the main fault for the Spitfire attack lay with the bombers for not identifying themselves. It pronounced that bombers and aircraft on coastal patrol aircraft should identify themselves to fighters when returning to their airfields.

It is perhaps not surprising that this verdict was controversial at the Air Ministry and elsewhere. Air Chief Marshal Dowding, AOC-in-C of Fighter Command, wrote in January, 'This is an intolerable doctrine and I am surprised that responsible officers should have set their names to it.' His view was that fighters should always be sure that an aircraft was hostile before opening fire.

Another disaster loomed and this time Gibson was at least a witness to what occurred. Following severe snow in the early part of 1940, which precluded flying for some weeks, No 83 Squadron was ordered to send aircraft and crews to Lossiemouth, near Elgin in northern Scotland, on an attachment to Coastal Command. Gibson went north and thus eventually achieved experience of flying operationally with three different RAF commands. Lossiemouth, close to the sea, had some resonance for Gibson, used to Porthleven, Folkestone and Saundersfoot, so the attachment was not entirely uncongenial though there were periods of boredom.

The next controversy arose on 27 February 1940 when the squadron was briefed to provide Hampdens for a sweep over the North Sea in search of a reported U-boat. Eight aircraft were involved, led by Squadron Leader Sam Threapleton. Accounts vary as to what happened and Gibson's own story, a mass attack on a submarine, does not accord with the official account or the squadron's operations record book.

It is recorded that the search area was changed, this information did not reach Threapleton and one aircraft following him bombed a submarine, despite the naval observer on the leading aircraft identifying it as friendly.

No harm was done but their lordships at the Admiralty were, understandably, furious and blame was handed out in various directions including to Sam Threapleton.

Air Vice Marshal Harris, recently arrived at No 5 Group, received a very stiff letter from Air Chief Marshal Sir Edgar Ludlow-Hewitt, Air Officer Commanding in Chief, Bomber Command, in which Ludlow-Hewitt wrote:

> 'This reflects great discredit both on the squadron concerned and on the group to which it belongs. I have again and again drawn your attention to the necessity for very thorough instruction and practice of an adequate and efficient briefing procedure and pre-flight preparation before departure. Your group have also been urged to improve the low standard of wireless communication efficiency which has been known to prevail in the group for some time. The incident clearly proves that insufficient attention is still being given to these important matters and neither the station commander nor the squadron commander seem to have any conception of the importance which should be attached to the proper preparation of crews before any operational mission, or any idea of what ought to be done. An operation conducted in so slipshod a manner can only be accounted for by assuming that officers of the unit have no idea of what constitutes efficiency.'

This came from a man who, some historians have argued, had the intellect for high command, though not the toughness. There is some background. Ludlow-Hewitt had been in post since 1937, fighting for resources for the bombers, against the greater priority given to Fighter Command. He was well aware that if he was asked to launch a full scale offensive against Germany his inadequate force would not last very long. Because he made this clear to his superiors he was accused of being pessimistic and even defeatist. He also had to defend Bomber Command against allegations of inefficiency and the fiasco of 27 February gave the Navy plenty of ammunition.

Very shortly after he wrote to Harris, Ludlow-Hewitt took up the more attractive post of RAF Inspector General, in which he remained until 1945, and Sir Charles Portal took control of Bomber Command.

Arthur Harris did not entirely accept the criticisms, pointing, in particular, to the failings of the Hampden as a weapon of war. However, at Lossiemouth, a training regime was instituted intended to ensure that No 83 Squadron would perform better when it was called upon again.

In the second half of March No 83 moved back to Scampton and now constant war was at hand – and so were more casualties.

Gibson did not fly on the night of 6/7 April when a patrol was mounted. In the early hours of the morning, nine hours after taking off from Scampton, Hampden L4054, skippered by Pilot Officer Wilfred Roberts, ran out of fuel and was abandoned over the North Sea. The aircraft hit the water near the St Mary's lighthouse which is on an island with a causeway close to Whitley Bay. None of the four-man crew was found before they succumbed to the water and the cold.

At the start of *Enemy Coast Ahead* Wilfred Roberts appears second in the list of 'pilots and their crews who fought with me against the enemy'. The man acting as navigator and bomb aimer of the doomed aircraft, Pilot Officer Keith Brooke–Taylor, comes first on the chronological list. There is no other evidence of particular closeness to the two men. The remaining two members of the crew, Sergeant Andrew McNicol and Leading Aircraftman Denis William Sharpe, are not included, though other aircrew who were not commissioned figure later.

Now the war turned less phoney with the beginning, on 9 April, of the German attack on Norway and Denmark. This was where the attention of No 83 Squadron would be focused for the time being. On Thursday, 11 April, 1940, with Denmark already defeated, Gibson joined this particular fray. He was tasked to undertake a diversionary reconnaissance, followed by minelaying, in the area which (with some disregard for the geography of the region) he described as 'Frederick-Middlefart-Little Belt-Kattegat'.

His aircraft for the sortie was L4070, which he had flown on operations from Lossiemouth and his, by now, regular crew consisted of Pilot Officer Jack Withers, who entertained in the mess by playing the piano, Leading Aircraftman McCormack and Pilot Officer Watson. It proved to be a long trip, but one without noteworthy incident. Six aircraft were despatched and all returned.

On the night of 14/15 April Gibson and his crew were despatched, along with three other aircraft on a 'gardening' (minelaying) operation in the vicinity of Middelfart, a place which Gibson's logbook entry demonstrates he was still unable to spell. Gibson's sortie was successful, despite coming under fire, though the other aircraft did not manage to lay their mines. Tragedy awaited at the end.

Gibson set down at the Kent airfield of Manston, close to Ramsgate, more than seven hours after he had taken off from Scampton. The Hampden flown by Flying Officer Kenneth Sylvester, 'Sylvo', a man on the outer reaches of Gibson's social circle, also attempted to make Manston.

Despite contact being made, things went wrong and it is believed that Sylvester flew on down the Channel until he and his crew went into the sea. No identified bodies came ashore on either side of the Channel and Sylvester and his crew are commemorated on the RAF memorial at Runnymede.

Nearly a week later, on 20 April, Gibson carried bombs to Denmark, as one of three aircraft with their target as German aircraft on the ground at Alborg in northern Denmark. There was an electrical fault with the allocated aircraft and Gibson and his crew had to transfer to a spare, with the result that they were flying half an hour behind schedule, knowing that the defences might well be on high alert when they reached the target.

The two other aircraft bombed their target, defying lots of light flak to do so, but Gibson became lost and had to give up with daybreak imminent. Gibson fumed on the return (to Lossiemouth) at the seeming incompetence of Withers, but the real culprit was a faulty compass. To some extent, this night came back to bother Gibson; the other crews would be decorated and the citations would refer to the Alborg attack. For Gibson and his crew who had not been so successful on the particular occasion, there was, of course, nothing.

More minelaying followed. During April and early May 1940 the activities of No 83 Squadron were regular, they resulted in loss (though enemy action was not a significant factor) and they made a contribution to the war effort, but this was hardly the level of warfare that had been predicted or was to come.

It was perhaps around this time that nose art came to the squadron. The credit for initiating the scheme was claimed by a member of the ground crew, Douglas Garton and it arose out of a session of fooling around which included reference to the Admiral Benbow, the public house depicted by Robert Louis Stevenson in *Treasure Island*. Aircraft were painted with admiral names, some pilots were less impressed than others, but Gibson took to the naming of his regular steed as Admiral Foo Bang and perpetuated the name on a number of future aircraft.

Chapter 5

Destroying the Barges

The tenth of May was the date when the war changed. In London Neville Chamberlain had been hounded from office as Prime Minister, after a two-day parliamentary debate, and the refusal of the Labour Party to serve in a coalition under him. The Conservative politician Leo Amery is now remembered as the catalyst with his assault on Chamberlain during the debate, using the words of Oliver Cromwell on another parliamentary occasion, 'You have sat too long here for any good you have been doing. Depart I say and let us have done with you. In the name of God, go.'

However obvious Churchill's place in history now, it was not in the least obvious at 1630 hours on 9 May as Chamberlain and the Government Chief Whip David Margesson met Churchill and the other, unwilling, candidate for prime minister, Lord Halifax. The peer was the man wanted by many. For Andrew Roberts, his biographer, Halifax was 'the calm, rational man of immense personal prestige and gravitas,' whereas Churchill was 'the romantic and excitable adventurer whose life was a *Boys' Own* story of cavalry charges, prison escapes and the thirst for action.'

Nonetheless, the outcome was that Halifax supported Churchill. 'It was perhaps Halifax's greatest service to his country,' wrote Roberts.

Hours before Churchill (around 1800 hours on 10 May) accepted the invitation from the King to form a government, German forces began their sweep across northwest Europe. The initiative was gained and held and the French and British air forces in France immediately began to suffer heavy casualties, as did the RAF aircraft operating from England.

At Scampton tension rose as evidenced by No 83 being called to readiness and personnel confined to the camp. In fact it was the beginning of the following week before even 'gardening' resumed. It was a week after the blitzkreig had begun, that Gibson, his regular crew and L4070, went on a bombing operation. By then nearly a thousand people had been killed in Rotterdam by Luftwaffe bombing and the war cabinet, seeking at least in part some positive news for home consumption, had lifted the embargo on bombing east of the Rhine.

Five aircraft were despatched to various targets and all returned, though with damage. The Operations Record Book (ORB) recorded of Gibson, 'Target A.8 at Hamburg (an oil refinery) attacked successfully. During the dive a balloon cable hit the starboard wing causing damage to a slat. Landed at Abingdon owing to fog at base.'

Quickly now the difficult road to the Channel ports was taken by the British Expeditionary Force and much of Bomber Command's task was to attack the German columns pursuing the troops and the roads, railways, transport infrastructure and other targets that might impede the pursuit. What was done did not and could not halt the German advance, but it was an heroic attempt to make a difference.

On 22 May Gibson and his crew smashed a railway bridge over the Schelde canal, returning to the Suffolk airfield of Mildenhall. Sergeant Stanley Jenkins and his crew did not come back that night. In poor visibility they were diverted from Scampton to Ringway, an order which required them to find their way over the Pennines. They crashed near the Yorkshire town of Holmfirth.

Four nights later Gibson reported blocking a railway tunnel near Aachen. A lighter note came about on 27 May, when the King came to Scampton to present decorations. This was not the kind of occasion that appealed to Guy Gibson, perhaps because he was not one of those to be honoured and therefore had no opportunity to play a leading part in the proceedings.

This ceremonial contrasted with what was going on elsewhere that day. The little ships were setting out for Dunkirk; the Isle of Man pleasure steamer, *Mona's Isle*, had been heavily bombed, while returning laden with troops and was towed into Dover with many dead and wounded on board. One of the tugs that brought her to safety was, as it happens, the *Simla*. Calais had fallen the previous evening, though the news did not immediately reach the RAF and Lysanders continued on 27 May to attempt futile re-supply missions. In the air, Hurricane and Spitfire squadrons of Fighter Command suffered heavy losses as they tried to keep the German air force away from the troops on the beaches.

It was at this time that the piano playing Jack Withers was given his own crew and the process of upgrading all aircrew to the minimum rank of sergeant was going on, though not all trades were dealt with at the same time. In addition some squadrons were less speedy than others with the administration of the orders involved and there are stories of some men flying on operations with sergeant's stripes in their pockets, as a means of gaining better treatment if they were shot down and captured.

Despite his reputation for being fully conscious of the difference between officers and other ranks, Gibson does not appear to have been strongly opposed to the situation. Many of the newly promoted men across the RAF did find that there was bitter resentment amongst the regular NCOs who had strived for many years to reach sergeant and above and now found, in some cases, 18-year-olds joining them in the mess, with, for one thing, doubtful ability to impose discipline or command respect. There are those who were quickly elevated though who would later recall no such animosity.

In the case of Gibson's crew and presumably the rest of No 83 Squadron, there was no hanging about. McCormack had become a sergeant when he flew with Gibson on a minelaying operation on 9 June.

During June the squadron flew a considerable number of sorties. It did not suffer any casualties though there was a growing realisation amongst the crews that they had entered a world where death – and perhaps a very unpleasant death – was highly likely. Demise did not just come in burning aircraft out of control. It was as necessary to force to the back of the mind what it must have been like for Sylvester and his crew lost over the Channel, having (though they may not have known this) only just missed the haven of Manston.

All military types live in their own world of shared action and other experiences. It is true of those who have been to Iraq and Afghanistan in the twenty-first century, as it was true for Bomber Command in 1940. For the outsider it is impossible to understand what being in such a situation is like. Historians might know more of the statistics and the strategy, but they can never know what it was like for those who can say, 'I was there'. Gibson felt keenly this impossibility of making somebody from a different world have any significant concept of what he and his comrades were doing.

What Gibson and his team were doing during June was attacking a variety of targets, as well as taking part in 'gardening' operations which were not an easy option. The German fighters saw to that and geography played a part in the degree of danger. Flying between the Dutch islands, for instance, flak could be coming at you from two sides. In another key area to lay mines, just as people in occupied Denmark looked across and fumed at the bright lights of neutral Sweden, so the Luftwaffe would seek to spot the silhouette of RAF aircraft out minelaying against the Swedish lights.

There was change at the top of the squadron. Wing Commander Snaith left No 83 Squadron, to Gibson's regret, though the two had had their differences with Snaith somewhat looking down on his subordinate's gung ho approach. The new man was Wing Commander J.C. Sisson, who flew more than Snaith, but was rather quiet.

Gibson noted Sisson's complete contrast to the forceful new CO of No 49 Squadron across the airfield. This was the well-known and noisier 'Downwind' Gillan who in 1938, as CO of No 111 Squadron, had earned his nickname flying one of the new Hurricane fighters from Turnhouse in Scotland to Northolt in a remarkable time. The Air Ministry's publicity machine stressed that the feat demonstrated the capabilities of the new weapon. RAF pilots were more inclined to consider the exceptional weather conditions and John Gillan was 'Downwind' for the rest of his service career.

On 1/2 July the squadron began a series of attacks on major German ships with the *Scharnhorst* at Kiel leading the way for Gibson. The target was one that had a particular significance for the British. The previous month the *Scharnhorst* had sunk the aircraft carrier HMS *Glorious*, following major misjudgements by the captain of the *Glorious*. More than a thousand men died in the carrier and two escorting destroyers, which were also sunk.

Wing Commander Sisson led twelve aircraft to Kiel in the first attack. Only one claimed a hit and one No 83 Hampden, flown by Pilot Officer Douglas Redmayne, was shot down in the target area, with the loss of all the crew. They are buried in Kiel war cemetery. The ORB recorded for Gibson's aircraft, 'bomb not seen to burst, though accurate dive reported.'

There were no losses when the squadron had another go at the *Scharnhorst* three nights later, though not much success either. In the intensity of the flak and the glare of the searchlights it was not possible to identify all the bomb bursts. Gibson made six attempts and finished by unintentionally dropping his bomb in the town – something that was still technically forbidden by British authorities.

On 9 July the target was the *Tirpitz*, a ship, then at Wilhelmshaven, which survived these attentions and was finally sunk by Bomber Command towards the end of 1944. This was the day on which the award of Gibson's first decoration was announced. His Distinguished Flying Cross was 'periodic', rather than immediate. The very short citation paid tribute to his gallantry and devotion to duty during flying operations and did not make reference to any specific incidents. Another pilot on the squadron, Jamie Pitcairn-Hill was similarly decorated at the same time.

Gibson was certainly cheered by this news as he took off for the *Tirptiz* at 2215 hours, though, in public at least, there was not the exaltation that Snaith, for one, might have expected from him, had the former CO been around to observe the situation.

L4070 brought Flying Officer Gibson and his crew safely back at 0350 hours on 10 July, but against intense opposition they had not been able to observe the fall of their bomb. According to the definition established after the war, the Battle of Britain had officially started at one minute past midnight while they had been in the air.

There was a six day interval before another operation for Gibson. When he took off for a bombing operation on 15 July he had a new crew member. Since the previous reorganisation of the crew, Sergeant Howard had been his second wireless operator/air gunner, now this role was taken by Sergeant Turner. A target near Dortmund was attacked after which they landed at Abingdon.

After two more bombing operations there was a break of nearly a month from the action for Gibson. He trained for a planned low-level attack on the Dortmund-Ems Canal, but then went on leave, spending it amongst the rather bare and rocky countryside at the fishing village Boscastle on the north Cornish coast, with his wife Eve.

Gibson therefore did not take part in the attack on the canal, missing the possibility of being one of the casualties suffered, missing as well being present as the RAF, for the third time in the war, earned a Victoria Cross. Possibly Gibson reflected later that he had missed both a close encounter with death and a chance for glory.

The specific plan was to destroy an aqueduct that carried the canal over the River Ems, to the north of Munster. From Nos 83 and 49 Squadrons, eleven Hampdens were detailed to take part, including four whose job was to attack diversionary targets. The operation was to be led by No 83's Jamie Pitcairn-Hill, now a squadron leader.

Pitcairn-Hill attacked first, plunging, like the men after him, into intense fire from mobile flak batteries, tracer and searchlights intended to blind the pilots. He bombed and survived, with his aircraft damaged. Two of the following three Hampdens were shot down and the fifth attack was made by Flight Lieutenant Roderick Learoyd of No 49 Squadron, a pre-war fruit farmer and motor engineer, who had then joined the RAF on a short service commission.

To avoid the trap of the blinding searchlights, Learoyd ducked below the windscreen and, in the final phase of the run, followed instructions from Pilot Officer John Lewis acting as navigator and bomb aimer. Flak and machine gun fire badly mauled the Hampden, causing major leaks in the hydraulic system, but the attack was completed. Inside the aircraft one of the homing pigeons laid an egg. On the return, Learoyd circled Scampton for a long time to effect a less risky daylight landing in the damaged aircraft. Later the operation was pronounced a complete success.

'Babe' Learoyd, a big man, much respected on his squadron, was awarded the VC and Jamie Pitcairn-Hill, the DSO. Learoyd would later command both the squadrons that had taken part in the attack.

For Gibson this was a period of significant losses of men he knew well. Amongst those who had already gone was Bill Tweddell DFC, who had failed to return from an attack on the Dortmund-Ems Canal on the night of 25/26 July. Tweddell and two of his crew were killed.

On the sortie that led to Learoyd's VC, the second aircraft to attack had been that of Ellis 'Rossy' Ross, an Australian who had been with Gibson when they were summoned for action on the first day of the war. His aircraft exploded during the bombing run and he died along with his crew.

Having witnessed that instant death, Flight Lieutenant Allen 'Mull' Mulligan, another Australian, was next to attack. This aircraft was shot down too, but Mulligan and Sergeant Younger survived to become prisoners of war. Sergeant Hill and Sergeant Abel were killed. Mulligan was awarded a bar to his DFC.

The key event of the summer and autumn of 1940 was foretold by Winston Churchill, the Prime Minister.

On 18 June Churchill made one of his series of defiant and inspiring speeches as Britain stood under threat of defeat and subjugation. On this occasion his peroration included the words:

'What General Weygand has called the Battle of France is over. I expect that the Battle of Britain is about to begin. Upon this battle depends the survival of Christian civilisation. Upon it depends our own British life, and the long continuity of our institutions and our Empire. The whole fury and might of the enemy must very soon be turned on us. Hitler knows that he will have to break us in this island or lose the war. If we can stand up to him, all Europe may be freed and the life of the world may move forward into broad, sunlit uplands.'

The words are famous and Churchill proved to be right. What came to be known as the Battle of Britain was fought. At the spearhead of the British resistance to invasion as it developed were the aircrew of RAF Fighter Command, who had to deny the Luftwaffe air superiority over the English Channel and southern England. Many others played their part in ensuring that a German invasion did not take place. They included the groundcrew and others who kept the fighters flying and directed towards the incoming hostile aircraft, the other RAF Commands, the Royal Navy, the Army, the civilian services and civilians in many walks of life who kept the country moving and often performed heroic acts when called upon to do so.

On 20 August 1940 in the House of Commons Churchill made another famous speech, in which he entered into legend the heroics of the RAF.

'The gratitude of every home in our Island, in our Empire, and indeed throughout the world, except in the abodes of the guilty, goes out to the British airmen who, undaunted by odds, unwearied in their constant challenge and mortal danger, are turning the tide of the world war by their prowess and by their devotion. Never in the field of human conflict was so much owed by so many to so few.

'All hearts go out to the fighter pilots, whose brilliant actions we see with our own eyes day after day, but we must never forget that all the time, night after night, month after month, our bomber squadrons travel far into Germany, find their targets in the darkness by the highest navigational skill, aim their attacks, often under the heaviest fire, often with serious loss, with deliberate, careful discrimination, and inflict shattering blows upon the whole of the technical and war-making structure of the Nazi power. On no part of the Royal Air Force does the weight of the war fall more heavily than on the daylight bombers who will play an invaluable part in the case of invasion and whose unflinching zeal it has been necessary in the meanwhile on numerous occasions to restrain.'

Later Churchill would write that his reference to 'so few' referred to the fighter pilots. Nonetheless, his meaning has been debated ever since and an individual interpretation of the meaning may depend on the layout and punctuation of the version of the speech that is being read at the time.

The demand for recognition and listing of the Allied airmen who had played such a major part in saving the country from invasion began during the war in Parliament and elsewhere.

The official debate included considering the extent to which the entire RAF, including personnel in staff jobs, had played their part in the victory. However, the main campaigners pushed the view that it was Fighter Command airmen who should be honoured. The announcement of the Battle of Britain clasp to the 1939–1945 star was made in 1945. The definition for qualification was tweaked over the years, but bomber crews were never included.

Indeed, the Air Ministry stressed in 1945 that, 'COs are not to admit claims for this highly-prized emblem which are open to any possible doubt. The clasp is not available for personnel who flew in aircraft other than fighters, notwithstanding that they may have been engaged with the enemy in the air during the qualifying period.'

A rather different line was taken in regard to the scroll containing names of those killed in the Battle of Britain which was presented to Westminster Abbey in 1947 at the time of the unveiling of the battle memorial there by King George VI. The scroll contained 449 names, including Bomber Command personnel and relatives of those men were invited to attend.

So Guy Gibson and his comrades did not take part officially in the Battle of Britain, though there is no doubt that what they did that summer and autumn played a major and heroic role in thwarting Hitler's plans.

In particular, as the fighters scrambled to meet German formations, the bombers were fighting the 'Battle of the Barges' as it came to be called. It can be argued that his gallant participation in this battle against the means of transport for the invading army was in fact Guy Gibson's greatest contribution to the war effort.

As the Battle of Britain started so did the attacks on targets associated with a possible invasion, though the intense period of action against the barges was in September. Constant sorties, by Bomber Command, Coastal Command and the Fleet Air Arm, were flown against concentrations of craft in ports across the channel. The targets included Le Havre, Dunkirk, Antwerp, the Dortmund-Ems canal, Ostend, Boulogne and Antwerp.

The need was desperate and even the Fairey Battles which had suffered so badly during the May and June fighting on the continent were thrown once again into the fray.

Wrote Gibson in *Enemy Coast Ahead*,

'Every port from Antwerp to Dieppe was packed like lumber floating in a river with thousands of these invasion barges. The Huns knew, of course, that our meagre bomber force would attack them. Light flak guns were brought from far and wide to put up a cordon of steel which would ensure that no bombs could be dropped within miles; flak towers were erected, balloon barrages were put up.'

Gibson also pointed out correctly that the Battle of the Barges, 'was a complement to the Battle of Britain; they were fought side by side by boys doing very different jobs.'

Now, after Gibson's return from leave, the Battle of the Barges moved towards its climax, though a mixture of targets was attacked and minelaying was still considered important in the circumstances of heightened fear of invasion.

Locations visited by Gibson during September included Ostend and Antwerp. Returning from Lorient, Gibson claimed to have attacked a Dornier

Do 17 travelling in the opposite direction, with a crew apparently too relaxed as they neared home. He said that he and his crew were credited with an enemy aircraft probably destroyed.

Gibson also recorded that he witnessed something of the action which led to the award of a VC. Heading for home from Antwerp, apparently having done a lot of damage to the barges, he flew alongside another Hampden which was on fire. Later he discovered that this was the aircraft of Pilot Officer Connor of his squadron, in which Sergeant John Hannah fought the flames and helped the pilot return home after the navigator had baled out. The 18-year-old Hannah received the VC and Connor the DFC.

Gibson's narrow escape came over Antwerp when a shell entered the aircraft, hit the toe strap on the pilot's rudder bar and flying debris knocked out Sergeant Houghton in the bomb aiming position.

Back at the airfield, damage was examined and produced the remark from the 'Chiefy' (flight sergeant), 'Cor sir, that's bloomin' providence. It missed your foot by half an inch.'

Sergeant Houghton was a party to this conversation and had the nerve to remark that he attributed the escape to Gibson's short legs.

The vital nature of the work of destroying the barges was rammed home before and after attacks. Gibson recorded how destroying fifty barges in a basin holding 400 was not considered nearly good enough. The flak was intense, the casualties across Bomber Command and the other commands were very high, but the barges had to go, otherwise the strong threat of invasion remained. The other vital ingredient, as Gibson was well aware, was the success of the fighters. They gave the Luftwaffe a very bloody nose on 15 September, though not nearly to the extent that was claimed at the time. The combined efforts of so many aircrew meant that the invasion threat was receding but nobody in Britain knew that for sure.

By now Gibson's time on his first operational squadron was coming to an end. He went out in considerable style, flying to Berlin, 'The Big City' as it would become to the bomber boys, on the night of 23/24 September, taking off from Scampton, according to his logbook, at 1930 hours and returning at 0400 hours.

In *Enemy Coast Ahead* he wrote,

'It was one of those trips which were so common in those days. Cloud all the way, flak all the way; no one knowing where Berlin was, our loop bearings continually being jammed by the enemy and general chaos all round.'

It is not surprising therefore that the propaganda value of the attack, and others like it, was considerably greater than the amount of damage done.

Gibson's target was the Potsdamer railway station, on the site of the first railway terminus in Berlin. The Nazis already had grandiose plans to close and replace it. By the end of the war there would be no choice in the matter. Gibson may or may not have hit the station and hastened its downfall.

By the standards of later trips, the losses on this Berlin raid were not substantial. A Whitley of No 77 Squadron, from Linton-on-Ouse, ditched in the sea; of the two survivors found by the Navy four days later, one died shortly after being picked up. The Polish crew of a Wellington of No 311 Squadron, based at East Wretham, all became prisoners of war.

There was a loss at No 83 Squadron as well and this involved more of Gibson's long-standing colleagues. The aircraft of Squadron Leader Anthony 'Oscar' Bridgman DFC was hit by flak and fell in Germany. Gibson and others waited for a long time, searching the sky and straining their ears for a returning Hampden. There was added poignancy because there had been some ill feeling between Gibson and Bridgman, his flight commander, before take off, over Bridgman and other pilots returning from a visit to Nottingham in a considerable state of inebriation.

The vigil was not rewarded, though news later came through that Oscar Bridgman was a prisoner of war. However, his crew had all died, including Pilot Officer 'Watty' Watson DFC, who had been purloined by Bridgman from Gibson at the time Gibson had returned from leave.

Immediately after this Gibson and a number of other No 83 aircrew were told they were being rested. At this stage of the war there was no firm number of operations that a man needed to do before the rest came, but later the normal figure for a first 'tour' would become thirty and Gibson had done rather more than that.

Perhaps the decision came at the right moment. Even the dashing and press-on skipper of Admiral Foo Bang was feeling the strain. He was having dreams about being on operations and, like most of his colleagues, could feel very tired. The squadron was being afflicted by early returns of aircraft and by what became known as 'creepback', when bombs were released just ahead of the target, whether deliberately or not, to speed the departure from the area of most danger. As more crews released even earlier, so bombs fell even further from the target. Other squadrons were no different, but certainly the men who had been ready for action since the start of the war and had, as autumn 1940 began, been flying with intensity for months, needed a break, whether they knew it or not.

What Gibson and his colleagues didn't know at this point was that Bomber Command was groping towards its strategic role in the war. Concentration bombing on a town, city or other large area was already being tried, as with Gibson's last operation of the tour, the one to Berlin. There was still an allocation of specific targets, but the evidence was growing that individual aircraft had little chance of finding and hitting a bridge, a factory, a railway station. Later the Butt report to the war cabinet would set out the failure rate starkly. Area bombing would become a fact out of necessity, as well as the belief in some quarters that it was the way to destroy German morale, impede its industry and win the war.

Chapter 6

Into the Night

Far from strategic considerations, Gibson made the short journey to No 14 Operational Training Unit at Cottesmore in the tiny county of Rutland and close to the A1 trunk road.

Cottesmore was one of the airfields built as a result of the RAF expansion plans in the thirties. It had been the home of bomber squadrons, first in No 2 Group and later in No 5 Group. In the early days of the war, an expansion of training during Ludlow-Hewitt's spell as AOC-in-C at Bomber Command had led to Cottesmore gaining a training role. Now No 14 OTU was in business to produce pilots and some other aircrew who were ready to fly on operations in the Hampdens of No 5 Group.

In the run-up to Gibson's arrival some of these trainee crews had been flying operationally, dropping propaganda leaflets over the continent. Long after Gibson's departure 14 OTU would provide aircraft and crews to ensure a maximum effort on the Thousand Bomber raids of 1942. Much later still, American airborne troops would take off from Cottesmore to go into action in Normandy, during the Arnhem operation and during the Rhine crossing.

For some, this would be the ideal posting, a more restful existence, without daily and nightly stresses of waiting for orders, though OTU accidents ensured that there was still some danger. At the same time people thus posted remained in the atmosphere of what some saw as an elite group and contributed to that group's war effort.

Gibson regarded things differently. He was distracted by his love and desire for his girlfriend Eve and they became engaged in early October. For some that might be an additional reason to take a rest, but Gibson was never good at being away from the action, or at training others. He was posted again, to No 16 OTU at Upper Heyford, but this too was a highly temporary arrangement. A chance to return to the action arose and was grasped firmly.

Even more closely this time Gibson's career development was linked to the actions of Fighter Command, the Battle of Britain and its aftermath. The first mass night attack on London had been made by the Luftwaffe, starting in the late afternoon of Saturday, 7 September, still sometimes referred to as

'Black Saturday' in the East End, and running through into the early hours of Sunday, 8 September.

The Fighter Command controllers had not immediately realised that London was the target, but in any case, the force unleashed could not have been halted by the fighter force. That night there were nine conflagrations (fires out of control in fire service jargon) on the east side of London. There were fires too officially rated at '300 pumps' and '200 pumps'.

When the last major daylight raid on London on 15 September was repulsed with considerable German losses, the Battle of Britain was effectively won, though it was a fact known at that moment to no-one, including the Prime Minister, the war cabinet and Air Chief Marshal Dowding, heading Fighter Command from Bentley Priory to the north of London.

Nonetheless, they all realised that the shape of the daytime aerial fighting was changing. In October the German fighters would come over at considerable heights and try to tempt the Spitfires beyond their effective altitude. They were tip and run raids and to some extent the bombing and fighter to fighter combat continued.

However, more and more, as the Luftwaffe could not sustain the losses it was suffering during the day, the emphasis was on attacks at night. Fighter Command was not equipped or trained to defend the country at night as it had been during the day. As well as the plotting and politicising that took place around the name of Air Chief Marshal Dowding at this time, there were sincerely held opinions as to why it was time for a change. The difficulty of fighting the enemy bombers at night, and what some saw as the unwillingness of Dowding to address this issue, added fuel to a fire.

Nonetheless, Dowding was very badly treated. On 13 November 1940 he was told by the Air Minister, Sir Archibald Sinclair Bt, that he was to leave. By coincidence, on the same day, Guy Gibson joined Fighter Command as a small, but not insignificant, part of the means of addressing the problem which had been identified.

The precise issue that brought this about was an appeal to Arthur Harris at No 5 Group, masterminded by Air Vice Marshal Sholto Douglas, Deputy Chief of the Air Staff. The request was for some of 5 Group's really top class bomber pilots to encourage, with their night-time experience, an improvement in the performance of the fighters in darkness. A few months previously, the flow had been in the opposite direction, with bomber and army co-operation pilots being invited to volunteer for Fighter Command.

Harris co-operated with the request he received and sent, 'a hand picked bunch of which Gibson was the best'. Gibson did not object in the slightest to the termination of his very brief rest, some of which he had spent on leave.

He set off for Fighter Command with a promise from Harris that service on night fighters would be followed by appointment to 'the best command within my power'. Very shortly afterwards Douglas replaced Dowding at Bentley Priory and Harris replaced Douglas at the Air Ministry.

So Gibson, with promotion to flight lieutenant, journeyed to No 29 Squadron then based officially at Wellingore in Lincolnshire, though he is recorded as having reported to Digby a few miles away, which the squadron was also using. It appears that with the intervention of his AOC he had narrowly avoided a posting to yet another OTU.

The squadron had been deploying the fighter version of the Bristol Blenheim, an aircraft seen as quite something at the time of its appearance in the 1930s, as a bomber, but now well outdated. Some of the Blenheims were fitted with airborne interception equipment (AI), but this had not been a factor in the few victories which had been achieved by No 29 Squadron.

More advanced Bristol Beaufighter 1s had started to dribble in to the squadron in September. Their AI equipment was an improved version of that on the Blenheims.

Some Blenheim/Beaufighter squadrons, including No 29, are officially considered to have taken part in the Battle of Britain, but their role was generally peripheral, including convoy patrols and escorting civilian and other non combat aircraft in and out of the UK, as well as the limited night time operations which were feasible at the time.

Gibson was part of a process of improving operations at night and he was also to play a major role in improving the performance of No 29 Squadron. The process was started four months before on 16 July when the squadron received a new CO.

Squadron Leader Stanley Charles Widdows (Charles to his family and intimates) was 31 years old and a graduate of the RAF College, Cranwell. His pre-war service as a pilot had included time with No 43 Squadron, 'The Fighting Cocks' and No 29 Squadron, as well as spells in Egypt and Palestine. As a test pilot at Martlesham Heath he reported on the first production Hurricane.

Following the command of RAF West Malling, Widdows would hold wartime staff appointments. He continued in the RAF after the war and played a major role in the early days of the Battle of Britain Fighter Association. He retired from the RAF as an Air Commodore in 1958 and had just passed his 100th birthday when he died in Guernsey in January 2010.

At No 29 Squadron Widdows found that he had inherited a mixed bunch of pilots. He was a man who knew what he wanted and set out to achieve his goals with not too much concern about being popular. His obvious record of achievement as a pilot earned him respect, perhaps grudging respect, as he rid himself of men he didn't want and demanded more training and less drinking.

There hadn't been very much glory in being a Blenheim pilot in the Battle of Britain and it showed in the attitude at Wellingore and Digby. The Spitfires and the Hurricanes stole all the publicity.

Interestingly, one well-known Battle of Britain pilot had been posted to Blenheims first, but had been transferred to a Spitfire squadron when he was found to be too short for his feet to reach the controls of a Blenheim. He flew Spitfires sitting on cushions and was certainly shorter than Gibson.

Widdows had an eye for talent. One of those he retained, who had flown in the Battle of Britain, was Flying Officer J.R.D. 'Bob' Braham. A former police force clerk in Lancashire, Bob Braham would become an outstanding night fighter pilot, amassing three DSOs and the same number of DFCs, finally being shot down and becoming a prisoner on 25 June 1944. His incarceration came about from an inability, like Gibson's, to keep away from operations, even when he had the chance.

After the war he received the AFC, before leaving the RAF to join the Royal Canadian Air Force. His most celebrated partner during his night time successes was 'Sticks' Gregory, so called for his prowess on the drums.

Variations in the quality of aircrew, and a lack of discipline, were not the only problem that Widdows faced as he strove to bring his new command up to what he considered scratch. The squadron had been moved around a fair amount, including detachments and would shortly move again. Airfields that had provided a home for all or part of the squadron since the outbreak of war included – as well as Wellingore and Digby – Debden, Wittering, Martlesham Heath, Ternhill and Drem.

The atmosphere on the squadron was apparent to Gibson as soon he arrived. The adjutant was guarded in his explanation of what was going on, thereby signalling that something was amiss. Richard Morris tells of how when Gibson arrived at the officers' mess he encountered cheerful log fires and sullen grunts in response to his entrance. One man walked out, slamming the door to indicate his view of new blood coming in. This would turn out to be Flying Officer 'Peter' Kells, a long-serving member of the squadron, having joined No 29 as a member of the Reserve of Air Force Officers in July 1938. Six months later he received a permanent commission.

Late in 1940 Kells went as an instructor to an OTU and then rapidly to the Aeroplane and Armament Experimental Establishment at Boscombe Down. He was still serving there when, on 21 February 1941, he was reported missing while flying a Hurricane at high altitude during petrol heating tests. His body was not found.

Despite their difficult start, Gibson included Peter Kells in the 'honour list' at the beginning of *Enemy Coast Ahead*, though he was mistaken over the type of aircraft Kells was flying and the month in which he died. Fortunately, as Morris recounts, some friendship was proffered by Pilot Officer Edward Graham-Little, as well as other recent arrivals.

The next night provided a considerably different experience for Gibson and one that impacted on him, on Bomber Command that he had just left temporarily, and on British public opinion. The Luftwaffe launched its Operation Moonlight Sonata against the city of Coventry. Now often represented as industrial and drab, Coventry, until the arrival of the enemy, had many historic buildings. The destruction included the ancient parish church of St Michael, since 1918 Coventry Cathedral. Though, in terms of what would come later in the war, the destruction and level of casualties in Coventry was relatively small, 'Coventry' in the twenty-first century, in many British minds at least, remains a word to evoke brutal bombing.

Gibson accompanied Widdows and they watched the raid unfold through the actions of WAAFs at the plotting table. Once again there was virtually nothing that Fighter Command could do to prevent what was going on in the darkness. Peter Kells was airborne and followed a hostile for some way before firing and missing. The operations room at Digby remains very much as it was on the night of Moonlight Sonata and visits are possible.

Like most aircraft types, the Beaufighter had teething problems and on Sunday, 17 November Widdows came close to losing his life in one, when an engine failed and the aircraft went into a steep dive. Widdows ordered the AI operator to bale out, but Pilot Officer Wilson could not open the hatch, so Widdows returned to his seat and managed to bring the aircraft down to a text book wheels-up landing in a field near Sleaford.

Two days later Gibson flew a Blenheim operationally, when, with a new-to-him Pilot Officer Watson, he completed an X-raid patrol, meaning that he was looking for unidentified aircraft reported by the defences. He found nothing.

A couple of days later and Gibson was airborne in a Blenheim again, but this time Widdows allowed him to use one to get to Cardiff for his wedding. A very short honeymoon followed at a hotel in Chepstow, from where, on the evening of the following day, the new Mr and Mrs Gibson found that they had a grandstand view across the River Severn as Bristol received its first major attack of the war. More than 200 people were killed and the Lord Mayor commented that, 'The City of Churches had, in one night, become the city of ruins.'

The sight probably intensified Gibson's desire to return to the war. He was back in Lincolnshire with Eve very quickly. On 1 December, as a member of No 29's 'A', or Beaufighter flight, he flew the type for the first time. His slight stature helped him cope with the space limitations of the Beaufighter and he perceived the potential of this new aircraft, conceived and built in a hurry as war threatened and then became reality. Despite the initial misgivings of many people the Beaufighter would go on to be a particularly successful and celebrated Second World War aircraft.

Four days later Gibson defied rotten weather to familiarise himself with the workings of the AI system. Perhaps the circumstances in which he found himself were good for Gibson's soul. In a bomber the pilot was effectively in the hands of the bomb aimer for a short part of the operation and to some extent in the hands of the navigator at every juncture, but still remained very much in charge of his destiny.

In a Beaufighter Gibson and the other pilots found themselves under the control of their AI operator for much of the time, until they were able to put their killer instincts to the test when they were actually upon the prey.

In the RAF, unlike the Luftwaffe, the pilot was always the skipper – the same is true today – but in a Beaufighter at night, the state of being skipper was often more theoretical than actual. The AI operators, quite often NCOs flown by a commissioned pilot, formed teams which sometimes went on, moving together to new postings.

If perhaps the relationship between a top golfer and his caddy has some of the aspects of a marriage in its intensity, then so too did the relationship in a Beaufighter night fighter. Gibson had to learn to be part of one of those teams, the more senior part, but still placing much trust and respect in the other member.

However, teams take time to develop and at first Gibson did not fly with one companion. On 10 December he took off a few minutes before 1000 hours with Sergeant Taylor and landed a little over an hour later. They had followed a blip on the radar set until the controller identified it as friendly.

The next morning Gibson was in the air again at 0750 hours, with Taylor once more, as a response to enemy air activity. The squadron operations record book states, 'Bandit chased out over the sea eventually shot at (the bandit), two short bursts at 800 yards range about sixty miles east of Mablethorpe. Enemy aircraft identified (as) Ju 88. No return fire from enemy aircraft and no damage observed as result of F/Lt Gibson's fire. Enemy aircraft lost in cloud. Height of combat about 1,500 feet.'

If all the logbooks of all the night fighter teams could be studied that would probably prove to be a typical entry of the second grade, the most common entry being where no sighting took place. During the night of 12/13 December Gibson flew two patrols with Pilot Officer Watson, with a complete lack of result.

Bad weather then closed in on Lincolnshire though Gibson, his mind firmly on the objective in hand, as it usually was, found opportunities to practise and gain mastery of AI operation.

He flew on further sorties in the run up to Christmas, with Pilot Officer Francombe, reporting that during a breakfast time patrol he had seen a Ju 88 shot down from around 150 to 200 feet by anti-aircraft fire from RAF Manby, east of Louth. Today RAF Manby has long ceased to exist, but one of the buildings on the site is the Guy Gibson Hall.

As the war dragged on, there would be many Bomber Command crews who found themselves attacked by Luftwaffe intruders, often in the moments when they seemed safely home from the continent. This experience came to No 29 Squadron on 22 December, when Pilot Officer Ken Davison was in the circuit at Digby in a Blenheim. His aircraft was fired on and hit, apparently by a Ju 88. Davison got the aircraft down safely and nobody was wounded, but one more hazard had been added to the list.

Gibson's logbook is uninformative about a patrol that started on the night of 23 December and took him into Christmas Eve, except that he wrote that the R/T packed (up). This was during the two nights of the 'Manchester Christmas Blitz' when nearly 700 people were killed and over 2,000 injured. The cathedral was hit and so badly damaged that demolition was considered. Another great Manchester landmark, the Free Trade Hall was wrecked, as were new Avro Manchester aircraft in the Metropolitan Vickers factory at Trafford Park.

Before the war the council in the neighbouring town of Stockport had defied Whitehall opinion and started a programme of building tunnels as air raid shelters. Now they found citizens of Manchester coming across the border to take advantage of this unusual facility.

In 2013 one place in Manchester Cathedral to seek out evidence of the raids is the statue of Humphrey Cheetham, the 17th century founder of Cheetham's school and library, although it no longer stands where it did in 1940. Both he and the child at his feet have pieces still missing as a result of bomb damage.

The R/T failure caused Gibson to break off his patrol and become hopelessly lost. He considered abandoning the aircraft. Eventually an Anson was spotted on 'finals' to an airfield, Gibson followed and found himself down at Upper Heyford.

Morris records that when Gibson got back to his digs in Navenby near Wellingore, he found Eve frantic with worry and contemplating widowhood. Her husband had not thought to try to get through to her and announce that he was safe and neither had anyone else.

Gibson's scare and his night's work generally had demonstrated the continuing gallant futility of what he and his colleagues were doing in terms of immediate results. They were striving to do better, the boffins were working to produce better equipment, based on the experience of pilots including Widdows and Gibson, but cities such as Manchester and Bristol were still in ruins.

In Manchester, the film unit of the Co-operative Wholesale Society made a defiant production called *Manchester Took it Too*. It showed night scenes of buildings burning and collapsing in the city centre, despite the efforts of the fire fighters. There were morning scenes too of Co-op workers battling through the rubble to get to their desks, displaying both awe at the carnage around them and a determination to carry on. One young woman would later typify the attitude of many by saying that her main concern was not to ladder her precious stockings on the wreckage she had to negotiate.

At the end of the year, the mood was summed up by the No 29 Squadron adjutant, Sam France. He wrote of the disheartening circumstances for a night fighter squadron in which constant endeavour produced few results and continued, 'We can only hope that the coming year will produce some new method, or improved equipment to enable our pilots to contact more enemy planes and shoot them down.'

Christmas brought a break in operations and Gibson did not fly operationally again for a month, with fog and snow predominant features of the local weather reports. Then he experienced new AI operators before coming together on 1 February with Sergeant Richard James, with whom he was compatible and would often fly.

Perhaps it helped that James was about six years older than Gibson. A Lancastrian by birth, he had only joined the Royal Air Force Volunteer Reserve in June 1940, volunteering for aircrew and going to Martlesham Heath in Suffolk to train to join the pioneering band of AI operators. He had arrived at No 29 Squadron on 20 October and flown his first operational sortie three days later, thus just qualifying for the Battle of Britain clasp, though of course he did not know that until much later.

Later in the war Richard James would have another association with someone who would become famous. At the Ground Controlled Approach Unit at Honiley near Coventry he would share duties with a chap called Nobby Clarke. 'Nobby' would later become better known as Arthur C. Clarke, the science fiction writer and would receive a knighthood. Richard James was released from the RAF in 1945 and died in 2005.

Success of a sort arrived for the new duo on 4 February, a night when bombs fell on Derby and there was also activity around Hull. The first contact turned out to be with another Beaufighter, but then a second contact occurred over the Humber estuary.

In the intelligence combat report for the night the story is told:

'By coming up behind and below a line of about six flares the enemy aircraft was seen above and ahead illuminated dimly by the flares below it at 1955 hours. Fire was opened at 500 yards range giving a two-second burst. Enemy aircraft was lost to sight when flares went out, but had been picked up on AI meanwhile and was held and followed for a few seconds. No apparent avoiding action was taken by enemy aircraft which was lost in turns. The flares seemed to ignite about 100 feet below the aircraft and burned for about fifteen seconds, being dropped in rows of six... The aircraft's type could not be determined as it appeared as a dull silhouette and distinguishing features could not be seen. Using similar tactics, the same or a second aircraft was picked up by sight at 2005 hours. A three-second burst from 200 yards range was given and the enemy aircraft was followed for a short period on AI. No return fire was experienced and no damage to enemy aircraft was observed during either of these attacks which were carried out between 7,000 and 10,000ft.'

To those who have read accounts of the triumphs in 1940 of the day fighter boys, this hardly seems to be a triumph. To a night fighter team, after months of largely empty black skies while British cities crumbled and burned underneath them and their comrades, this was a sign that things were moving in the right direction. Certainly Gibson was excited by his experience and liked to think that he had frightened one of his quarries to the extent that bombs were jettisoned. Within hours, Gibson and James had made another contact through the AI screen, though with no sighting.

With better weather there was plenty of flying, but the rest of February produced little excitement in the air for Gibson and James, though plenty more in the way of opportunities to become a team and improve their skills.

On one night, flying with Sergeant Austin, Gibson came upon an aircraft, but it turned out to be a Blenheim bomber. Sergeant James had returned to the back seat on 2 March, when there was no 'trade' to be had, so they practised interceptions with another Blenheim.

Charles Widdows was a demanding man, but he had a human side. He organised a party in Lincoln at which (unsurprisingly) much heavy drinking was done, entertainment was enjoyed through the alcoholic mist and there was considerable damage done to the venue and its stock of glasses. It was reprehensible no doubt, but it was a classic way for aircrew to escape from danger and frustration and perhaps it worked. More success awaited.

On 12/13 March Liverpool and Wallasey were attacked. In Liverpool city centre there were a number of incidents. The main post office and the telephone exchange were both hit. Gibson claimed an enemy aircraft destroyed, but he was not credited with it and the evidence is not supportive.

On the following day Liverpool docks were targeted but the main incident occurred with the bombing of St Ann's School, Chatham Place and an air raid shelter in Adlington Place. Among the deaths at the school were firewatchers, police and ARP wardens. Gibson did not achieve a victory on this day, but Bob Braham did, shooting down a Dornier Do 17.

In addition there was success at last for Charles Widdows, who destroyed a Junkers Ju 88. It broke up in the air and the pieces fell in the Louth area of Lincolnshire. Much congratulation and celebration awaited the returning heroes.   .

Three weeks later Widdows was awarded the DFC. It is arguably possible to read much between the lines of the announcement which appeared in the *London Gazette* on 4 April 1941.

'This officer has commanded the squadron since July 1940, and, under difficult circumstances, has maintained a high morale among the personnel. Wing Commander Widdows has carried out a large number of difficult patrols in bad weather and has shown extreme keenness to engage the enemy. He has flown a considerable number of hours of operational flying at night, and succeeded in destroying a Junkers 88 one night in March, 1941.'

So although the March victory is mentioned, this was not an 'immediate' award of the DFC, as has sometimes been claimed. One victory would not normally qualify a fighter pilot for such a decoration. Widdows was being rewarded for an outstanding job in bringing his squadron back to operational efficiency and for his own persistence in trying to perfect his technique and achieve success, night after night. Perhaps he had not been in all that much danger from the enemy in the preceding months, but he had survived the weather and incidents that might well have killed him.

'Gongs' can be earned in a momentary rush of blood, or at the other extreme, in gallantry which involves having considerable opportunity to think about the dangers involved. The award to Charles Widdows came firmly into the latter category, though perhaps it took imagination for authority to recognise him with the DFC at that point. It was a good month for Widdows. He had been promoted to wing commander on 1 March.

How much of the leadership style of Widdows rubbed off on Gibson can be debated, but it seems to have been a significant amount. There were certainly similarities in their approaches to commanding a squadron.

With the victories of Widdows and Braham the squadron had momentum and sadly the opportunity to exploit it. This was the time of the two-night Clydebank blitz, as the Germans targeted the docks, but often struck the packed tenements nearby. Clydeside's suffering does not seem to be as well remembered as that of some other locations, even though the *Glasgow Herald* wrote a few days after the event that, 'The cool, unwavering courage of the people is evident and when the full story of their heroism in the face of the Luftwaffe is told they will take their place alongside the citizens of London and Coventry.'

One of the German bombers, a Heinkel He 111, did not reach the target. Sergeant James, picked it up on his set and Gibson closed in from behind and below. At 100 yards distance he opened fire, only to find that very quickly the cannon jammed. With the Heinkel taking evasive action the armament came back to life and the bandit disappeared into the sea. There were no survivors.

Now beyond dispute Gibson had lost his virginity as a night fighter pilot and the inside of the Beaufighter became a very happy place, though Gibson did claim to have spared some thought for the men he had just killed. One account at least suggests that Sergeant James, despite his exhilaration, was exhausted by the effort required to restore the cannon and achieve the victory.

Some crewmen had been disappointed to find that the Beaufighter was fitted with a turret, so that they could display their skills in air gunnery. They were impressed with the cannon though, but found themselves hauling 60lb drums of ammunition out of racks and fitting them into the cannon, in the dark, wearing full kit and perhaps while the pilot was executing a tight turn.

Those finer feelings about the deceased German crew did not prevent Gibson travelling to Skegness and acquiring the dinghy from the Heinkel as a souvenir. He wrote that one body had been recovered, that of a Hauptmann (approximately a squadron leader) the man's watch and Iron Cross had been stolen and the police claimed to be searching for the thieves. The tail assembly from the Heinkel became a squadron trophy and later Gibson used the dinghy when relaxing in Cornwall.

The victory would not be immediately followed up. As is sometimes the case in March, winter weather came back and there was no flying for a time. Gibson was determined and got as far as the Beaufighter on one occasion, only to be told firmly by the station commander that he was not going anywhere.

James was absent for a time and other partners for Gibson came and went. The ORB records that on 8 April he was assailed by an intruder, as he landed, and Sergeant Bell was hit in the leg. For a seasoned Battle of the Barges man, this was all in a day's march.

Gibson did not always show disregard for danger. Richard James came back and they had some excitement during the night of St George's Day, 23 April. They lost a Junkers Ju 88, but then closed in on a Dornier Do 215. Gibson attacked twice and scored hits, but each time broke away as there was accurate return fire from the German. No victory could be confirmed. Gibson's approach to this combat is interesting in view of a misfortune which would befall Wing Commander Widdows shortly afterwards.

Meanwhile Charles Widdows had been cultivating Air Vice Marshal Trafford Leigh-Mallory, the Air Officer Commanding Fighter Command's No 11 Group. History has not been kind to the memory of Leigh-Mallory. He is often accused of not being 'one of us' amongst the pilots and to have been misguided in his decisions and pompous in making them known. He had been a pilot in the Great War and did not survive the Second World War to write his own account. The debate continues, but this was a time when Leigh-Mallory took the right decision, at least as far as Widdows was concerned.

Chapter 7

Closer to London

On 25 April 1941 No 29 Squadron was informed that it should move to the fairly new, but properly appointed, airfield at West Malling, near Maidstone in Kent. Here they would be relatively near the attractions of London and with plenty going on in the air. Widdows and Gibson immediately hopped into a Beaufighter and went down for a look. They liked what they found.

Many on the squadron had had enough of the Lincolnshire countryside, the lack of entertainment and the sometimes unfamiliar, even inexplicable, ways of people in a remote rural area. The squadron made sure that the locals noticed them going. Gibson recorded in his logbook the formation flight to their new home and noted of Wellingore, 'Everyone very pleased to leave.' They arrived at their new abode in the garden of England in some style.

A bonus for the aircrew of Fighter Command was that the people of Kent had watched from the grandstand the year before as much of the Battle of Britain had been fought overhead or off the coast. The impact had of course been far greater than around No 29's previous home. To many 'Men of Kent and Kentish Men' (and perhaps more importantly maids of Kent and Kentish maids) the 'fighter boys' were still heroes. West Malling was west of the River Medway, so No 29 had alighted in the territory of the Kentish men and maids.

No 29 Squadron settled in at West Malling at a time when a climax of a sort was going to be reached in the sky overhead, leading to plenty of targets to be found. The London Blitz would have an intense finale in mid-May. No 29 had arrived in Kent just in time for a burst of intense action.

Gibson destroyed an unidentified hostile in early May, by what he regarded as a 'lucky burst', but generally, in the months ahead he came to feel that others were moving ahead of him in terms of achievement in his present task.

Bob Braham, who had received his first DFC from the King early in the year, was soon into his stride, being credited with the destruction of a Heinkel He 111 on 8 May. His partnership with the NCO peacetime drummer 'Sticks' Gregory would begin in June. For seven months, until Braham was rested as an instructor, they scored victories steadily amongst the German bombers venturing to England.

There were other highly successful night fighter teams, who were achieving considerable results at this time. On No 604 (County of Middlesex) Squadron, Flight Lieutenant John Cunningham and his partner, Sergeant Cecil Rawnsley, a pre-war electrical engineer, aged thirty-seven, were on the way to becoming perhaps the most famous night fighter pairing of the war. The press dubbed Cunningham 'Cat's Eyes', to his displeasure and suggested that he was an enthusiastic eater of carrots. There was no benefit at the time in drawing attention to the advancing technology which he and Rawnsley were putting to outstanding effect and so he had to put up with his nickname.

Even the Boulton Paul Defiant, much derided as a day fighter and lacking AI, was proving its worth at night. One successful pairing was Flight Lieutenant Christopher 'Jumbo' Deanesly and his New Zealand air gunner, Sergeant Jack Scott, of No 256 Squadron. This unit was based at Squires Gate, Blackpool and defended Liverpool and Manchester. One of their triumphs is claimed to be the only enemy aircraft to fall in the Greater Manchester area in the course of the Second World War. During the night of 7/8 May, the Heinkel He 111, abandoned by its crew, crashed at the village of Hazel Grove, on the edge of what is now Stockport Golf Club. At this point, another Defiant night fighter squadron, No 264, was sharing West Malling with No 29 Squadron.

In contrast to the achievements just outlined, Widdows suffered a tragic experience early in the morning of 7 May. With him, as AI operator, was Sergeant Browne Ryall, who had partnered Gibson. Over the English Channel they attacked a Junkers Ju 88, but return fire from the bomber badly damaged the Beaufighter. At first Widdows considered that the aircraft was finished and ordered Ryall to bale out, which he did. Eventually, though, the pilot managed to coax the stricken machine back to West Malling and get it down in one piece. The 25-year-old Ryall was never found and he is commemorated on panel 51 of the Runnymede Memorial. It is assumed that he drowned in the Channel.

In the major German attack on London of 10/11 May 1940, the most remembered victim is the chamber of the House of Commons, which was destroyed. Elsewhere in the Palace of Westminster, the roof of Westminster Hall, scene of the trial of King Charles I, amongst many great events, was set alight, but the hall was saved.

Gibson claimed that, in seeking to defend London that night, he sighted four Heinkels, but failed to destroy any of them because his cannon kept on jamming. In contrast, the logbook of Richard James records only two sightings.

Gibson's version of events was, 'And the reason? Not the cannons at all but a simple electrical solenoid in the firing button becoming unserviceable.

Sergeant James who had, of course, been responsible for the interceptions, was furious! Four Huns! For months we had stooged around, thinking ourselves lucky if we saw one. Then we had seen four fat ones with bomb loads on, and they had all got away. We saw them – unlike most things that got away.' Nobody is going to establish the truth of those efforts now, but frustration was showing.

Intelligence officers could be a source of annoyance on squadrons. Gibson thought that the one who belonged to No 29 was better than many. However, IOs as a breed were people you argued with over claims. Those who had flown themselves, perhaps in the First World War, could be respected. Others, including those who had been school teachers in peacetime, were not normally admitted to the club of flyers.

Some had realised that they had been too generous in allowing claims at first and toughened up. All kinds of reasons could be found for denying a claim, especially at night when the crew itself was less likely to have seen the outcome and a shortage of other witnesses was to be expected. There were even political reasons for denying an addition to someone's score, such as that the aircraft had fallen in another sector and so must have been shot down by their chaps.

There was less opportunity for anyone to improve his score from the second half of May as the intensity of the blitz abated. Visits to the dentist did not help Gibson's mood. At the time the pilots attributed the quietness in the sky to the need for the Germans to send aircraft to the Mediterranean area, for the invasion of Crete. The forthcoming launch of Operation Barbarossa against Russia was a bigger factor.

As summer started, Charles Widdows was posted away, though only as far as the West Malling station commander's desk. His replacement as CO of No 29 Squadron was 27-year-old Wing Commander Edward 'Ted' Colbeck-Welch, who Gibson would come to like and respect. Once again, aspects of a leadership style would transfer to the subordinate.

Squadron commanders had many duties to attend to besides flying, some taking those other duties rather more seriously than others. On occasions when Colbeck-Welch couldn't lead the squadron it fell to Gibson to do so. His experience was steadily expanding.

Colbeck-Welch was a regular officer. He was not yet decorated, something that some people could look down on at this stage of the war. On the other hand he had relevant experience, arriving from No 219 Squadron, at Tangmere, which also flew Beaufighters. He had started his operational career in 1934, flying the Vickers Vildebeest bomber and army co-operation aircraft.

Colbeck-Welch would receive the DFC in 1942 for his performance while in command of No 29 Squadron. His citation praised his 'tenacity and a fine fighting spirit' on over seventy night sorties and also drew attention to an occasion in January 1942 when, 'after a pursuit lasting nearly twenty minutes, he shot down a Dornier 217 into the sea some seventy miles from the coast.' This was said to be the second enemy aircraft that Colbeck-Welch had shot down at night far out to sea.

Edward Colbeck-Welch was an air vice marshal when he retired from the RAF in 1963 on medical grounds. He died in 1994.

There was training and there were patrols that produced nothing to cheer about for Gibson and James, who was still sitting beside him, though occasionally Pilot Officer Willis stood in; 'patrol and searchlight co-op', 'X-raid patrol', 'no contacts', 'stooge patrol' read the entries. The Germans were minelaying and mounting what were effectively nuisance raids – Bomber Command under Harris would do much the same with the intention of keeping German factory workers awake – but this didn't amount to rich pickings.

A notable exception came on 7 July, shortly after Gibson achieved his 'scraper ring' by being promoted to squadron leader. A Heinkel He 111 was found minelaying over the Thames Estuary near Sheerness and exploded after a two second burst. There were no survivors. Generally though the minelaying aircraft were hard to find and despatch.

The new rank for Gibson brought with it full responsibility for the squadron's 'A' flight. Bob Braham also became a flight commander, having charge of 'B' Flight. In September he was awarded a bar to his DFC. The citation said that he had destroyed three enemy aircraft and damaged another.

Gibson had acquired a Labrador puppy and called it Nigger. He reckoned to take his new companion with him frequently on patrol.

Gradually the point arrived when Gibson would be considered due for a rest and a new posting. Would he suffer what, for him, would be the unwelcome (as well as usual in the circumstances) fate of being posted to an OTU? Or could the promise made to him by Arthur Harris be resurrected and implemented?

The posting that came up was to No 51 OTU at Cranfield, south west of Bedford, where he would become chief flying instructor. This was despite some lobbying by Gibson, including a visit to No 5 Group headquarters at Grantham, where Harris had long departed for Whitehall and subsequently on a mission to the United States.

Bob Braham went to Cranfield too, though he was a rather different man to Gibson and enjoyed the experience just a little more.

For Gibson, the experience was deeply unpleasant. He hated being away from the action, he missed West Malling and returned there when excuses arose, he was away from Eve (no point in finding a joint home in Bedfordshire, he felt, when he was determined that his stay would be short), all in all, he was a man of action and not a man to smooth the path of others to the action. There were various types of aircraft to fly, though plenty of bumpf to deal with, and the danger, in a different way, was probably just as great as his previous posting given the number of accidents. The situation, though, offered little consolation for a squadron leader with two DFCs and a feeling that perhaps he had not yet quite justified them.

Chapter 8

Back to Bombers

In February 1942, a momentous point in the history of the RAF in the Second World War arrived, with the appointment of Arthur Harris as Air Officer Commanding in Chief, Bomber Command. Harris replaced Air Marshal Sir Richard Peirse, a man with some presence, who was, nonetheless, presiding over failure. Despite their losses, the bombers were not achieving anything like the impact which was expected of them.

Peirse suffered from lack of resources and perhaps a lack of the willingness displayed by his successor to fight for those resources. Peirse went off to the Far East, where he eventually impressed Lord Louis Mountbatten, as a key member of his South East Asia Command. He was removed again after he began an affair with Lady Auchinleck.

Now Harris was in a position to keep his promise to find a top command for Gibson. In addition, he needed men like Gibson to beef up the leadership of a command that had performed with great gallantry, but had not achieved great success and was therefore under extreme scrutiny from those who could influence or decide what part it would play in the future war effort.

It was in March that Harris contacted Air Vice Marshal Slessor at No 5 Group and quickly Gibson was removed from the hell, as he saw it, of Cranfield. Before writing to Slessor, Harris had summoned Gibson by telegram to the Bomber Command headquarters at High Wycombe and given him some idea of what was afoot.

Harris wanted Gibson to command one of the squadrons now taking on the new Avro Lancaster four-engined bomber. The chief left Slessor with room for manoeuvre though and that officer's decision was to send Gibson to No 106 Squadron at Coningsby, where it had only just discarded Gibson's old aircraft the Hampden. The replacement for that now well outdated type was not yet the Lancaster, though Gibson knew that they would soon arrive. Gibson had to convert to the Avro Manchester, a disastrous aircraft, alleged to be more dangerous to its crews than it was to the enemy. Not for the first time he had arrived on a squadron in transition from one type to another.

So Gibson was now highly visible to Harris, though nowhere near directly reporting to him. Gibson's immediate boss was the station commander,

Group Captain 'Daddy' Rowe, a pipe smoking dahlia lover, to whom Gibson immediately warmed.

Now, working at Coningsby, almost in the shadow of Tattersall Castle, one of the favourite Lincolnshire aids for sprog navigators, Gibson had the opportunity to put into practice his own ideas on leadership, mixed in with what he had learned from the COs of his previous squadrons.

He listened to his new adjutant, Charles Martin and he listened to the aircrew who would now serve under him. He defended his new charges too against demands from group (and indirectly from Harris) that maximum numbers of aircraft should be sent on operations.

In Gibson's view there was still a very good case for allowing newcomers to play themselves in as second pilots or, in the case of whole crews, on 'gardening' trips. Thus he resisted some of the instructions he was given. This placed this 23-year-old on the credit side as far as his men were concerned. In the opposite column though were entered various temperamental outbursts and snap judgements, felt to be very unfair on some of the men singled out.

The management theory is sometimes put forward that a new boss has until lunchtime on the first day to make the impression on his staff that will stay with them for good or bad. In the large family of a bomber squadron, the new CO perhaps had longer. Early assessments were mixed and the views held of the CO would remain mixed. A new nickname for Gibson was not long in coming – 'The Boy Emperor'.

Despite being somebody who was so keen to return to action, Gibson sensibly exercised restraint and, in terms of operations, played himself in gradually. Aircraft, as well as crews, were allowed to work up to the big occasions. The first Lancaster operation had been flown by No 44 Squadron on 3/4 March when mines were laid off the German coast. On the same night there was a considerable boost to bomber morale when well over 200 aircraft (at the time a very large number for a single target attack) set out for the Renault lorry plant at Billancourt, to the west of Paris, where the company had placed its main operations since 1898.

The concentrated attack wrecked much of the factory. Bomber Command had demonstrated that it could hit a target and do damage to the German war effort (the plant produced 14,000 vehicles a year for the German forces), though the later estimation was that less than two months of production had been lost. Equally good news was that there were no mid-air collisions, despite the number of aircraft involved and casualties were extremely light.

As with Gibson, the new man at the top of the command was inducting himself. For Harris, though, there was more haste. He certainly did not have much time to make an impression before the course of Bomber Command's war might be changed. The command's performance had to improve.

Harris also had new instructions to follow. A few days before he took command, an Air Ministry directive, based on war cabinet decisions, had been sent to Air Vice Marshal Baldwin the acting commander-in-chief of Bomber Command. Harris inherited this directive, which instituted area bombing by authorising the use of bombers 'without restriction' and listing primary industrial areas for attack, including Cologne, Dusseldorf and Essen. There was a list of other industrial areas to be considered for attack, including Lübeck, Bremen, Kiel and Schweinfurt.

The next day, Sir Charles Portal, Chief of the Air Staff, apparently wondering whether the directive had been sufficiently to the point, issued a further instruction, using the words, 'I suppose it is clear that the aiming points are to be the built-up areas, not for instance the dockyards or the aircraft factories.'

At the end of March nearly 250 bombers took the area policy to the medieval north German town of Lübeck, 'built more like a fire lighter than a human habitation,' to quote Harris. It was also lightly defended. The crews watched the bonfire from above and many would remember the sight for the remainder of their lives.

This was the background against which Gibson took command of No 106 Squadron and he would immediately find inspiration in the deeds of the Lancasters that, in mid-April, carried out the daylight attack on the *Maschinenfabrik Augsburg Nurnberg AG* (MAN) diesel engine factory at Augsburg in southern Germany. The leader of this operation, Squadron Leader John Nettleton of No 44 Squadron, survived and was awarded the Victoria Cross.

Gibson's logbook tells us that his first operation with his new squadron was a minelaying sortie on 22 April. Accompanied by Warrant Officer Boyce, Sergeant Greenwood, Pilot Officer Wickens, Sergeant Carter, Sergeant Jordan and Sergeant Youngs, he flew to the Baltic and dropped four mines in the required positions.

Before the end of the month Gibson participated in a main force attack with 106 Squadron for the first time, with Rostock on the Baltic as the objective. This was a frequent target at the time.

May came and Lancasters started to appear on the squadron, though, despite the excitement generated, their arrival and the conversion of crews to fly them was a slow business. Not only was the Lancaster, in the view of many, the greatest bomber of the Second World War, it was a vast improvement on the Manchester. If you were on a bomber squadron in the spring of 1942, this was a very pleasant set of circumstances to find yourself in. Gibson was taken up in one by one of the flight commanders, as his initiation on the type.

It would be July before Gibson had the opportunity to fly the Lancaster in anger. One reason for the delay was a mystery illness, followed by recovery leave, which caused him to spend time away from the squadron and to miss the publicity coup achieved by Arthur Harris, which would launch him into the public mind.

If nicknames imply character, Harris was larger than life. To his peers, he was 'Bert', a common service appellation for people named Harris. Quickly to the man and woman in the street, he would become 'Bomber', after a short period when newspapers, to his considerable displeasure, referred to him as 'Ginger'. He also came to be known as 'Butcher' or 'Butch', among the men and women who served under him. This perhaps implied that they felt that he did not have regard for their lives, or those of the Germans whose bombing he was leading – yet at the same time he generated tremendous loyalty.

At High Wycombe Harris understood the value of public opinion in ensuring the future of the command. He railed against what he saw as idle criticism by politicians and others, which inevitably surfaced in the press and what he saw as the lack of interest shown by Air Ministry publicity types in the achievements of his men. This was not only an issue about the future of the command, but a danger to morale, in the Harris mind. Stories with immediate impact were needed to create the right public climate, not merely pronouncements on long gone raids, after all the intelligence information had been properly studied.

A bald statement of what was to come appeared in the *Daily Express*, which had previously enthused about Harris as a commander in a good English tradition which encompassed Wellington. Now the paper quoted Harris as saying, 'If I could send a thousand bombers to Germany every night, it would end the war by the autumn. We are going to bomb Germany incessantly... the day is coming when the USA and ourselves will put over such a force that the Germans will scream for mercy.'

It was wishful thinking to a large extent, but the thousand plan was indeed brought to reality. On 30/31 May Cologne became the first target to be hit with this size of force. Originally the intended target had been Hamburg, but the advice of the meteorologists intervened.

There was a scramble to achieve a force of 1,000 bombers, particularly after 250 from Coastal Command were withdrawn late in the planning. Mainly due to Harris's Senior Air Staff Officer, Air Vice Marshal Robert 'Sandy' Saundby, it was possible to claim four figures on the night.

This could not be done though without involving aircraft and crews from operational training units and others with non-operational status. One of the aircraft that failed to return was an elderly Vickers Wellington 1A from the Central Gunnery School, shot down by a night fighter, with only one survivor.

Another feature of the operation was the introduction of a full 'bomber stream' with all aircraft using the same height and speed, and individual aircraft being given individual height and timing instructions to minimise the risk of collisions.

When crews were being briefed prior to the attack they, including men at No 106 Squadron, received a personal message from Harris which read:

'The force of which you form a part tonight is at least twice the size and has more than four times the carrying capacity of the largest air force ever before concentrated on one objective. You have an opportunity, therefore, to strike a blow at the enemy which will resound not only throughout Germany, but throughout the world. In your hands lie the means of destroying a major part of the resources by which the enemy's war effort is maintained. It depends, however, on each individual crew whether full concentration is achieved. Press home your attack to your precise objective with the utmost determination and resolution in the foreknowledge that, if you individually succeed, the most shattering and devasting blow will have been delivered against the very vitals of the enemy. Let him have it – right on the chin.'

Forty aircraft, plus an intruder Blenheim, did not return from the operation, and a number of others were lost in accidents on their return. Some pundits had feared a much higher cost.

Gibson, laid low, would learn of the loss of two of his Manchesters, both of which had been loaned to No 50 Squadron. One was flown by Flying Officer Leslie Manser, aged 20, rejected by both the Army and the Royal Navy before he joined the RAF, who had collected his aircraft from Coningsby on the day of the raid. He was killed when he remained at the controls of the doomed Manchester, hit by flak, long enough for the rest of the crew to escape. The co-pilot reported that in the last seconds before the crash he had attempted to clip on Manser's parachute and had been dismissed with the words, 'For God's sake get out'.

Five months later the award of a posthumous Victoria Cross to Leslie Manser was announced. Five of Manser's crew had reached home, aided by the French Resistance, to bear witness to his heroism. Shortly after the

Cologne operation, further 'thousand' raids were mounted against Essen and Bremen.

On his return to the squadron Gibson encountered, and began his close association with, one of the men who would follow him to the German dams in 1943. Pilot Officer David Shannon, RAAF, had arrived in No 106 Squadron while Gibson was away and had participated in the thousand bomber trip to Bremen. On that operation the remarkably youthful looking 'Dave' Shannon (he was actually aged twenty) had flown as second pilot to Squadron Leader John Wooldridge, Officer Commanding 'B' Flight.

Shannon had enough confidence and brashness to impress Gibson and he was competent too, not least in a Lancaster. In addition, Gibson was impressed that the Australians and the other 'colonials' had come to Britain to fight when they didn't have to. Shannon joined his CO on a training flight and found himself hired as second pilot and flight engineer for Gibson's first Lancaster operation.

There were aircrew who were Gibson's type and who would be admitted to a developing inner circle. There were others, often non-pilots and the less obviously aggressive, more intellectual sorts (and, of course, those who weren't commissioned) who just weren't his cup of tea, or, actually, pint of beer.

Richard Morris points out that Wooldridge, a music lover, was one of those who did not join the circle. He wasn't Gibson friendship material – and there was an incident where Wooldridge managed to scheme his way into taking Gibson's preferred aircraft on an operation, to the CO's extreme displeasure – but it would seem that Wooldridge, in any case had no desire to be one of the chosen ones.

Morris also notes that Gibson was in the habit of picking up hitch-hiking ground crew returning to the station. This was more to do with getting the men back as quickly as possible to their contribution to the war effort, rather than any great desire to break down the barriers between officers and other ranks. The point was illustrated by an NCO rear gunner who recalled walking into a pub in Boston with some pals. Gibson was already there and ignored them. They quickly found a better atmosphere in another pub.

At this time, as part of his crash course on Lancasters, Gibson had flown with another man, far more experienced than Shannon, who would join him at No 617 Squadron; Flying Officer John 'Hoppy' Hopgood was a public schoolboy (Marlborough) who would earn two DFCs during his service with No 106 Squadron.

Soon after midnight on 8 July Gibson lifted off from Coningsby in Lancaster R5681, bound for the submarine yards at Wilhelmshaven. As well as Dave Shannon he had with him Flying Officer Vivian as navigator, Pilot Officer Ruskell as bomb aimer, Sergeant Jordan (wireless operator), Flight Lieutenant Combie in the mid upper turret and Pilot Officer Wickens in the rear turret. Ruskell and Wickens were among those who qualified to socialise with Gibson in addition to flying with him.

Gibson recorded that he bombed from 12,000ft and was confident that his bombs had fallen in the dock area, though he could not be sure that the submarine section had been hit. It was a 'good prang', despite the opposition being fairly accurate.

It was probably a night fighter that disposed of the one No 106 Lancaster that did not come back from Wilhelmshaven. Pilot Officer Broderick and four of his crew have no known grave. The other two were buried, one each in the Netherlands and Germany.

Submarines were on the agenda again on Gibson's next op, still with Shannon alongside him. They flew in daylight and bad weather to Danzig and failed to bomb the target. Instead they scored a near miss on a ship and the gunners let fly at a flak ship.

In mid-July Gibson took part in an intended operation to Essen which was recalled as he crossed the enemy coast. For the first time there were three future Dam Busters in the aircraft, the third being a new wireless operator, Pilot Officer R.E.G. Hutchison, known as 'Hutch', who, despite a lack of enthusiasm for alcohol, would become one of Gibson's friends.

Progress was being made in improving the performance of No 106 Squadron. July closed with a trip to Dusseldorf in which light opposition was encountered and the city was set 'well alight'. Bombs were dropped on the city centre from 12,000ft.

Gibson found the opposition light, but for many it was a night of drama. More than 600 bombers took part and a lot of damage was done. There were a good many casualties too, including amongst crews despatched by OTUs, though this was not a 'thousand' operation.

From No 106 Squadron one aircraft did not make it home. The Lancaster flown by Warrant Officer Merralls, who held the DFC and the DFM, crashed near Cologne. He and his crew – Sergeant Gaskell, Sergeant Cooper, Flight Sergeant Smith, DFM, Sergeant Holmes, Sergeant Ellis-Buxton and Sergeant Grimshaw – all died.

There was a sequel to the Dusseldorf raid and one that provided evidence that Gibson was getting somewhere with the squadron. The Air Officer Commanding No 5 Group, Air Vice Marshal Alec Coryton, wrote to the station commander at Coningsby congratulating the squadrons under his command on their efforts on the raid, saying it was worthy of the highest praise.

Shortly after this Coryton would reveal to Gibson an aspect of his character which would eventually lead to his removal from his post and his replacement by Ralph Cochrane. Alec Coryton went back a long way with Arthur Harris. Coryton had served under Harris in India and his CV also included teaching Prince Albert, the future King George VI, to fly. It was no coincidence that he was now serving Harris again. The AOC had great regard for Coryton and had chosen a number of men he knew well and found impressive to work closely with him – on the occasions when he could get his way with Sir Charles Portal on such matters.

However, Coryton was deeply concerned to avoid casualties, to an extent perhaps greater than a senior commander in wartime can afford to be. He found himself in growing dispute with Harris over some of the operations he was ordered to carry out. Probert says that the breaking point came early in 1943 when there was a requirement to send a small force of Lancasters to the Ruhr. It was one of those attempts to keep German workers from their sleep rather than do direct damage to the enemy's industry. The weather was very poor and Coryton objected to the instructions he was given, in terms of the risk involved, compared with the benefits to be obtained.

In an unusually personalised, 'more in sorrow than in anger', letter to his old colleague, on 23 February 1943, Harris praised Coryton's enormous contribution, high sense of duty and outstanding efficiency, as well as his group's many achievements, but said that he could not put up with the persistent disputing of operational instructions.

'I have repeatedly reminded you that it is for me to say what shall be done and when and broadly how; and for you to accomplish it. The responsibility for the outcome is mine and mine alone... where you fail is through your inability to divest yourself of a moral responsibility which is not yours.'

Thus Harris opened his heart a little in despatching Coryton. He stressed that he had no intention of making an adverse report about his subordinate. He also accepted that Coryton might be right; however, he was not the commander-in-chief.

After this Coryton went to the Air Ministry and then to the Far East, eventually retiring from the RAF as Air Chief Marshal Sir Alec Coryton. He died in 1981.

The contact between Gibson and Coryton came over the development of a new bomb, and bombsights to go with it, designed to beat the armour plating of warships and do catastrophic damage inside. With some similarity to the Dams raid to come Gibson's squadron was required to test two bombsights.

At first delivering the bombs from low level was a possibility, however Gibson (perhaps without too much difficulty) convinced Coryton that attacking capital ships from low level was not on. The casualty rate would be enormous.

Training came to concentrate on the Stabilized Automatic Gunsight, (SABS), which would be used from around 8,000 to 8,500ft. Meanwhile Gibson fitted in more minelaying sorties and a visit to the Roman city of Mainz on the west bank of the Rhine, where the result of the bombing could not be observed because evasive action was taken. There was considerable light flak.

The opportunity to try out the new found expertise with SABS arrived on 27 August. Squadron Leader D.S. Richardson, a bombing specialist who had been sent to Coningsby in a training role, took part in the attack, acting as Gibson's bomb aimer. According to the logbook, this was Gibson's sixth different bomb aimer in six successive operations. There were a variety of other crew members at this time, including the fact that Dave Shannon had moved on to fly on his own account in the squadron. Hutch was back at the wireless set, having not been part of Gibson's crew since they had been to Dusseldorf.

Nine aircraft set off for Gdynia in the Baltic, under a full moon, where they were briefed to seek out the not yet completed German aircraft carrier, *Graf Zeppelin*, as well as the capital ships *Scharnhorst* and *Gneisenau*. Despite concern about it at the time, the *Graf Zeppelin* never went into operational service. It fell into the hands of the Russians at the end of the war and was eventually deliberately sunk, having been used for target practice. The German Navy was never able to deploy an aircraft carrier during the Second World War.

For the British there was unfinished business with the *Scharnhorst* and *Gnesienau*, not least because just over six months earlier they had been allowed to dash through the English Channel, with a totally inadequate effort made to stop them. They had been attacked by Fleet Air Arm Fairey Swordfish, all of which had been shot down, a fate that could easily be predicted by their crews before they took off. Five men were rescued from the Channel and all were decorated, the four officers with the DSO and the one rating with the CGM.

Lieutenant Commander Eugene Esmonde who led the attack was awarded a posthumous Victoria Cross. Most unusually, the initial signature on the recommendation for the award, was that of an RAF officer, Wing Commander Tom Gleave, Officer Commanding RAF Manston, from which the Swordfish had set off. The German war diary for 12 February 1942 included the words, 'the mothball attack of a handful of ancient planes, piloted by men whose bravery surpasses any other action by either side that day.'

Now Gibson and his men could make another effort to eliminate these sharp pains in the side of British forces. 'Going round again' was not a popular pastime for many in Bomber Command. With haze over the target though, Gibson made around twelve runs, with Richardson straining to get a sight of the *Gneisenau*. He didn't manage it, but they bombed and missed. Nobody hit the target that night, although higher authority accepted that an excellent effort had been made both in terms of training and the determined attempts to complete the operation successfully.

On the same night a much bigger force of Bomber Command aircraft had struck at Kassel, doing considerable harm to its industrial output, but with a large number of Wellingtons, Stirlings and Lancasters, plus one Halifax and one Hampden being lost.

This was the time when the Pathfinder Force was being formed, after much opposition from Arthur Harris, who thoroughly disliked the concept of an elite being created within his command. An early setback for the new force occurred on 1 September, when the target was Saarbrucken, but Gibson and others dropped their load on Saarlouis instead, misled by inaccurately placed markers.

The squadron had developed tremendously under Gibson's leadership and continued to do so. There was a blow, however, to Gibson and many others in the middle of September. On the night of 15/16 September, bombers were sent to Essen and Gibson did not fly. This was another operation that produced high casualties. Again the OTUs suffered. The crews they put out were usually a mixture of screened veterans and men still under training.

Personnel watching at Coningsby for the return of No 106 Squadron aircraft waited in vain for three crews, those of Squadron Leader C.M. Howell, Pilot Officer W.O. Williams and Pilot Officer D.J. Downer, all well known faces. None came back and nobody survived the crashes of the three Lancasters. The mix of nationalities to be found in Bomber Command crews is illustrated by the fact that, as well as the RAF, the Royal Australian Air Force, Royal New Zealand Air Force and Royal Canadian Air Force all lost men amongst the twenty-one who were killed.

Now administrative and physical upheaval arrived, with the news that No 106 would move from Coningsby to Syerston in Nottinghamshire.

In a paper presented in 2006 to a reunion of the Royal Air Force Airfield Construction Officers Association, Sebastian Cox, head of the Air Historical Branch (RAF) explained the situation.

Airfield construction in the 1920s ensured that the RAF pointed south towards France. German and Japanese militarism was the catalyst for a change in the 1930s, when new construction in such counties as Norfolk, Suffolk,

Huntingdonshire and Yorkshire ensured that the RAF now pointed east, of much more use if Germany was to be the main target.

Now, three years into the war, the problem was that the airfields were struggling to cope with the latest heavy bombers. Existing runways needed to be lengthened, new ones built and all the infrastructure to sustain the bombing campaign had also to be developed.

So, Gibson and his squadron were to move. The traditional shoot up of Coningsby as they left got a little out of hand, complaints were made and Gibson was furious. As a result, two pilots were placed under station arrest when they reached Syerston. Gibson's desire to send people to war against Germany quickly overcame his anger and the pair were let out and sent back to the cockpits of their Lancasters.

Chapter 9

Gus Walker at Syerston

O ne benefit at Syerston was a station commander to whom Gibson could relate very well. Group Captain Augustus 'Gus' Walker had played rugby for England (though he had missed his blue at Cambridge) and had the boisterous approach to life often associated with the rugby clubhouse, as well as a determination to hit the enemy as hard as possible. He had entered the RAF from Cambridge University, five years before the war and was a former CO of No 50 Squadron, where he had earned the DFC and the DSO.

Gibson recalled that Walker, 'used to lead us around the countryside practising navigation at nought feet.' He was a great man, thought Gibson and, 'I know that all of 106 would like it to be said that he was one of the finest station masters that they had ever served under.' Walker would rise to be Air Chief Marshal Sir Augustus Walker, but long before that he and Gibson (on the fringe) would be involved in a blood curdling adventure.

Losses on Gibson's squadron mounted again. On 15/16 October Cologne was the target. Gibson returned just before midnight and noted the high wind which he encountered. The ORB entry reads,

'Cloud over the target at 6,000ft, visibility was good. Identified bridges over the river and dropped bombs from 10,000ft – they were believed to have burst on the east side of the river. Flak was very heavy and the aircraft was hit. Bomb load, 1 x 4000lb, 12 SBC (4lb).'

After bombs had demolished walls and smashed open windows and doors, incendiaries were then intended to have more opportunity of doing their job. The hollow aluminium SBC (small bomb container) had unsurprisingly been designed to carry small bombs. Now Gibson and many others were taking SBCs, after some modification, to the Reich with stacks of incendiaries.

Despite the damage to his aircraft, Gibson returned to Syerston. Three Lancasters from his squadron did not; one was flown by one of the flight commanders, Squadron Leader Charles Hill, DFC, the others by Pilot Officer Crowfoot, DFC and Pilot Officer White, RCAF.

The circumstances of the loss of Hill's aircraft are unclear and there were no survivors to give an account. Crowfoot's aircraft was hit by flak shortly after bombing. This killed two of the crew and eventually four men survived to become prisoners of war. White's aircraft fell to a night fighter over the Netherlands on the return journey. He and three of his crew survived as prisoners, but Pilot Officer Marshall, RNZAF, the navigator and the two air gunners, Sergeant Garbett and Sergeant Piddock did not. For the commanding officer there was the task of writing twenty-one letters, or at least supervising that task and it was something that Gibson normally took very seriously.

The wireless operator of Hill's aircraft, 26-year-old Sergeant John Ernest Bellamy, was one of those and the letter would have gone to his widow, Mrs Olive Mary Bellamy who was living in Yorkshire at the end of the war.

Flight Sergeant Benjamin George Stretch, the navigator, was a 24-year-old Welshman. Like his comrades he was buried in the Rheinberg War Cemetery. He is somebody whose name can also be found on the war memorial in his home town – Fishguard in Pembrokeshire. His parents would have received the letter.

The point is often made that the Bomber Command aircrew were young. Many were, the youngest member of Hill's crew was the 19-year-old flight engineer, Sergeant Cecil Bruce Horne. Dangerous though the work of Bomber Command was, it was also a means by which much older men could go to war.

Chorley in *Bomber Command Losses* notes that, in a Halifax of No 103 Squadron, which also failed to return that night, the rear gunner, Sergeant B.W. Vaughan was forty-three. He was far from being the oldest man to lose his life flying in a bomber in the Second World War. Poignantly, three weeks later an award of the DFM was promulgated for Sergeant Vaughan. It was 'in the pipeline' at the time of his death.

Two days after this attack, members of the squadron were flying in daylight in an operation that continues to be quoted today as one of the RAF's achievements.

The RAF website explains:

'This famous raid was carried out against the large Schneider factory at Le Creusot, situated more than 300 miles inside France. The factory was regarded as the French equivalent to Krupps and produced heavy guns, railway engines and, it was believed, tanks and armoured cars. A large workers' housing estate was situated at one end of the factory. Bomber

Command had been given this as the highest priority target in France for a night attack but only in the most favourable of conditions. (Air Chief Marshal) Harris decided to attack by day, at low level, despite the fate of the force sent to Augsburg exactly six months earlier, when seven out of the twelve Lancasters dispatched were shot down. The task was given to Air Vice Marshal Coryton's 5 Group and its nine Lancaster squadrons carried out a series of low-level practice flights over England.'

The force of ninety-four Lancasters (eighty-eight of them to bomb the main target) was led by Wing Commander L.C. Slee of No 49 Squadron. There was no fighter escort for the force and equally no intervention from hostile fighters as the bombers skimmed the trees across France; two men were, however, injured by bird strikes. The target was reached at sunset. Some bombs fell short, but many hit the target. Much credit for the generally successful outcome was given to Slee's navigator, Pilot Officer A.S. Grant.

The only aircraft lost was one from No 61 Squadron, also based at Syerston and tasked to bomb the nearby Montchanin transformer station, which flew too low and crashed in the target area. The mid upper gunner survived.

Gibson and Hopgood flew two of the other five aircraft to attack this target. Hopgood too flew over enthusiastically low and was caught by the blast of his own 500lb bombs. He got back, but the aircraft suffered plenty of damage.

Although the crews who took part had undertaken some special training, there was a disappointed air at High Wycombe when it came to analyse the results. Perhaps more training would have enabled a categoric claim to be made that no civilians had been killed, as well as more damage inflicted.

Two more attacks followed for Gibson in October. They gave him and his men new scenery to inspect in the middle of very long flights. First they went to Genoa and then they returned to Italy to strike at Milan. November too would be taken up with the assault on Italy, with raids on Genoa and Turin.

Politics at the highest level influenced the choice of these targets. A debate raged between the leaders of Great Britain, the United States and Russia, over how the defeat of Germany was to be pursued. An early assault on Germany through northwest Europe was nowhere near a possibility at that stage, whatever the Russians might demand.

Finally there was an agreement on a joint American and British invasion of French North Africa to sweep 'the Hun' away, make the Mediterranean more hospitable and build a platform for an Allied entry into southern Europe the following year. At first it was to be Operation Gymnast, then Super Gymnast.

When it took place from 8 November 1942 it was Operation Torch. Bomber Command mounted its Italian campaign at this time in support of Torch.

The reaction at Syerston was a mixture of concern at the length of the flight involved and an opinion that these would not be dangerous targets. The popular view of the lack of calibre of the Italian armed forces when compared with the Germans, seemed to some to have been confirmed when the Italian Air Force failed to show a great deal of enthusiasm for a fight.

A remarkable success was the verdict on the first raid in the series, that on Genoa. There were no losses, which was a considerable achievement, even if the opposition was not of the sternest. Arthur Harris, though, was far from happy. Sending his men and aircraft to Italy meant that they were not being despatched to Germany, where the war would be won. Things became worse for the commander-in-chief when he was required to submit to the prime minister and the chief of the air staff proposals for taking further steps to take Italy out of the war.

A few hours after No 106 Squadron returned to base, the opening shots were fired in the second, more famous, battle of El Alamein. The battle of Stalingrad was already exacting terrible casualties and perhaps had a greater impact on history, but El Alamein had a major impact at macro and micro level. Rommel, the German commander, was decisively beaten and at last the British Army had a major success to trumpet. At home, the prime minister led the celebrations. On 10 November the annual Lord Mayor's banquet in the City of London (as a wartime measure a lunchtime occasion) he was able to say, 'Now this is not the end. It is not even the beginning of the end. But it is perhaps the end of the beginning.'

Churchill also harked back to traditional post-war Britain, by ordering the Sunday morning ringing of church bells in celebration. As Roy Jenkins noted in his biography of Churchill, 'Early in the Churchill government they had been silenced, except in the event of invasion when their peals would give a series of linked local warnings. Churchill typically missed these familiar sounds of an English Sunday, although there is no known instance of his responding to their summons when at Chartwell.'

As Britain enjoyed the glow of success, the battle of Stalingrad began to turn in favour of the Russians and Operation Torch began.

The Italian campaign waged by Bomber Command continued. On 18 November, for example, there was a 'good trip' to the Fiat works at Turin, after which Gibson landed at the fighter airfield at Middle Wallop in north Hampshire, now the headquarters of the Army Air Corps. Here John Searby, one of the 106 Squadron flight commanders, and a man growing in stature in Gibson's eyes, witnessed his boss start a row with night fighter personnel over the cushiness of their life. To Searby this was a sign of increasing strain.

'Johnny' Searby was described by Gibson as 'a little older than the average, rather taciturn – sometimes severe – but a very good-hearted fellow.' Searby, a former aircraft apprentice at Halton, would go on to his own fame in the RAF. He would command both No 106 and No 83 Squadrons and, while in the latter post, he acted as master bomber on the vaunted attack on the German research station at Peenemünde in the Baltic. The citation for his immediate DSO for that operation stressed his 'faultless leadership, great courage and resolution throughout.'

Turin again at the end of the month, with take off at 1900 hours on 28 November. A 'grand prang' according to Gibson, and in the ORG it can be read that

> 'Bombing conditions very good. Target in bombsight when bombing from 8,000ft and bombs seen to burst in centre of town. Flew around over target for thirty minutes taking a movie film of the bombing – this turned out to be very successful. Passenger taken on this trip – Major Mulloch, the 5 Group Flak Liaison Officer. Bomb load: 1 x 4,000lb, 12 SBC (4lb).'

Italian operations continued into December and on Tuesday, 8 December occurred the incident that changed Gus Walker's life and had a considerable impact on Gibson too, though he did not take part in the attack on Turin. The pair watched the Lancasters of Nos 61 and 106 squadrons taxi-ing before take off. Walker saw that burning incendiaries were falling from a 61 Squadron aircraft, being used as a reserve that night, which happened to be close to the airfield's main bomb dump.

Walker's reaction was to run from the control tower to his car and drive to the spot, where he took charge of the attempts by firefighters to deal with the situation. Gallant attempts to move the lighted incendiaries were still going on when the 4000lb bomb on the Lancaster exploded. Injuries to those nearby were inevitably severe. One of the firecrew died later, another lost a foot. Gus Walker was hurled away and very badly injured, though he remained conscious.

At No. 4 RAF Hospital Rauceby Walker's right arm was amputated just above the elbow. At first, given his precarious condition, the surgeon who arrived at Syerston had considered performing the amputation at the airfield.

While Walker was being treated in the sick quarters at Syerston, before being removed to Rauceby, the remains of his right arm were held for a time by a Rauceby theatre nurse, who had came with the hospital's mobile surgical team. Corporal Margaret, 'Maggie' or 'Butch' North found herself in an awkward and uncomfortable position and asked for help. Gibson stepped forward and supported her back with his legs.

Walker had recently married a WAAF who was the widow of an officer lost on bombing operations in 1941. When Corporal North came to Walker's bedside after his operation she found Mrs Walker there and the 'boyish-looking' Gibson. Thus a relationship started between North and Gibson.

Gus Walker not only recovered, but was back at his post two months later and flew again, attaching his newly-acquired false arm to the control column of the aircraft. He became base commander at Pocklington (when a new system had been established of grouping a number of airfields together in the command structure) and was senior air staff officer at No 4 Group.

After the war his posting included officer commanding RAF Coningsby and, while commandant of the RAF flying college at Manby, he flew the Handley Page Hastings transport and troop carrier aircraft on polar navigation exercises. He converted to jets and flew the English Electric Canberra. He played golf and refereed rugby at the top level. He died in 1986. In recent years a blue plaque was placed on Gus Walker's childhood home in the Yorkshire village of Garforth.

At the beginning of 1943 Essen was seen as a key target, assisted by the advent of Oboe, a major blind bombing system using two ground stations and a pulse repeater in aircraft (Mosquitos of No 109 Squadron at this stage). Gibson flew to Essen, taking off in the late afternoon of 11 January. He had a new bomb aimer, Sub Lieutenant Gerard Muttrie, a Navy type flying on attachment with Bomber Command. Muttrie would fly with Gibson on further occasions and was lost, still with the squadron and by now a lieutenant, after Gibson's departure, on 15 April 1943. He was part of Flight Lieutenant Brodrick's crew on an operation to Stuttgart. The Lancaster crashed in France during the homeward flight. Brodrick and two others survived to become PoWs.

For Gibson, the image of the highly efficient bomber captain took a slight knock on this trip. He came back 'the wrong way' and the radio was left on transmit, something he found 'very embarrassing'.

In the squadron ORB it was recorded that the wing commander's aircraft had experienced:

'10/10ths cloud. Target located by skymarker technique. Bombed at 19.35 hours from 2,000ft when the red and green warning flares were seen, the bombing being carried out [on?] the white flare. Trip did not seem to be too successful. Flak heavy. Bomb load 1 x 4,000lb, 12 SBC (4lb).'

Muttrie was also in the crew on Gibson's next operation to the 'big city', Berlin on 16/17 January. So Essen was not the exclusive target and, anyway, naval pressure would soon ensure that resources were diverted to attack the French Atlantic ports as well.

For Berlin Gibson entertained more newcomers. One came in the not inconsiderable shape of the BBC war correspondent Major Richard Dimbleby. Here was a sign that Bomber Command was starting to gain some public credit for its efforts.

At this time, 29-year-old Dimbleby was already a well-known figure. He had reported from the royal tour of Canada in 1939 and had been briefly in Spain, witnessing some of the horrors of the civil war. He became, officially, the BBC's first war correspondent, as soon as Britain went to war with Germany. He spent time with the British Expeditionary Force, before the fighting in earnest began. Then he went to the Middle East, observing much action in various countries and eventually being recalled, in part because the BBC had little idea of how his role should be performed and he had been sucked into a row between the corporation and the government.

Now he was becoming the BBC air correspondent, despite claiming to dislike flying and to be sick when he did it. He would also say that he approached his flight with No 106 Squadron and Gibson with no excitement and considerable fear. It was the first time that a BBC war correspondent had flown on a bombing raid. If there was any time for relaxation before or after the flight, the war correspondent and the pilot had at least one subject of interest in common. Dimbleby had spent his honeymoon in Cornwall, beloved of Gibson.

The other fresh face in Gibson's crew this time was Sergeant McGregor, another in the line of new pilots gaining experience in the 'second dickey' position, acting as flight engineer. He had a lot to cope with. There was the CO to impress and the unwieldy war correspondent impinging on the flight engineer's territory. In addition, Dimbleby was very sick and passed out at one point through lack of oxygen. McGregor sorted that situation out.

As the aircraft crossed the coast into occupied Europe, Dimbleby gained his first taste of anti-aircraft fire from the receiving end. The listening world was later told by Dimbleby, 'It was bursting away from us and much lower. I didn't see any long streams of it soaring into the air as the pictures suggest. It burst in little yellow winking flashes and you couldn't hear it above the roar of the engines. Sometimes it closes in on you, and the mid – or tail – gunner will call up calmly and report its position to the captain, so that he can dodge it.'

Dimbleby would, in later years, be accused (despite his own vehement denials) of pomposity and remoteness from ordinary lives. Here in 1942 he was a man from outside the bomber family, overcoming his fear to experience and describe that world.

As they approached the target the war correspondent saw the criss-crossing searchlights, 'a tracery of sparkling silver spread across the face of Berlin.' The flak seemed intense – 'one burst lifted us in the air as though a giant hand had pushed up the belly of the machine.' Dimbleby had a cine camera with him but it jammed.

Weather, thick haze in particular, made life difficult. Muttrie wanted to go round again and they bombed on the second run (temporary relief was provided for Dimbleby's nerves in the apparent safety of the darkness), dropping their 8,000lb bomb near the red marker flare. The result was not observed, but Gibson believed that the bomb did fall in Berlin. Moments later, Dimbleby was overcome by nausea, turned away from the pilot, but only just missed Muttrie with his vomit. Overcoming all his tribulations, the correspondent was exultant. He pictured Hitler and the other Nazi leaders cowering below in some shelter.

Dimbleby's night was certainly successful, despite his discomfort and despite the haze. He had observed the spectacular show put on by Bomber Command on such attacks and broadcast it later in vivid detail. Gibson was delighted that someone, particularly of Dimbleby's stature and public visibility, had experienced what Gibson and his men experienced all the time and had explained it well to a huge audience away from the closed atmosphere of a bomber squadron.

Some at the BBC were very pleased too. There was a traditional view against this kind of 'at the front' positioning of correspondents. There was also a feeling amongst some of the correspondents that progress was being made in reporting the 'actuality' of war, but that more use could have been made of Dimbleby's vivid report.

A number of military leaders, including Harris, were grasping the power of press and radio to shape the perception of events. Even in conflicts much later than the Second World War, it was a lesson that had still not been learned by every leader.

This flight to Berlin and back with Gibson was the first of about twenty operations which Dimbleby would fly. He later headed the war reporting unit, described the crossing of the Rhine and what the allies found at Belsen.

He became associated as a broadcaster with many great state events in the years following the war and died in 1965.

Now 'media' considerations, in today's language, were coming to the fore. Gibson's next sortie was to Milan on 14 February and Sergeant Cartwright, a camera operator, joined the crew. This was a 'good trip', as far as Gibson was concerned and the ORB entry reads,

> 'No cloud, very little haze. Target easily identified in the moonlight and a straight run was made across the target at 11,000ft, bombs being released at 2241 hours and seen to burst near the aiming point. Flew around for twenty minutes taking movies. Enjoyable and successful trip.'

That a summary based on Gibson's report could include the word 'enjoyable' for a bombing operation, perhaps demonstrates a man at the height of his professionalism, as well as the fact that the 'movie making' was again spreading the deeds of the bomber crews around the world. On the same night Bomber Command also attacked Cologne.

By now Gibson was both nearing the end of his time with No 106 Squadron and finding himself more and more in meetings at group and elsewhere. As a highly experienced squadron commander, one of the 'bomber barons', as they were called, and somebody whom Harris was keeping an eye on, his opinion was both sought and valued.

Nonetheless, he was still flying from time to time and his next operation was the long haul to Nuremberg on 25/26 February.

It was a 'good but frightening trip'. He and many others were forced to hang around waiting for the Pathfinders, but the target was found visually and Gibson bombed from 12,000ft, contributing to a good concentrated attack.

A good trip, but it also involved the loss of another of Gibson's friends, an American serving as a pilot, in the RCAF, Flight Lieutenant Don Curtin DFC (and bar) crashed close to the target; all were killed. In his list of comrades, fallen and missing, in *Enemy Coast Ahead*, Gibson is a little out with the date of Don Curtin's death. Cologne on 26 February was a 'wizard prang', with the return recorded in the ORB at 2359 hours. Heavy flak in barrage form was encountered.

At this time one of the players in the drama of the dams took the stage. Air Vice Marshal Coryton departed from the leadership of No 5 Group and was replaced by the aristocratic and austere, Air Vice Marshal, the Hon Ralph Cochrane. Gibson had naturally come to know Coryton well and found himself dealing with a new and very different character.

Early in March one of the major phases of the bomber war began – the Battle of the Ruhr, 'happy valley' to the airmen. This phase of the campaign would last until nearly the end of July, though there were attacks on targets outside the Ruhr as well.

Gibson did not fly on the first sortie of the Battle of the Ruhr, which was an attack on Essen on the night of 5/6 March. It was considered highly successful, with sixteen aircraft becoming casualties from almost 450 which set out. In particular the headquarters of the Krupp industrial conglomerate suffered considerable damage. Krupp's contribution to the Nazi war effort included the manufacture of tanks, naval guns and armour plate.

From Syerston, Edward Hunt of the *Sunday Express* observed the launch of the Battle of the Ruhr. The copy he filed awarded himself the honour, certainly not true, of being the only civilian on any Bomber Command station during the first operation and led to the headline in the paper, 'This Was It! – Three Tons of Bombs on Essen Every Four Seconds for 35 Minutes'.

Gibson was quoted as regretting that he was not available to take part, but indicating his pleasure at the success of the raid and at the relatively small scale of the losses. Losses to Bomber Command, that is. As well as the damage inflicted on Essen's industrial strength, almost 500 people had been killed on the ground.

Now Gibson would fly his last sortie, to Stuttgart, one that produced differing accounts of what took place. Yet again the man who joined the Gibson crew as flight engineer was an inexperienced pilot, Pilot Officer Walter Thompson. Years later Thompson wrote of his wartime experiences in a book called *Lancaster to Berlin*. When he met Gibson for the first time Thompson found him, 'Not a tall man, but firmly and squarely made, his smile lit up the day.' Gibson was also happy to introduce him around.

As far as Gibson was concerned, he flew to the target with three good engines and one that was hardly functioning. He dropped his bombs from 12,000ft and they were seen to burst near a concentration of fires. Flak was light, but the main attack fell southwest of Stuttgart.

In Thompson's view (and he was the man charged with looking after the engines) two engines were lost to flak, not malfunction. Touchdown back at Syerston was, for Thompson, 'more in the nature of a controlled crash'. He found it encouraging that there was a certain infallibility about a man of Gibson's high reputation.

The squadron's diary gives one version of what happened next. On 14 March it notes that Wing Commander Gibson had been posted away to form a new squadron (the 'new squadron' may have been added with hindsight) and continues:

'He commanded 106 Squadron for eleven months and during that period some notable successes were achieved. The squadron completed conversion from Manchesters to Lancasters and under Wing Commander Gibson's command it was and retained the reputation of one of Bomber Command's leading squadrons, figuring conspicuously in most of the more important and spectacular raids – the '1,000' raids, Danzig, Le Creusot and Milan to mention but a few. His own personal record is remarkable. With the squadron he flew on twenty-nine raids, winning the DSO in October [actually November 1942] and his operational sorties, in figures, are seventy-two bombing raids and 199 fighter hours.'

Now at the end of Gibson's tour, Group Captain Bussell, Officer Commanding Syerston, recommended him for a bar to his DSO. This was one of those recommendations that was written on by various increasingly senior officers, expressing their own views as it journeyed through the pipeline. The award of the Victoria Cross to Flight Lieutenant 'Nick' Nicolson in Fighter Command in 1940 is another example that comes to mind.

At group, Cochrane, not a man to become effusive, thought that a third DFC might be suitable for Gibson, so soon after his DSO.

Then it was the turn of Arthur Harris at High Wycombe. He wrote, 'Any captain who completes 172 sorties in outstanding manner is worth two DSOs, if not a VC. Bar to DSO approved.'

Here was a foretaste of a decoration to come. Harris was probably to some extent tongue in cheek with what he wrote about the VC on this occasion. He must have realised that the chances of gaining approval for such an award for Gibson at that stage were virtually nil – the recommendation would have to go considerably higher up the command structure. Monarchs were not content to be figureheads in the process and King George VI made telling interventions on some Second World War VC matters.

Possibly, the King's most noticeable intervention was the part he played in the exchange for the VC of the DCM awarded to Company Sergeant Major Peter Wright of the Coldstream Guards for his actions at Salerno in Italy. In the case of Gibson, Harris certainly disclosed the way in which his mind was working.

During the Second World War (unlike the Great War) only one airman was awarded the VC for the totality of his performance on operations, rather than for heroism isolated in terms of its extraordinary manner. That was Leonard Cheshire. Even so, DSO and bar was a rare award. Sporting that and two DFCs on a uniform made anybody stand out in a crowd.

Now comes the matter of how Gibson made the transition from officer commanding No 106 Squadron to the same role in what would become No 617 Squadron. Many subtle variations of the story have appeared in public.

It seems safe to dismiss the account given by Gibson himself, that he was posted to No 5 Group under instructions to write a book for up and coming bomber pilots. Morris favours 15 March as the date of Gibson's being told of the requirement for a new squadron that he would form and lead. As Morris says, 'All sources agree on the question which had preceded this invitation. Cochrane had leaned forward and asked, 'How would you like the idea of doing one more trip?'

Plans for leave and a holiday in Cornwall were abandoned, so that Gibson could continue with flying on operations, perhaps the actual love of his life at that point. Aged twenty-four, Wing Commander Gibson set off on the great adventure that would bring enormous responsibility, more great danger and long lasting fame.

Chapter 10

Why the Dams?

At the Imperial Defence College (IDC) in the early to mid 1930s, students undertook exercises in which various possible enemies were considered. Italy, Germany and Japan were all treated as likely candidates for hostile action. As it became clear that the major threat was presented by Germany, so the focus, both amongst students at the IDC in Buckingham Gate and amongst those seeking to dictate real events at the Air Ministry and elsewhere, concentrated on the Nazi regime.

Stanley Baldwin had caused much concern with his speech in the House of Commons in November 1932 when he had used the words, 'The bomber will always get through'. He was not the first person to draw attention to this theory, but it was his reference to it that woke up the British public to the threat. He was not in fact saying that such a situation was inevitable. He was presenting the possibility of abolishing bombers, as an awful new weapon of war and the control of civil aviation, to prevent airliners being converted into bombers when the fighting began.

He declared, 'Up to the time of the last war civilians were exempt from the worst perils of war. They suffered sometimes from hunger, sometimes from the loss of sons and relatives serving in the army. But now, in addition to this, they suffered from the constant fear not only of being killed themselves, but, what is perhaps worse for a man, of seeing his wife and children killed from the air. These feelings exist among the ordinary people throughout the whole of the civilized world…'

With hindsight, the German use of civil aviation as a means of developing its interwar fighting capability without incurring international intervention brings extra force to Baldwin's views.

Inevitably, as war came closer, much thought was given in Britain to the extent that the RAF could use its own bomber force against Germany and the targets whose destruction might create the biggest impact. Indeed, at the end of the First World War, Trenchard, as chief of the air staff, had stressed that a part of the future would be long distance aerial attacks against the 'sources of supply' of the enemy, whoever that might be.

As another war approached work was done inside and outside the RAF through a range of committees and sub committees, on the possibilities for disrupting German industry. Perhaps the first official mention of attacks on the dams that six years later would feature in the operation by No 617 Squadron, came a little under two years before the outbreak of war.

What was known as the Air Targets Sub Committee argued, as did others, that the concept of a devastating blow against the German industrial heartland, over a very short period and with relatively small cost, was unrealistic. As an alternative the sub committee drew attention to what it saw as the enormous potential for causing German industrial turmoil by a successful strike against the Möhne and Sorpe dams. Their destruction would lead, it was argued, to the destruction of many other structures and a significant reduction in the ability of the Germans to generate electricity.

Bomber Command immediately pointed out the substantial nature of the construction of the dams. The weapon was not available to strike the blow, nor the means of delivering it to the targets. Neither then, nor for a considerable further time, does it seem to have been realised by 'top brass' that in at least one sense, the destruction of the dams would not provide the desired result. Germany was only dependent on waterpower for the generation of electricity to a limited extent.

The difficulties were clear, but the seed had been sown and work was done to establish how the destruction of the dams might be achieved. In July 1938 a meeting of the Air Ministry's bombing committee was chaired by the assistant chief of the air staff, a recently created post, the first holder of which was Air Vice Marshal Sholto Douglas, who during the war to come would be air officer commanding-in-chief of both Fighter Command and Coastal Command at different times.

At the meeting he chaired Douglas said that he regarded dams in both Germany and Italy as an 'achilles heel' for the war effort of those countries. Much detailed discussion followed.

So, the dams remained as active targets, even though the difficulties that would have to be overcome remained very clear to most of the decision makers.

Sholto Douglas would, much later, write two volumes of memoirs. In *Years of Command*, covering the relevant period, he makes no mention of his early support for the dams as targets, though his interest in technology is well covered, including the credit he could claim for his part in the bringing of radar to operational use.

As these tortuous discussions were going on in Whitehall, so at Weybridge in Surrey other thinking was being applied to the problems. At Weybridge, Barnes Wallis, a Vickers chief designer (there was more than one) was putting his brilliant mind to some of the issues being confronted if the German dams were to be destroyed. His idea, developed with his colleague Rex Pierson, for a huge bomber with six engines had not found favour. However, he was also convinced of the need for deep penetration bombs, though there was no means of carrying them successfully.

Early in the war Wallis's thinking turned also to the destruction of Germany's economic power. This concept and those of a big aircraft and a big bomb all became interwoven in his thinking. For Wallis, size meant a great deal. Scattering small bombs about (as the RAF had against rebellious people in various outposts of the world before the war), or even somewhat larger ones, was not a way to ward off the threat posed by Hitler.

The waters became much muddied over time, not least by the accounts Wallis himself gave. His biographer, J.E. Morpurgo, writing while Wallis was still alive, referred to 'the considerable body of mythology [which] has grown up around the true story of Wallis during the Second World War', and went on, 'it cannot be denied that to that body Wallis had added a few delightful fables of his own.' Morpurgo rightly went on to point out that history as well as fairy tale were demonstrations of his subject's genius.

Wallis and others created the belief that he had developed the idea of attacking the dams and had fought against official obstruction to achieve it. There was not nearly as much obstruction as Wallis liked to think and the idea of an attack had been around for a long time. Gradually, though, with Wallis giving considerable attention to relevant matters all the elements that would lead to Operation Chastise were coming together. Lord Beaverbrook, the minister of aircraft production, played a part, after Wallis had seized the opportunity of a meeting with the minister, on another topic, to explain some of his ideas.

In parallel, at Bomber Command, Sir Charles Portal, then the commander-in-chief, was in favour of finding a way to attack the Möhne. He would soon be chief of the air staff. At this point, Portal's ideas on how the destruction of the dam might be achieved included the proposition that consideration be given to converting Hampdens to carry torpedoes. This proposition was put forward at the beginning of July 1940 between two Hampden sorties flown by Gibson to attack the *Scharnhorst*.

The Admiralty naturally wanted the German capital ships out of the way and, as well as encouraging the RAF to bomb them, was working on its own plans for projectiles to threaten such targets. All kinds of threads were now converging.

Naturally there was indeed opposition to Wallis's thinking. He was supported in much of what he argued by the eminent scientist Sir Henry

Tizard, who amongst many other appointments and distinctions acted as an adviser to the ministry of aircraft production.

Sadly one drawback to being supported by Tizard was that it made the support of Frederick Lindemann far less likely – and Lindemann had more influence. They were extremely different men, Tizard sometimes displaying an impish sense of humour, while Lindemann lacked humour of any variety.

More importantly they were scientific rivals who had fallen out spectacularly and publicly in the 1930s. Before that things had been different. Tizard had been a leading advocate of Lindemann's long-standing appointment as professor of Experimental Philosophy (actually Physics) at the university of Oxford.

Known as 'The Prof' by many, Lindemann had been a close friend of Winston Churchill for many years before the Second World War. With Churchill now Prime Minister, Lindemann, created Baron Cherwell of Oxford in 1941, rarely moved from his metaphorical right hand.

Lindemann appears to have taken a dislike to Wallis and his ideas, before he had met the man, though perhaps not before he had heard details of some of the ideas. His dislike was not, of course, eventually fatal, but it delayed matters and probably contributed as much as most things to the Wallis idea that he had found obstruction to be fought and overcome at every juncture.

In the late summer of 1940, permission was granted for Wallis to use the wind tunnel at the National Physical Laboratory at Teddington, Middlesex. During the winter of 1940/41 he was allowed to carry out experiments at the Road Research Laboratory at Harmondsworth, also in Middlesex. There Wallis talked of the Möhne and Eder dams and also an Italian dam as likely targets. It was clear to those who assisted him at Harmondsworth, using models, that, in particular, it was the destruction of the Möhne that he cherished.

Experiments on a model of the Möhne dam were also conducted, at the request of Dr W.H. Glanville, who headed the Road Research Laboratory, at the Building Research Station, Garston, Hertfordshire. Laborious work in constructing a model of the Möhne was carried out in such secrecy that gossip was caused and security threatened. Those involved felt that less secrecy might have meant more security.

Glanville (knighted in 1960, long before Wallis) was a good contact for Wallis to develop. He was much respected and had spent many years gaining an insight into the workings of the bureaucratic mind. In addition, he and his team were already working with the air ministry and the ministry of aircraft production on the programme of airfield expansion, advising on concrete runways and other wartime demands of the RAF.

At this stage Wallis envisaged that dams would be attacked using a very large bomb dropped from a very great height. He continued his lobbying of authority with a paper, also large, titled *A Note on a Method of Attacking the Axis Powers*. This discussed various kinds of structures that served to supply energy to the enemy, including power stations, coal mines and oil fields. He pointed out the impossibility of dispersing many such structures and claimed that destruction on a considerable scale would make the enemy utterly incapable of continuing the war. Though he ranged widely in this paper Wallis had the dams right at the heart of his thinking. For practical purposes, big bombs and big aircraft didn't work. Neither existed and there was no prospect of bringing the two together in any kind of reasonable timescale.

Now a subject that had long interested Wallis came to the forefront of his thinking again; this was the performance of spheres. It has been claimed that Wallis could have changed cricket for ever had he been allowed to. He had wanted to design a cricket ball which appeared no different to other cricket balls, but which batsmen would be unable to cope with. If this is true, it would seem that the MCC was not encouraging. Batsmen continued to amass centuries.

The experiments conducted by Wallis with his children in the garden of his home, as depicted in *The Dam Busters*, did actually take place.

Progress was made. A breach was achieved (at the second attempt) in the disused Nant-y-Gro dam across a tributary of the River Elan, near Rhayader in mid-Wales. Not many disused dams could have been available in wartime Britain. This one was because it had been constructed as part of the great dam building operations in that part of Wales. One of its main purposes was to supply water to the temporary village used by the workforce. It became redundant with the completion of the dam construction. Once breached it was left to be enveloped in woodland and remains so today.

Sweetman wrote of the Nant-y-Gro experiment, 'It resulted in a spectacular success: a flash of water whitened the surface of the reservoir before water at the point of the explosion was drawn upwards into a huge spout... Then the centre of the dam was punched out.'

Wallis was allowed to use a Wellington for experiments along with 'Mutt' Summers, chief test pilot at Vickers and his number two, R.C. Handasyde, son of the aviation pioneer, George Handasyde. The first test drops at Chesil Beach, Dorset, did not provide much encouragement, though things improved. It has been claimed that naval gunners at Portland, a breed traditionally quick to assume any unidentified aircraft was hostile, had opened fire, but Handasyde denied it.

At the same time the navy was showing interest, something that Wallis, rather cunningly, had encouraged. Plans emerged which envisaged 'Upkeep', to be carried by Lancasters to the dams and 'Highball', a smaller version which was to be carried by Mosquitos, used to attack major enemy ships.

A further paper was produced by Wallis, with the title, *Air Attack on the Dams*. Even Cherwell was thawing now. With the Navy and Ministry of Aircraft Production keen to press ahead with Highball, Wallis sought to persuade his adversary to take up his case with the RAF, perhaps exaggerating the results somewhat. He claimed for instance that successful experiments had been carried out with more than one dam in Wales.

There was now increasing RAF interest and Wallis met Arthur Harris, suffering a hostile reception. Ministry of Aircraft Production permission came through for the modification of two Mosquitos for Highball trials. Portal authorized the modification of Lancasters for Upkeep development. There was continuing pressure from the top of Vickers to deflect Wallis away from his passion, but the tide now flowed for him towards the dams. At the end of February 1943 he was instructed to deliver in eight weeks the weapons to attack the dams at their fullest in May.

Chapter 11

Preparing the Way

There is always much confusion over ranks held in wartime, 'substantive', 'wartime substantive', 'acting' and 'temporary' are just some of the categorisations that may apply. Matters become worse in relation to the attack on the dams, because a number of the aircrew involved received promotions around the time of the operation. Indeed, some took off from Scampton not knowing of their elevation.

Amongst those to be promoted at that time were Flight Sergeants Anderson, Deering and MacLean, who were commissioned. The ranks used in this book for those and other personnel are those that seem most appropriate for the time being referred to.

It is also worth pointing out that the official name for Flight Lieutenant Martin's aircraft was 'P for Peter'. However, the crew referred to the aircraft as 'P for Popsie' (a slang expression at the time for an attractive young woman) and this is the appellation that has gone down in history.

Gibson arrived at Scampton, the appointed home for the new squadron, on Sunday, 21 March, accompanied by Nigger. He did not find old friends from amongst the aircrew fraternity awaiting him in the officers' mess. That is a fiction of *The Dam Busters* film for creative effect.

Administrators were arriving for 617 Squadron. There was an adjutant, who Gibson did not take to (fairly or unfairly, it is difficult to be sure with Gibson) and then there were Flight Sergeant George Powell and Sergeant Jim Heveron, two men who would play leading roles in the creation of this new bomber squadron from a piece of paper. Both had come across the airfield from No 57 Squadron, a Lancaster unit, resident at Scampton since September 1942.

Like most flight sergeants Powell was sometimes 'Chiefy', a tradition that dates back to the amalgamation in 1918 of the Royal Naval Air Service and the Royal Flying Corps to form the Royal Air Force. When the new RAF ranks were announced in 1919, flight sergeant was the equivalent of the naval rank of chief petty officer. Powell was also known by his peers as 'Sandy' and this was most likely to be a reference to the comedian, Sandy Powell (1900–1982), associated with the catchphrase, 'Can you hear me, mother?'

Powell and Heveron put in an enormous amount of work to bring the squadron to reality, finding personnel and equipment. Their boss was working hard too and was often not to be seen.

One person who Gibson did talk to himself was Section Officer Fay Gillon, who also came from No 57 Squadron, but in an intelligence role. This manifested itself, in particular, as a role facilitating the programme of training in low flying that would be needed and liaising with group about it.

Gillon would recall that Gibson made clear at the meeting that he rather doubted the ability of women to contribute to important matters, but his sexism was a benefit when he ensured that her new office received some basic equipment and decoration.

Gibson needed a crew and the work of assembling that had been going on. Only Hutchison had joined him from No 106 Squadron (via a heavy conversion unit to which he had been posted). Whether other potential crew members from No 106 were invited to No 617 is not clear.

No 50 Squadron provided a firm basis for the new crew. The navigator, Pilot Officer Harlo Taerum, RCAF, had gone from 50 Squadron to Wigsley, where Hutchison was also newly arrived. It may have been 'Hutch' or it may have been Mick Martin who put forward the name of the Canadian who would be 'Terry' in 617 Squadron.

Taerum was from Alberta, the eldest son of a Norwegian immigrant farmer who had died young. According to his mother, Harlo was determined to join the RCAF following the invasion of Norway by the Germans and after hearing reports of the ill treatment of its citizens.

The bomb aimer selected was 24-year-old Pilot Officer Frederick 'Spam' Spafford, DFM, an Australian friend of Taerum's from No 50 Squadron. Spafford had been born with the name Burke but had been adopted by his grandfather, bringing about a change of name. His grandfather died before Spafford enlisted in the Royal Australian Air Force and he gave as his next-of-kin his uncle, Walter James Spafford, who was then the director of agriculture for the state of South Australia. 'Spam' had spent short spells with other squadrons including No 83.

The rear gunner, Flight Lieutenant Richard Algernon Dacre Trevor-Roper, DFM was another from No 50 Squadron and was deeply experienced. He was also the man referred to by Morris as figuring in Burke's Peerage. His father, Captain Charles Cadwaladr Trevor-Roper had served with the Hampshire Regiment in the First World War and had died of wounds on 3 August 1917, being buried in Belgium. His son was born on the Isle of Wight and was two years old when he lost his father. The historian, Hugh Trevor-Roper (later Lord Dacre of Glanton) was a second cousin of Richard. At the time of Operation Chastise Hugh was working for MI6.

Now we come to the two NCO members of the crew and, perhaps in his usual fashion, the two with whom Gibson appeared to be rather unimpressed.

Flight Sergeant George Deering who would take the front turret on the attack, was Canadian and a veteran of more than thirty operations. Despite this, Gibson regarded him as 'pretty dumb' and not competent in handling the guns.

The flight engineer, Sergeant John Pulford, was recruited from No 97 Squadron. Gibson stuck with him despite claiming to regard him as not very bright. Morris points out that, 'This may say more about Gibson than Pulford, for Gibson never listened to him long enough even to notice that he came from Yorkshire, rather than London', which is where Gibson placed him. Pulford was from Hull. Assuming that he had not striven to lose any hint of the East Riding in his voice, it was a remarkable example of lack of observation, or hearing, given the closeness of the relationship between pilot and flight engineer, both in terms of jobs and proximity in the aircraft.

The aircrew who flew in the Lancasters of No 617 Squadron in the spring of 1943 offer a most interesting study. Many inaccuracies have appeared about them. Richard Morris made an attempt to get at the truth in a study, published in the autumn/winter 2010 edition of *Everyone's War*, the journal of The Second World War Experience Centre.

In doing so, Morris commented on the value of personal memories of those 'who were there', but also considered the dangers of extreme reliance on this form of evidence.

He made a very important point. An historian might be able to quote the strategy and the tactics, the names, the squadrons and much else that the veteran had forgotten or never knew. Only the veteran can know what it was like to go to Berlin (or the dams) in a Lancaster, be in a Hurricane or Spitfire diving into a vast German formation, fight house to house at Arnhem or face the Chinese hordes at the Imjin River.

Over many years memories blur, events merge into one another and original insights are tampered with by what others say and what is read. The experience of being in action is always buried somewhere in the mind. It is vital to record the memories of action, but so many other sources need to be considered.

Morris addressed the issue through the use of prosopography – the analysis of data about social groups whose members are not easily studied through available historical sources. In the case of the dam busting aircrew he studied data on fifty. Noting the smallness of the sample and the lack of comparative data on aircrew in other squadrons in No 5 Group, he, with considerable modesty, if perhaps strict scientific correctness, described his results as 'tentative and impressionistic'.

Analysing the backgrounds of the captains, Morris wrote:

'Of the eleven RAF and Volunteer Reserve captains, almost all were ex-public school, and from professional backgrounds. Hopgood and Maltby had been to Marlborough. Young was an alumnus of Westminster. Astell had been educated at Bradfield, Ottley at Hurstpierpoint. Gibson had attended St Edward's Oxford. Maudslay was an Old Etonian. Townsend was educated at Monmouth School. Only two appear to buck the trend: Pilot Officer Geoff Rice who attended Hinckley Grammar School, and Flight Sergeant Cyril Anderson, who went to Lawefield Lane School (later the Grammar School) in Wakefield and left it at the age of fifteen.

'Looking to background, Young's father was a London lawyer, his American mother Fannie coming from a Connecticut family that had amassed wealth through developing property. Maltby's father was a headmaster who came from a clerical family. Maudslay was the son of a midlands industrialist who in turn came from an industrial-entrepreneurial background. Gibson's father had been a senior officer in the Indian Forest Service, his mother the daughter of a Cornish sea captain. Astell's father Godfrey was company director of a Manchester cotton mill. Again, Anderson is the exception: his father was a colliery byeworker* and his grandfather had been a labourer. The census of 1911 finds the family living with grandparents in Sandal Magna.

'The milieu of the British captains, then, was strongly middle class, and characterised by teaching, law, industry, technology and empire.

'If we now assimilate Australian, New Zealand and Canadian captains to this picture, we find it partly reinforced and also subtly transformed. Those from Australia and New Zealand came from professional classes or agriculture. Martin, twenty-five years old at the time of the raid, was the grammar school educated son of a Sydney doctor. Shannon, twenty in May 1943, was the son of a South Australian MP. Robert Barlow had been educated at Melbourne Grammar School and had then gone into the motor trade. At thirty-two he was among the oldest captains to fly on the raid.

'Les Munro grew up on a New Zealand sheep station, and after high school had worked on dairy and sheep farms.

---

* A definition of a byeworker offered by the National Coal Mining Museum for England is 'a person who worked underground, but not at the coal face, was paid by the day and performed tasks such as processing coal and making repairs.'

'The Canadian captains show a varied profile. Twenty-five-year-old Lewis Burpee was a graduate of Queen's University, Kingston, Ontario, where he had studied English literature. Ken Brown and Vernon Byers were countrymen from Saskatchewan, Brown from Moose Jaw, Byers from Star City. Joe McCarthy grew up in the New York Bronx. The son of a fireman, he had learned to fly as a teenager and had joined the RCAF in Ottawa before the United States entered the war.

'McCarthy was not alone in having had pre-war flying experience. Apart from Gibson himself, Cyril Anderson had been in the RAF since the mid-1930s, although he had started as ground staff and did not transfer to flying until after the war had started. Barlow had learned to fly as far back as 1928. Young had been in the Oxford University Air Squadron. Astell had learned to fly in the Reserve. John Sweetman long ago disposed of the legend that 617 Squadron's aircrew were all hand-picked veterans, although such is that legend's power that there are many who continue to believe it. Nonetheless it is interesting that all but three of the captains were commissioned (this is a higher proportion than one would find in other 5 Group squadrons at this point in the war), and that several of those with long flying experience were at the upper end of the age scale – Young was twenty-seven at the time of the raid, Anderson twenty-eight, Barlow thirty-two. Another 32-year-old pilot was the Canadian Vernon Byers, who had completed only five operations before joining 617. In due course it would not be surprising to find that he, too, had flown before the war. As a footnote to the question of experience, it is worth noting that while both Astell and Young were seasoned pilots, much of their experience had been in the Mediterranean theatre, on Wellingtons, in Malta and the Middle East.'

Morris noted the inevitable tendency to 'blue collar' amongst the other members of the crews, with plenty having worked in jobs that needed technical skill. There was a considerable number too who had worked in retailing or office jobs, as well as some who had gone straight into the RAF after their education. Teaching was also a favoured pre-service occupation.

A conclusion reached by Morris is that 617 Squadron aircrew in the main represented the middle class.

'One clear finding is that 617's aircrew were not a cross-section of mid-20th-century British and Commonwealth society. Notable absences from the social spectrum are members of the aristocracy – only one family appears in Burke's Landed Gentry and one other in Burke's Peerage – and of the labouring working class,' he wrote.

One of the teachers was Sergeant John Nugent, the navigator in Anderson's aircraft. He came from the village of Stoney Middleton in the Derbyshire Peak District. His specialist subjects were maths and music. After qualifying at St Mary's Training College, Strawberry Hill, near London (now St Mary's University College) he had taught in London, moving when his school was evacuated to Brighton. He joined the RAF in 1940.

Another navigator who had been a teacher was Flying Officer Ken Earnshaw, RCAF, part of Hopgood's crew. He had been born in Yorkshire, but the family moved to Alberta when he was young.

If some of Gibson's own crew fell foul of him, the same was true of other crews. Sergeant Ray Lovell and his team returned to No 57 Squadron, Lovell's flying not considered to be up to the standard for No 617.

A difficulty arose too in the case of a crew, from No 57 Squadron, headed by Flight Sergeant Lanchester, RCAF. Lanchester wasn't the problem, it was his navigator, Flying Officer Cleveland. It may have been 'Dinghy' Young who decided initially that Cleveland's navigational skills weren't good enough and passed a recommendation to Gibson. The CO told Cleveland to go and this led to a revolt by the rest of the crew. They all packed their bags as a result, including Flight Sergeant Clifford, who had proved himself an excellent bomb aimer.

Another indication of the far from hand-picked nature of the 617 Squadron aircrew as a whole is that it was not until late April that all vacancies were filled and all who were not suitable for whatever reason were weeded out.

Gibson's arrival at Scampton on 21 March was followed by a trip to Surrey on 24 March, when he met up with his old contact Mutt Summers, who introduced him to Barnes Wallis. This was the famous occasion when, to his embarrassment, Wallis was unable to tell Gibson what the target was, because Gibson's name did not appear on the right list. Wallis was able to talk about the Upkeep weapon and show Gibson some film of trials with a version that was half the intended size.

The previous day (23 March) the first reference to No 617 Squadron occurred in an Air Ministry memorandum, though this was perhaps not communicated to the squadron until 25 March. The squadron therefore fitted in after the highest numbered of the pre-war Auxiliary Air Force squadrons, No 616 (South Yorkshire) Squadron, which flew Spitfires in the Battle of Britain and was later the first unit to go operational with Gloster Meteor jets.

On Saturday, 27 March Gibson was given 'most secret' orders which did not name the target, but referred to moonlight, an objective that was lightly defended, a specific low height and a precise speed. Practice over water would be 'convenient' and precision in the release point would be required. Flight

Lieutenant Bill Astell was ordered to fly over nine lakes that might be suitable for training and obtain pictures.

On Monday, 29 March Cochrane called Gibson to group and the target was at last disclosed to him. He was shown models of the Möhne and Sorpe dams. For Gibson and others when they found out, there was relief that they were not being asked to launch an attack on the German battleship *Tirpitz*.

Shortly afterwards there was another trip for Gibson to the temporary office that Barnes Wallis was using in Surrey, close to the Vickers works and the two men could have a frank discussion for the first time. It has been claimed that at this point Wallis was contemplating a daylight attack and that Gibson dismissed the idea. It is unlikely that Wallis did believe that the operation could be carried out in daylight.

Probably on Sunday, 4 April, the Derwent reservoir was flown over for the first time, with Gibson flying and Hopgood and Young accompanying him. Sweetman says that the flight took place earlier at a date when Hopgood had not arrived on the squadron. They found meeting the requirements in daylight was not a problem, but it was much more difficult when dusk arrived.

While the training for the dams operation continued, so did the Battle of the Ruhr, as well as other operations, and No 57 Squadron's involvement in it. While its aircrew watched an apparently inactive 617 Squadron across the airfield at Scampton, they themselves were flying into action and suffering losses.

On the night of 4/5 April for example, Squadron Leader Wallage and his crew – Sergeant Harbottle, Pilot Officer Weldon, Sergeants Spicer, Haddow, Evans and Woods – did not return from Kiel. Their names are on the Runnymede Memorial. Six nights later the target was Frankfurt and Flight Sergeant Lemon, RCAF and his crew fell in Germany. On 20/21 April another RCAF pilot was lost from 57 Squadron. Pilot Officer Collins and his crew disappeared during an attack on Stettin. Inevitably there was banter, even ill feeling, about the, for the time being, apparent difference in the contributions to the war effort being made by the two squadrons.

During March there had been much planning carried out at various levels – No 5 Group, Bomber Command and at the Air Ministry – to put into place the training requirements for the attack. At first it was envisaged that the Wellington modified for the Upkeep tests would be used for training, but this never happened. Modified Lancasters started to become available.

There was great pressure to produce a proficient attacking force very quickly. In May the dams were holding the peak amount of water, following the melting of water in the surrounding hills. After 19 May the amount of water held would decline as supplies were released into the industrial system.

Discussion took place about selecting lakes for training that were relatively close to Scampton, though in the event, the training spread across a large area of England and Wales.

A major issue, that in different ways had plagued Bomber Command in the early days of the war, was the question of bombsights. A range of ideas and designs were considered for Operation Chastise, with the 'boffin', Wing Commander Charles Dann, the tame expert at the centre of affairs. After much consideration and experiment, a device using triangulation sighting was agreed upon, though No 617's bomb aimers were able to devise the precise method of delivery to the target which suited them best.

Dann was also involved in determining how the aircraft could approach their targets at the right height, eventually decided as sixty feet. A weighted cable descending from the aircraft was one of the ideas considered. Famously twin spotlights, with their beams converging, when the Lancaster was at the right height, were used over the dams. Among the accounts of how this device came about, the ones that can be rejected are those from the film and Gibson's book, involving inspiration coming from the spotlights during a theatre visit.

Robert Owen has pointed out that the idea had originated in the First World War, with the 'Night Height Projector'. In theory, any height could be worked out up to 500ft and later 1,000ft.

Trials at Orfordness threw up difficulties and the concept was not proceeded with at that time. It remained under consideration between the wars and during the Second World War. It is likely that Ben Lockspeiser of the Ministry of Aircraft Production conceived its use by No 617 Squadron.

Less impressed than the 617 Squadron crews was Arthur Harris whose annotation of a Bomber Command document included the words, 'I will not have aircraft flying about with spotlights in defended areas. Get some of these lunatics controlled, if not locked up. Note – beams of spots will not work on water if glassy calm. Any fool knows that.' For once, an order from Harris was not implemented. Low level navigation in moonlight was one of the issues and, with the 19 May deadline in mind, 10 May was set as the date for competence to be achieved.

Despite its depiction in the film, one thing that did not take place was the actual dropping of bombs for practice at the Derwent or any other dam, though this was an idea that was contemplated. Practice weapons were dropped at the Wainfleet bombing range on The Wash.

Charlie Williams and Gwen Parfitt

During the run up to Chastise, Flying Officer Charlie Williams, Barlow's Wireless Operator, was writing letters to his fiancée, Gwen 'Bobbie' Parfitt in Nottingham. They intended to marry when Williams was given leave after the operation. Charlie Williams did not return. In the 1990s, Gwen sold the letters and other papers to the State Library of Queensland, Charlie's home state.

These extracts are reproduced by courtesy of the State Library's, John Oxley Library.

'22 April 1943
Got chipped today by my Flight Commander [Squadron Leader Young]. I was late getting up this morning and did not have time to shave, and really meant to shave at lunchtime, but was late coming over and forgot about it.

I was standing quite close to him about three o'clock and he looked at me and said 'Did you shave this morning?' I said, 'Yes Sir! I was late and had a very hurried one', he said, 'yes, I think you must have'. Later he turned to me again and said, 'My how you must have had a rough shave, see that you use a new blade tomorrow. I said, 'Yes, Sir!'

14 May 1943
They were very excited at home the other day to hear over the news that F/Lt Norm Barlow and self had taken part in the big Berlin raid and no doubt they will be interested to learn that the same Norm Barlow is now my skipper.

15 May 1943
Norm is very thrilled about his DFC and he has every reason to be, he certainly has earned it as he has done thirty-two successful trips.'

And later in the same letter

'I am very glad darling that you were there for the take off and the return, and now you will fully realise what a strain we are under the whole time, without the actual operations, and you will not now wonder why our nerves are bad at times. You will have an idea what we feel like every time some of our pals or even just aircrew acquaintances fail to return, we get hardened to it to a certain extent but cannot help feeling depressed every time some of them fail to return.

Many of the chaps I knew well who did not return were some of the finest chaps I have ever met and there are many more of them in every RAF station in England.'

Light flak, particularly effective between 250 feet and 2,500 feet was seen to be one of the most likely causes of casualties on Operation Chastise. Hence the decision to fly very low (in theory under the flak) to the targets, though this was at the cost of greatly increasing the difficulty of map reading.

Losses would be sustained as a result of the very low altitude used. Air Vice Marshal Cochrane reflected on that fact in his post-operation assessment, though further losses would be sustained by the squadron later at low level.

Gibson meanwhile was clearly unwell as the deadline approached. There were various symptoms and hereditary gout was diagnosed. The medical advice that the CO should have a rest from flying was of course dismissed completely. Gibson had an objective and he was going to lead the way in meeting that objective whatever might happen.

At the last moment, there was almost a postponement of Chastise. Trials of Highball, the naval version of Upkeep, had not progressed well and a case was being made in some quarters that to use one weapon when the other could not be used would present the concept of Highball to the enemy. The Royal Navy was for putting off the use of Upkeep until Highball could be put right.

Gibson visited a sealed off area at Reculver near Herne Bay in Kent on a number of occasions. Here, where there had once been a Roman fort and an Anglo Saxon monastery, he saw for himself the struggles of Barnes Wallis to perfect the weapon to be used against the dams.

The late possible delay was averted. The chiefs of staff were in Washington with Churchill, but, urged on by an assessment from London, prepared by Air Marshal Sir Douglas Evill, Vice Chief of the Air Staff, they ordered the separation of Upkeep and Highball. This message was decoded and ready for reading on the afternoon of Friday, 14 May. Now the race was on to take advantage of favourable weather, the full moon and the fullness of the lakes.

The final preparations were made in an atmosphere of national rejoicing. On Thursday, 13 May Axis forces had surrendered in North Africa. The tide of the war could now be seen to be firmly with the Allies. The outcome of Chastise would be announced to a British people now coming to expect good news.

It was a good juncture for Bomber Command too. Harris compiled for Churchill a list of the 100 German towns most important to the war effort and on 14 May the joint chiefs of staff also approved the plan for a joint offensive against Germany from the UK by the RAF and the USAAF. The terms of the agreement clearly showed a belief that the USAAF was capable of precision bombing by day, while the RAF was not nearly so capable during the hours of darkness. Operation Chastise presented the opportunity to paint another picture.

Chapter 12

To the Dams

On Friday night a dress rehearsal, involving only some of the crews, was flown with mock attacks on Uppingham lake and the reservoir near Colchester. Whitworth accompanied Gibson who, otherwise, would have invited the WAAF intelligence officer, Fay Gillon, to come along. By this time she almost counted as 'one of the boys' to Gibson. Instead she flew with Martin and his crew in 'P for Popsie'.

Now there was to be a weekend of frantic activity. The Lancasters were checked and bombing up began on the Saturday. Even so, some flying was still taking place. Photo reconnaissance sorties were flown over Germany by Spitfires. The dams were of course an objective of this reconnaissance, but the net was deliberately spread much wider.

The major participants in the drama were assembling at and around Scampton, including Barnes Wallis. The details of the operation began to spread outwards. On Saturday evening Wallis joined Gibson in briefing Maudslay and Young, the two flight commanders, as well as Hopgood, the deputy leader for the attack on the Möhne and Bob Hay, of Martin's crew, the squadron bombing leader.

It was on this evening too that an incident occurred that claims a sad chapter all of its own in the Dam Busters legend. Gibson's labrador, Nigger, ran in front of a car in which both local occupants were injured as the driver attempted in vain to miss the dog. Nigger was killed. The news was passed upwards and it was Group Captain Whitworth who informed Gibson.

Two parts of the Gibson personality now came into operation. He was devastated by the loss of a dog he loved – his planning of the funeral arrangements is some indication of this – yet focused on a clear and vital objective, he was not a man to allow a personal tragedy to deflect him from his task. A determination to maintain security which had marked Gibson's entire approach to the operation was maintained to the last. On instructions from his boss, Humphries, the adjutant marked the order of battle, as 'night flying programme', though all the signs of preparation for something rather different ensured that only the more naive inhabitants of the airfield would have been taken in.

On Sunday, Gibson's day started with a visit to the doctor to seek advice on pains in his feet. The MO, understanding the situation, did not prescribe painkillers which might have made a pilot less alert. Gibson carried on suffering from gout.

First pilots and navigators were briefed by a team including Gibson and Wallis. Then they were joined by bomb aimers and gunners. Gibson stressed one of the major reasons why it was vital that the operation should succeed. If it didn't they would have to go back immediately and try again. The prospect of surviving two such attacks was slim.

At 6pm the final briefing was held for all the men of the nineteen Lancasters that would take part. Gibson, Wallis and Cochrane all spoke. There was still time afterwards for final preparations or for waiting and thinking. David Shannon would later say that John Hopgood clearly did not believe that he would return this time.

Three waves of aircraft would fly that night. The first (nine aircraft), including Gibson and what he later said he considered to be the best bombing crews in the squadron, would attack the Möhne, followed by the Eder. The second wave (six aircraft) would aim to divert enemy attention from the first wave, while attacking the Sorpe – a dam of different construction to the Möhne and Eder and for which particular plans had been laid. The third wave had four aircraft that would act as a reserve, being diverted by radio to the most appropriate target. Group Captain Whitworth would decide on the targets for these aircraft.

Two crews did not take part, those of Flight Lieutenant Wilson and Pilot Officer Divall. Officially there was illness in both crews, but Gibson quite possibly believed that one or both were not up to scratch. In any case, there were not sufficient specially modified aircraft available for twenty-one crews.

Humphries described the scene before take off in the squadron diary, though perhaps his assessment of the level of ignorance on the station was optimistic.

'This was *Der Tag* [The Day] for 617 Squadron. Hardly a soul, with the exception of the crews knew the target. Very few people outside the squadron knew we were operating – not even the WAAFs. From eight o'clock onwards the scenes outside the crew rooms were something to be remembered. It was not like an ordinary operational scene, all the crews on this occasion being aware of the terrific task confronting them. Most of them wore expressions varying from the 'don't care a damn' to the grim and determined. On the whole I think it appeared rather reminiscent of a crusade.

'Dave [Shannon] was late, leaving the crew room quite a while after his own crew was in the plane, and I anxiously wondered if our David, in his usual light hearted manner, had forgotten all about it. The wing commander turned up in his car prompt to time with crew. How they all got into that car beats me. He looked fit and well and quite unperturbed. Our favourite Yank, Flight Lieutenant McCarthy caused quite a disturbance. He arrived at his aircraft and after finding she had hydraulic trouble came dashing back to our only reserve aircraft. When inside he noticed he had no compass card and came rushing back to the Flights frantically screaming for one. He had also pulled his parachute by mistake and the white silk was streaming all over the ground, trailing behind him. With perspiration dropping off his face good old Mac ran back to his aircraft with everyone behind him trying to fix him up with what he wanted. He got off just in time.'

Martin's navigator, Flight Lieutenant Leggo, would be another to have compass problems. This was after he was airborne and he had to make allowances in his calculations.

At 2128 hours the signal was given from the control caravan to begin the attack on the Ruhr and Weser dams and the second wave aircraft skippered by Flight Lieutenant Barlow became the first aircraft to begin its take off.

Part of the talent of author Paul Brickhill, on whose novel *The Dam Busters* the film was based, was to create the atmosphere inside a Lancaster, a place much more cramped and difficult to move around in than many suppose. Brickhill wrote of Gibson's cockpit as the aircraft prepared to take off.

'G for George waddled forward with the shapeless bulk under its belly ("like a pregnant duck." Gibson had said), taxied to the south fence, swung its long snout to the north, and waited, engines turning quietly. P for Popsie turned slowly in on his left, and M for Mother on the right.

'Gibson rattled out the monotonous orders of his final check. "Flaps thirty." Pulford, the engineer, pumped down 30 degrees of flap, and repeated, "flaps 30." The instructions were given regarding the radiator and the throttles. Pulford confirmed that the radiators were opened, checked the nut on the throttle unit and confirmed "Throttles locked."'

Gibson was airborne at 2139 hours, quickly followed by Hopgood and Martin. Young, Maltby and Shannon followed. They lumbered into the air and immediately headed into the distance, rather than circling to gain height. At this point the third wave had two hours to wait before their take off time.

A surviving document from this night is the logbook of Sergeant Vivian Nicholson, the navigator in Maltby's aircraft. He noted, on becoming airborne, the switching on of the IFF (Identification Friend or Foe) device. The aircraft passed over Woodhall Spa, crossed The Wash, flew over East Dereham in Norfolk and, at Southwold, Suffolk, began its journey over the sea.

It was about forty minutes after take off that Gibson's flight left the coast and headed across the North Sea, very low and very much together. Spotlights were tried out successfully.

Problems were encountered but did not prove fatal. The auto pilot in G for George was u/s and strong wind led to navigational error. The flight crossed the island of South Beveland, but escaped attention from the defences. Bomb aimers had a key role in the navigation process over enemy territory and Pilot Officer Spafford in that position in Gibson's aircraft was using a roller 'like a roll of lavatory paper' to spot landmarks and avoid power cables.

Gibson wrote, 'We were flying low. We were so low that more than once Spam (Spafford) yelled at me to pull up quickly to avoid high tension wires and tall trees. Away on the right we could see [a] small town, its chimneys outlined against the night sky; we thought we saw someone flash us a 'V', but it may have been an innkeeper poking his head out of his bedroom window. The noise must have been terrific.'

Navigation was still a problem. They used the Rhine to regain course and came under some fire. Near Dulmen, Hopgood's aircraft was hit by flak. He was wounded, as were other members of the crew. In fact Pilot Officer Gregory in the front turret may have died at this point.

Opposition encountered included armed barges on the Rhine. Gibson's gunners returned their fire. The last turning point, near Ahlen, was relatively easy to spot from the abundance of converging railway lines. The track was to the north of another easily identifiable, but heavily defended, railway landmark – the marshalling yards at Hamm.

Gibson and his wave continued almost due south, came over the hills, with Martin now in the lead and found the Möhne lake. To Gibson, the dam looked 'squat and heavy and unconquerable'.

Young, Maltby and Shannon arrived safely, though some men noted a tendency of Young to fly rather high – a natural temptation when looking for a navigational feature – but one which affected chances of survival.

In Knight's aircraft, N for Nuts, one of the final group of three aircraft, from the nine of the first wave, Johnny Johnson, the bomb aimer, thought the outward flight was reasonable, 'No real trouble, some flak, some searchlights.' However, one of these three Lancasters was lost.

Running twenty minutes behind Gibson's group, Flight Lieutenant Astell's aircraft hit high tension cables at Marbeck, north east of Raesfeld. The Lancaster struck the ground and the Upkeep exploded. There were no survivors.

Later Gibson would describe Bill Astell as 'a grand Englishman from Derbyshire'. For Gibson, the first part of that compliment was from the top reaches of his scale.

At the Möhne lake, Gibson made a dummy run through the flak and then launched his attack, a straight run from the southern arm of the Möhne lake, over the Heversberg (hill) and direct to the dam. He flew into heavy flak, was not hit and released his weapon at 0028 hours. The great wall of water which erupted caused some of those present to assume that the CO had smashed the dam. He had not, the water subsided and the dam wall was still there.

It took several minutes for the water to calm sufficiently for another attack to be made. At this point, the two surviving aircraft from the third section arrived.

Hopgood in M for Mother, the deputy leader for this part of the operation, was next to attempt to breach the Möhne Dam. The German anti-aircraft gunners of course knew what to expect now. They scored several hits, including on at least one engine, probably two and the starboard wing. The mine was dropped late and bounced over the dam. Pilot Officer Fraser, the Canadian bomb aimer, would later say that he was considering going round again when the aircraft was hit and that was the point at which he pressed the release button. He also said that the intercom exchanges indicated that Sergeant Brennan, the flight engineer, had tried and failed to extinguish the fire.

The watching crews saw M for Mother, badly on fire and struggling to gain height. Then it exploded and the wreckage lay burning on the ground. Gibson took the optimistic view that some of the crew had survived and indeed they had – Pilot Officer Burcher from the rear turret, taking the exceptionally low height into consideration, broke the rules by releasing his parachute inside the aircraft. He suffered a severe back injury but lived. Fraser did the same with his parachute and survived unhurt.

According to Burcher's own account he had opened the parachute of the badly wounded wireless operator, Sergeant Minchin and pushed him out of the aircraft. Minchin, however, was found dead. Hopgood and his crew had achieved one thing at least. Their Upkeep had written off the dam's power house.

Over the history of the Victoria Cross there has been frequent debate over whether 'hot blooded' acts are as worthy of the ultimate recognition as 'cold blooded' feats. Now Gibson clearly displayed cold blooded heroism.

Five minutes after the demise of Hopgood's M for Mother, P for Popsie, skippered by Flight Lieutenant Martin, began its attack. Gibson flew ahead of him and to starboard, to distract the gunners. The effect was added to by fire from the gunners in G for George, Flight Sergeant Deering in the front and Flight Lieutenant Trevor-Roper in the rear.

Martin's Lancaster was hit by the flak, including damage to the, fortunately already empty, starboard outer fuel tank, but dropped its mine and came through. Still the dam held, although some of the anti-aircraft gunners on the ground thought momentarily that a breach had occurred.

Next came Squadron Leader Young and his crew in A for Apple. This time both Gibson and Martin flew with him. The spotlights on the wing commander's aircraft were flicked on and off as a further distraction for those on the ground.

At last there was success, though the fact was not realised immediately. Young's wireless operator, Sergeant Nichols, sent the codeword 'Goner', meaning an Upkeep released and his message was received in a gloomy atmosphere at the No 5 Group operations room at Grantham. This was where Harris, Cochrane and Wallis had gathered to follow events. Great disappointment was welling up inside Wallis. The Möhne should have gone by now.

While the fifth aircraft, J for Johnny, attacked, again accompanied by Gibson and Martin, the pilot, Flight Lieutenant Maltby, and members of his crew could see, as they released their Upkeep, that the wall was already crumbling, following Young's effort.

Still it was not obvious to everyone and apparently Maltby did not immediately report what he had seen. Gibson ordered Flight Lieutenant Shannon, his old comrade from No 106 Squadron, to make an attack.

Then came the revelation; a voice over the RT shouted, 'It's gone, it's gone'. Gibson told Shannon to wait. There was now a babble of voices which Gibson had to hush.

The CO flew closer to see what was happening. The Möhne Dam had been smashed. Gibson found a great breach which he estimated at 100 yards across. Water, looking like 'stirred porridge' was pouring through and heading into the Ruhr Valley. 'Hutch', the wireless operator in G for George ignored the general celebration over the air, instead causing a celebration to break out at Grantham when he sent the message, 'Nigger' indicating success at the Möhne.

At Grantham Wing Commander Wally Dunn, the Group Signals Officer, demanded, and received, confirmation. Witnesses recorded Barnes Wallis jumping in the air and pumping both arms.

Legend, and it can be believed, tells how Arthur Harris shook the boffin's hand, with the words, 'Wallis, I didn't believe a word you said when you came to see me. But now you could sell me a pink elephant.' The words that night were well remembered, but Harris would later deny that he had regarded Wallis in such a totally dismissive way at the initial meeting.

Over Germany Gibson was excited, in pain from his feet and firmly in control. He ordered Martin and Maltby to return to Scampton. Young, Maudslay, Shannon and Knight would accompany Gibson to the Eder Dam, less than a quarter of an hour's flying time away. Young, like Gibson, no longer had an Upkeep to deliver, but would take over as leader if Gibson were incapacitated.

Nothing happened on the short flight to cause a difficulty, the German night fighters had not intervened as they might well have done by this time, but the Eder Dam proved difficult to find. It was tucked away and mist was spreading across the waters of the reservoir. Initially Shannon found the Rehbach dam to the west and thought it was the target, though he was puzzled by the absence of the other Lancasters. He was put right by a red Very light fired from G for George.

Around five minutes were lost before Gibson was able to order Shannon to make his attack. The youthful Australian now faced a very tough challenge. His attack involved flying down the side valley to west of the impressive Waldeck Castle in the hills above the lake, turning tightly to port and crossing a spit before the final run to the target. At least the defences for the Eder were confined to soldiers with rifles. Such was the situation of the dam, deep in the valley, that the German view had been that air attack could be discounted.

The problems were not immediately overcome. Shannon made multiple unsuccessful attempts and so did Maudslay. Shannon eventually released his mine and caused an explosion of water, but no obvious damage to the dam.

On Maudslay's third run in Z for Zebra, the bomb aimer, Pilot Officer Fuller, released the Upkeep. It was late though and some of those watching, including Gibson, thought that the aircraft had been caught in the explosion. Others felt differently. The idea that Maudslay and his crew died as a result of their own explosion gained ground from the faint message which was heard from the aircraft in answer to a demand from Gibson to know if he was OK. A voice said, 'I think so, stand by'. To Sergeant O'Brien in the rear turret of Pilot Officer Knight's aircraft, the voice sounded unnatural, not human.

However, Z for Zebra did survive the explosion, though the Lancaster was probably damaged, and flew away from the Eder towards base. The survival was only temporary. Approaching the Dutch border, the aircraft was hit by flak and set on fire at Emmerich and crashed in a field to the north of the town. Maudslay, a veteran of the thousand bomber raids, and his crew now lie in the Reichswald Forest War Cemetery. Awards for three of the crew, for their service before 617 Squadron were gazetted after their deaths. In the case of Flying Officer Urquhart, RCAF, the navigator, this occurred as late as July 1945.

Gibson paid emotional tribute in *Enemy Coast Ahead* to 'Henry, the born leader.' He was, 'a great loss, but he gave his life for a cause for which men should be proud. Boys like Henry are the cream of our youth. They die bravely and they die young.'

At the Eder, with Astell and his crew long dead, there was only the New Zealander, Pilot Officer Knight in N for Nuts to come. Knight made one dummy run, with much advice coming over the air. Then, with Flight Sergeant Kellow having switched off the radio on the instructions of his skipper, another run was made, the Upkeep was released, the aircraft stood on its tail to climb out of the valley. O'Brien in the rear turret and Kellow, standing at the astrodome, both saw a hole appear in the Eder dam and the water start pouring through it.

Shannon's bomb aimer, the big ex-guardsman, Flight Sergeant Len Sumpter, would remember seeing the headlights of a car which was gradually being overtaken by the water. The lights dimmed and then vanished as the vehicle was submerged.

The code word 'Dinghy', meaning that the Eder had gone was transmitted to Grantham and confirmed. It was at this point that Harris phoned the Chief of the Air Staff, Sir Charles Portal in Washington and gave him the news for onward transmission to the Prime Minister and then the President of the United States. The propaganda machine which would be attached to the Dam Busters was already under way.

Unfortunately there is no truth in the delightful story that a nervous WAAF at Grantham, instructed by Harris to get him the White House, phoned a nearby pub of that name, the landlord of which, grumpy at being woken up, then gave the AOC-in-C an earful.

Now, with no aircraft from the first wave available to attack the Sorpe dam, the task was to get back to Scampton as quickly as possible through the thoroughly wide-awake German defences.

One more did not make it. Perhaps 'Dinghy' Young was flying rather too high again. As he came out over the Dutch coast, his Lancaster was hit by flak and came down on a sandbank just off the beach at Castricum-aan-Zee. Local witnesses say that wreckage remained where it fell until broken up by the storms of 1953.

Shannon's aircraft was the first to land of those that had gone to the Eder, a few minutes ahead of Gibson, who had flown over the Möhne and studied the results there of the night's work. Gibson's wheels touched Scampton at 0415 hours. Ahead of all the survivors was debriefing, partying, reflection on the losses and celebrity, before operations claimed their attention again. For Gibson there were onerous additional prospects including reporting on the operation and ensuring the despatch of letters to the next-of-kin of those who were missing. His rigorous attention to the letters showed a softer side in an outwardly tough man. So did his comforting of Wallis who, initially elated at the triumph, had become distraught when he realised the extent of the casualties. The thought of the losses haunted Wallis for the rest of his life, his daughter Mary has said.

The second wave of aircraft had been tasked to attack the earthwork Sorpe dam, though the Upkeep weapon was much more suitable for structures such as the Möhne. Flight Lieutenant 'Norm' Barlow's aircraft, E for Easy, had been the first to set off on Chastise, unsticking from Scampton just before 2130 hours. Just after crossing into Germany the Lancaster struck power cables near Rees and crashed, killing all on board. The Upkeep did not explode and therefore fell into enemy hands. The book *Dambuster Crash Sites* says that a large piece of wreckage was used by a farmer to cover the access to a farmyard sewage pit, until he sold it to the authors of that book in 2002.

Flight Lieutenant Munro's aircraft, W for William, crossed into the Netherlands, but was hit by light flak in the area of Vlieland in the West Frisian islands. The damage, as assessed by Sergeant Frank Appleby, Munro's flight engineer, was severe including the loss of the ability of the crew to communicate with each other by intercom, or with other aircraft. From then on, recalled Appleby later, Munro used handwritten notes and Appleby as runner, as a new means of communication.

After much heart searching the skipper decided to return with his mine. He would receive an unfairly frosty reaction from Gibson. Years after, Les Munro said of having to return, 'I was bitterly disappointed, but I suppose that is why I am alive today.'

Pilot Officer Vernon Byers was one of the older aircrew on Operation Chastise and also one of those who was relatively inexperienced. He was 32 years old and had flown on four operations with No 467 Squadron. The crash site of this aircraft in the sea in the area of Texel and Vlieland is still disputed. Byers was brought down by anti-aircraft fire and was off course at the time. Only one body was discovered. Flight Sergeant James McDowell, believed to have been in the rear turret, is buried in Harlingen General Cemetery.

Yet more problems for the second wave occurred to the aircraft flown by Pilot Officer Geoff Rice. Approaching Vlieland the crew witnessed an aircraft going down and this may have been Byers. Soon afterwards, Sergeant Smith, the flight engineer, spotted that the altimeter was registering zero. Before he could warn the pilot, the aircraft shuddered and shuddered again as Rice fought for height, and water poured through the fuselage. The mine was torn from its mounting and disappeared. In the rear turret Sergeant Burns found himself swamped by water and disinfectant and whatever else was in the smashed Elsan toilet.

A very depressed Rice turned back. Sweetman records one of those classic wartime misunderstandings of a signal. As Scampton was approached, Warrant Officer Gowrie, wireless operator, informed control, 'Aircraft damaged, possibly no flaps'. The crew assumed crash positions and Rice landed on the front wheels, the tail wheel having gone. In doing so he had a near miss with Munro who had also returned and had no means of reporting that fact. Later a WAAF operator enquired of Rice as to what he had meant by his report that the aircraft was damaged and 'without a clutch'. Whitworth commiserated with Rice, Harris told him he was very lucky and, according to Rice's own account, Gibson was relatively sympathetic on his return.

Only the much delayed McCarthy of the second wave was therefore still pressing on towards the dams. He came under fire from flak, saw night fighters and the gunners exchanged fire with a heavily armed train. There were navigation problems as well, though that did not prevent them flying over the Möhne Dam and seeing the breach. The Sorpe dam was reached, where, for the pilot, a particular problem was the church spire at the village of Langscheid.

Sergeant Johnson, in the bomb aimer's position, was something of a perfectionist and, despite some unrest amongst the crew, it was not until the tenth pass over the dam that he released the mine. At the time, McCarthy claimed that a small breach had been achieved, but later intelligence reduced this to some damage.

After midnight, the reserve wave left Scampton. Each of the five crews had been given one of the alternative targets and each needed to be prepared to attack the Möhne or the Eder if one or both of those were still standing and they were so directed.

Pilot Officer Warner Ottley's C for Charlie met its fate near Hamm. Perhaps flying too high, the aircraft was coned and shot down. Remarkably, Sergeant Fred Tees, the rear gunner, survived, though badly injured. He later said that immediately before disaster struck, Sergeant Guterman, the wireless operator, had reported the destruction of the Möhne. The Lister Dam had therefore become C for Charlie's target. According to the No 617 Squadron operations record book, the order to go to the Lister was acknowledged. However, another change of plan was transmitted immediately – to head for the Sorpe – and this was not acknowledged.

Other crews in the reserve formation saw Ottley crash as probably did Gibson, from a considerable distance, and on his return journey. Fred Tees died in 1982. His ashes were placed in the Reichswald Forest War Cemetery, alongside the graves of his comrades.

Comrades also witnessed the death of the crew of S for Sugar, Pilot Officer Burpee's aircraft. Hit by flak while off course, it exploded and crashed in the vicinity of Gilze Rijen airfield, the bomb detonating too. Shortly afterwards Group attempted to send S for Sugar to the Sorpe. Gibson would recall Lewis Burpee, about to become a father at the time of his death, as, 'slow of speech and slow of movement, but a good pilot.'

F for Freddie, flown by Flight Sergeant Brown, did reach a target. In this aircraft a last minute change of personnel was made when one of the air gunners, Sergeant Buntaine, reported sick. Sergeant Daniel Allatson from Divall's crew took the front turret.

Brown found the familiar situation of the difficulty of navigating in all the circumstances, as well as missing power lines and finding plenty of flak exploding close by. He later recalled almost flying through the front door of a German castle.

Then the aircraft received the signal 'Dinghy', indicating that the Eder had gone and the Sorpe was to be the target. At the dam Brown found that the mist had worsened since McCarthy had attacked the same target two and a half hours before. He was also conscious of the difficulty caused by the church spire. A number of attempts were aborted, one pass in particular nearly culminating in disaster, before Brown told Sergeant Hewstone, the wireless operator, to drop incendiaries to guide the subsequent run. The mine was released and more crumbling of the dam wall achieved, but the Sorpe was not breached.

Brown was another to observe the devastation at the Möhne. He reported that a flak gunner opened up from below, but stopped after intense fire from Flight Sergeant McDonald, the rear gunner. As they continued, incendiaries were tossed at suitable targets and then there was the ordeal of crossing the coast through the flak, very low and very fast and with dawn well broken. They came through. Flight engineer 'Bas' Feneron relieved the very tired pilot, and took the controls over the sea, remaining in control until the sight of the twin towers of Lincoln Cathedral confirmed that it was almost time for landing.

Heading back to England half an hour after Brown, even more exposed by the approach of daylight, was O for Orange, skippered by Flight Sergeant Bill Townsend, which had been ordered to attack the Ennepe. Three times Sergeant Charles Franklin called 'dummy run', before releasing the Upkeep on the fourth. Its fall was slightly short and the dam wall survived the explosion. John Sweetman put forward the theory that O for Orange in fact attacked the Bever Dam – a point on which the discussion continues.

For this crew too, there was the chance to be amazed at the sight of the destruction at the Möhne before a return to base packed with danger. Bill Townsend was an outstanding pilot, a fact that played a major part in a safe arrival.

However, he was now exhausted, had only three engines and an oil-smeared windscreen. In those circumstances he made a rotten landing in front of the large crowd of all ranks who had gathered to welcome the last aircraft home. He then was rather crotchety to Arthur Harris, whom he did not recognise. Townsend survived that experience too.

Y for Yorker, captained by Flight Sergeant Anderson, was sent to the Sorpe. The aircraft became seriously lost, the rear guns were not functioning, the time was moving towards dawn and Anderson took the decision to turn back to Scampton with his Upkeep still on board.

Immediately now, Guy Gibson and the men he commanded were national heroes. Gibson, a person who had demonstrated his ability to inspire others to follow him into great danger and die in the process, was still only 24 years old. He had survived a great many operations and now and in the months ahead, he would move into new worlds. He would become a celebrity and a figure of national importance, used in a new form of inspiration to encourage the prosecution of the war effort.

The impact of the destruction of two dams on the German war effort was hardly what the pre-war planners had hoped and supposed. The Möhne and the Eder were rebuilt, with the Germans finding it a puzzle that the RAF did not make great efforts to prevent that work.

However, the material damage inflicted on the German war effort is almost immaterial. The propaganda and the morale value of what No 617 Squadron – and Gibson above all – achieved was beyond dispute and remains so. This was the foundation of their fame and a major justification for that fame lasting seventy years.

In addition the Dam Busters had staged a demonstration of the ability of Bomber Command to launch a precision attack and Gibson had, in effect, become the command's first pilot to act as a master bomber.

The public glory was not long in coming. The story was in many newspapers, and not just in Britain, on Tuesday 18 May, as many in 617 Squadron set off on leave. Gibson went on leave too at the end of the week, travelling to south Wales, to Eve and her family. He was there on Sunday, 23 May, when Sir Arthur Harris telephoned to tell him of the award of the Victoria Cross. This was a moment that Gibson, more than many, should have cherished, but there is no doubt that he was also deeply troubled by the loss of so many comrades.

Perhaps John Hopgood was the one he felt most saddened about. After all, they were very close and he had persuaded 'Hoppy' to come on the great adventure with him. There were other friends too though and even more who he had known only briefly, or hardly at all and who he had also led to their deaths. There was a party, but the losses, even that of Nigger, weighed heavily.

Over the next few days the award of the VC and the thirty-three other decorations for the attack were announced in a supplement to the *London Gazette* and reported in the press. Then on Thursday, 27 May, the King and Queen came to Scampton, met survivors and had the attack explained to them.

Following that honour, there was a trip to Sheffield for Gibson, the new celebrity, to support Mrs Churchill in promoting 'Wings for Victory' week, more leave with Eve at St Ives in Cornwall and a return to his old school. More public exposure and celebration came with the investiture at Buckingham Palace, when the Queen presented all the 617 Squadron awards together and before all the other awards due that day. Adding to Gibson's mixed view of his situation was the fact that, unsurprisingly, he was forbidden to fly on further operations.

No. 617 Squadron,
RAF Station,
Scampton,
Lincs.

20 May 1943
My Dear Mrs Tees,
It is with deep regret that I write to confirm by telegram advising you that your son, Sergeant F. Tees, is missing as a result of operations on the night of May 16/17th 1943.

Your son was front gunner of an aircraft detailed to carry out an attack against the Möhne Dam. Contact with this aircraft was lost after it took off, and nothing further was heard from it.

It is possible that the crew were able to abandon the aircraft and land safely in enemy territory in which case news will reach you direct from the International Red Cross Committee within the next six weeks. The captain of your son's aircraft, Pilot Officer Ottley, was an experienced and able pilot, and would, I am sure, do everything possible to ensure the safety of his crew.

Please accept my sincere sympathy during this anxious period of waiting.

I have arranged for your son's personal effects to be taken care of by the Committee of the Adjustment Officer at this Station, and these will be forwarded to you through normal channels in due course.

If there is any way in which I can help you please let me know.

Yours *very sincerely*

Guy Gibson

Wing Commander,
Commanding,
617 Squadron,
RAF.

Mrs. E. Tees,
23, St. James Rd.,
Chichester,
Sussex.

The words in italics were handwritten.

In fact, Sergeant Tees was the rear gunner of C for Charlie and survived as a prisoner of war.

This is the letter that, according to legend, was sent to *The Times* immediately after Operation Chastise by No 617 Squadron officers. It was not published:

Dear Sir

In international bird watching circles the bombing of the Möhne Dam has caused grave concern. For three years previous to the outbreak of war a pair of ring-necked whooper swans nested regularly on the lake. They are almost the rarest of Europe's great birds. The only other pair known to have raised a brood during recent years were a pair of the Arctic sub species which were photographed by the aunt of the late Professor Olssen of Reykjavik on their nest on the shore of Lake Thongvallavatn, Iceland, in 1927.

Has anything been heard of the fate of the Moehne pair, probably the last in Europe? And, in view of the rarity of these beautiful birds, why was bombing of their home permitted? Furthermore, assuming that this operation was necessary, could it not have been deferred until the cygnets, if any, were fully grown.

Yours faithfully, etc.

Chapter 13

Two Very Different Debates

What happened in M for Mother?

Of all the mist and fog shrouding some elements of Operation Chastise, perhaps more than most attaches to what went on inside M for Mother. From the two men who survived, Pilot Officer Burcher gave various accounts of what happened. Sometimes they seemed to conflict and sometimes they seemed to claim knowledge of what was going on at the front of the aircraft that a rear gunner was unlikely to have.

It has been suggested by at least one historian that Hopgood was recommended for a posthumous Victoria Cross. His claim to one being that he had been wounded by flak on the outward flight, had pressed on, concealing his difficulty from his crew, had pressed home his attack and had then remained at the controls, fighting for more height, in an attempt to allow his crew to escape. A further claim has been made that, on their return from imprisonment, Burcher and Fraser were interviewed about what had happened and asked if they would sign witness statements. This was quite normal in cases where a VC was being considered, but surviving witnesses had become prisoners.

The allegation from one historian is that Burcher was prepared to sign, but Fraser was not. This hardly accords with the fact that Fraser's eldest son was given the names John Hopgood, his daughter received the name Shere (the Surrey village in which 'Hoppy' was born) and a younger son was named in tribute to Guy Gibson.

Robert Owen, historian of the No 617 Squadron Association, commented on these and other suggestions. 'There are other enigmas in respect of this crew and the stories of the survivors that simply do not add up. Conflicting evidence, though not disproving absolutely, creates areas of uncertainty. I am wary of "the facts" as variously claimed, and whilst keeping an open mind, fear that it is now too late to get to the truth in many cases.'

Untrue though the story may be, it is worth airing as an instance of the kinds of tales that have developed around the Dam Busters.

The treatment of Cyril Anderson and his crew

Cyril Anderson and his crew had failed, for whatever reason, on Operation Chastise and their treatment is normally presented in terms of 'instant dismissal' and return to where they had been. This is broadly true, though they were not officially posted until early June and Anderson managed to look cheerful in some versions of the photographs taken of the surviving pilots hours after their return.

It may be no more than unfortunate coincidence that the pilot who was deemed to have put up the least worthy performance was also the one who stood out because of his social background. In terms of 'class' Gibson and Anderson had nothing in common and the older man was only just in the process of becoming an officer. That thought has to be set against the clear fact that the crew of Y for Yorker had not accomplished their task and had not achieved even the 'glorious failure' of some crews or the clear reason for failure of Munro and Rice.

So much faith is placed in the navigator of an aircraft. There are moments when the rest of the crew, including the pilot, is very much reliant on him. Eyes, at least metaphorically, are watching him and waiting for a decision. Sergeant Nugent must have felt the pressure very much that night.

Robert Owen Official Historian of the No 617 Squadron Association in a letter to the author in 2012 wrote,

'With regard to Anderson's return and dismissal from the squadron; this is understandable if one puts oneself in Gibson's shoes. He had completed a stressful and demanding operation and seen one of his best friends (Hopgood) go down in flames, with little chance of having survived. Others too had died. Gibson's own 'press on' spirit may have been affronted by this apparent lack of determination (as he saw it) and he may have also allowed personal emotions, and fatigue to influence his decision.

'He may also have considered (if so, erroneously in my opinion) that one more Upkeep on the Sorpe might have made the difference. Perhaps also there was an element of "to discourage others".

'That is not to say that the decision to post Anderson from the squadron was necessarily wrong, but a fuller examination of the circumstances (now impossible since none of the participants are available for comment) would be needed to make a dispassionate assessment.

'In reality, given the problems facing Anderson, it must have been a difficult decision for this captain to make, more so knowing Gibson's likely response to such a decision to return. Some might think that fear of the consequences of returning, having failed to reach the target, was almost as great as that of trying to continue the operation. As it is, Anderson saved both his crew and a valuable, modified aircraft.

'Recent works have stated that Gibson accused Anderson not only of lacking determination, but that he is also reported as saying that "Anderson flew up and down the North Sea all night". Despite cited attribution, I cannot believe that this was the case. The "quote" may be mis-remembered, or taken out of context – "For all the good they did they might as well have flown up and down the North Sea all night", or similar, might be the actual wording. It is inconceivable that had he proof of any deliberate shirking of task, Gibson would not have had the crew court martialed – not simply returned to their original unit.

'Were this accusation true, then to fake navigation logs etc to construct a scenario that they had got part way to the target and then decided to return with their Upkeep, knowing that this would trigger the CO's ire, seems out of the question. The risk of the concocted logs being identified as such would be great. It would make as much, if not more sense, if the crew did want to avoid this operation, to have dropped their Upkeep in the North Sea and then used the briefed flight plan to fudge a log to make out that they had reached and attacked their target, but failed to breach it. Alternatively they could have returned with an account of an assumed or fabricated mechanical or equipment failure.

'Thus I prefer to believe the official explanation and do not consider that these conspiracy theories stand up to close examination.'

Conspiracy theories rarely do provide the answer to controversy. Further argument against them is provided by the rest of the brief career of Cyril Anderson and his comrades.

In all the circumstances they were happy to return to No 49 Squadron at Fiskerton, where they were given a short rest. They then resumed operations. On the night of 22/23 September 1943 Pilot Officer Anderson and his Dams crew were tasked to attack Mannheim. They reached the target and bombed, but soon afterwards, were intercepted by a Luftwaffe Messerscmitt Bf 110 flown by Leutnant Heinz Grimm. The Lancaster was shot down and there were no survivors. Two weeks later Leutnant Grimm was fatally wounded in a friendly fire incident.

Dom Howard, a great nephew of Cyril Anderson, has worked to establish the truth in his relative's story. With the help of a German team of researchers, he has located the crash site and recovered some items, with more activity planned. He talked to Cyril Anderson's widow, Rose, and was told that Anderson, 'did not like Gibson at all, it seems the feeling was mutual.'

Howard feels that Anderson suffered because he was too honest. He wrote, 'If they had just dropped Upkeep on what they thought was the dam I think things would have been completely different but their honesty in bringing Upkeep home and saying they were unable to locate [made them suffer]. Gibson took the decision that this was not good enough.'

Chapter 14

Anti-Climax

After the hard work, the danger, the success, exuberance, congratulation and celebration came the let down for Guy Gibson. He was not to fly on operations and so, although he remained commanding officer of the squadron and so a part of his favoured world, he was only largely a spectator within it. To some extent that must have been worse than being sent away.

Both flight commanders had failed to return from the Dams. Their replacements not only ran their flights but largely ran the squadron given Gibson's non-operational status.

Neither of the new flight commanders would survive very long and the pair have been treated very differently by history. David Maltby had been newly-promoted to squadron leader, had played a major part in the Dams attack and has come down to us, quite rightly, as part of the legend. In the short history of the squadron he was an insider.

Since 2008 he has had his own biography, *Breaking the Dams*, written by his nephew, Charles Foster, who also provides moving detail of the men who flew to the dams with David Maltby and later died with him. A picture emerges of a big cheerful man from an immediate close family, who made friends easily.

Flight Lieutenant Harry Humphries, the 617 Squadron adjutant, described Maltby as having, 'a natural aptitude for being popular' and in the mess, 'always like a big schoolboy, always ready for a practical joke'. In other words he was Gibson's type, sharing some of his leader's attributes, while achieving a more rounded personality.

He also achieved an obituary in *The Times*, which Foster suggests might have been written by Maltby's uncle, Aubrey Hatfeild. In this he is said to have insisted, when his DSO was announced, that all the credit should go to 'his very fine crew, his grand ground staff and magnificent Lancaster.'

Even accounting for the possible origin of the tribute from within the family and the emotion of the time towards a Dam Buster, David Maltby comes across as a man rather unlike Gibson, yet a man of the sort whom Gibson wanted to have around him. Certainly, the story of the Dams cannot be told, whether in fact or legend, without placing David Maltby in a leading role.

George Holden, on the other hand, a post-dams arrival, is not so fondly remembered. He does not seem to have been popular, he lasted a very short time after eventually taking over the squadron and when he died some of Gibson's legendary crew died with him. One of those who has been quoted as not liking Holden was John Pulford. The Yorkshireman seems to have been rather unlucky with his 'choice' of skippers, given that Gibson made obvious his lack of respect for his flight engineer.

There is at least one story about Holden's time with 617 Squadron which places him in focus as a bully and as somebody lacking respect for the lower orders. So there is perhaps a hint of similarity to Gibson there.

Holden was thirty when he died, so he had more of an opportunity to mature than Gibson. He also died as a holder of the DSO, DFC and bar and with at least one Mention in Despatches to his name. A few hours before he was killed and, while planning the raid on which he would be killed, Holden fulfilled the deeply unpleasant duty of visiting Mrs Nina Maltby to talk to her about her husband's death. Some COs would have found a way of dodging that task.

So there are things to be said in favour of George Holden, but the verdict of most accounts is against him.

Replacements generally posed much the same issues for the squadron as the original recruitment of aircrew had done. Considering this issue, Robert Owen wrote,

'As far as replacements go, the same difficulty existed within No 5 Group, exacerbated by having already trawled to form the squadron.

'Thus (there was) the casting of a wider net to include other groups – not ideal, since, whilst this would catch operationally experienced crews, they would not have experience on type.

'Post-Chastise, the squadron's reputation worked both for and against it. Seen by some as a glamour unit, it attracted some volunteers who were not suitable and who were not selected, whilst some who had the desired qualities possibly looked upon it as an "on op", suicide squadron and did not wish to become part of what might be a short-lived posting. In some respects, in the light of events of September 1943 they may be considered to have foresight.'

Gibson was seeking to fulfil the role he had acquired of national and public hero, while also being a bystander. He flew, for example on what seems to have been an exercise to test smoke defences in the Upper Derwent Valley. There was much concern that the enemy might try to launch its own version of the Dam Busters.

From now on there remains regular difficulty in tracking some of Gibson's movements (unless he was doing something that others were recording in detail) in part because of the careless way in which he maintained his logbook. This was never a document of great precision. Now its value as an historical record declined some more.

There is sometimes debate on why Guy Gibson was not promoted above the rank of wing commander in the sixteen months between Operation Chastise and his death. There are a number of possible reasons for this which appear reasonable.

Gibson was an 'operational type'. Administration and paperwork were not his strengths, therefore to become a group captain and be placed in charge of a station would have been a considerable trial for him. As a station commander, the temptation would have been overwhelming to find reasons to fly on operations.

A consideration here must have been that to capture Gibson would have been a gift for the enemy. Here was the man who had commanded Chastise, had met Churchill and Harris and held the highest British decoration. He could be interrogated and used, however much he might resist, for purposes of propaganda to the detriment of British public morale and negotiation. Alternatively, the Germans might have decided that Gibson warranted much harsher treatment than the typical PoW.

Equally, a staff role, even further removed from the front line, would not have been a good use of his talents. In addition, he spent so long removed from the operational environment that he was 'behind the curve', to quote Robert Owen, in terms of operational equipment and tactics, reducing further his suitability for a posting to Group or Bomber Command HQ duties, where staff were employing increasingly sophisticated techniques.

Arguably too, his status as a 'celebrity', a public relations ambassador for the British war effort, had overtaken any requirement for a higher rank. In a normal RAF career progression, higher rank is one passport to more respect. With Gibson his rank had largely become irrelevant.

Finally, there has to be the thought that those in authority considered that, as a wing commander, he had reached his appropriate rank. A fundamental requirement of developing managers in any environment is to know when not to promote further, thus avoiding losing a high performer at one level and acquiring a low performer at the next level up.

A portrait of Wing Commander Guy Penrose Gibson VC, DSO & Bar, DFC & Bar. Gibson's decorations are displayed at the RAF Museum, Hendon.

Wing Commander Guy Gibson's office at RAF Scampton was on the first floor of the annex to the right of the No 617 Squadron hangar entrance – the top right window in this view. The final resting place for Gibson's dog, Nigger, can be seen in the foreground. (Martin Mace/HMP)

Wing Commander Guy Gibson's office at RAF Scampton, recreated by volunteers of the RAF Scampton Museum as it would have appeared during the war. (Martin Mace/HMP)

Guy Gibson, on the right, pictured about to board a Lancaster with his Wireless Operator on the Dams raid, Flight Lieutenant R.E.G. "Hutch" Hutchison. Gibson is wearing a German life-jacket which he picked up as a trophy from one of the aircraft he had shot down earlier in the war. (ww2images)

A photograph said to have been taken from Guy Gibson's Lancaster over the Derwent Dam. (Courtesy Vic Hallam, Derwent Valley Museum)

Wing Commander Guy Gibson and his crew board their Avro Lancaster, ED932/G, for the Dams raid. Left to right are: Flight Lieutenant R.D. Trevor-Roper DFM; Sergeant J. Pulford; Flight Sergeant G.A. Deering RCAF; Pilot Officer F.M. Spafford DFM RAAF; Flight Lieutenant R.E.G. Hutchison DFC; Wing Commander Guy Gibson; Pilot Officer H.T. Taerum RCAF. (Imperial War Museum; CH18005)

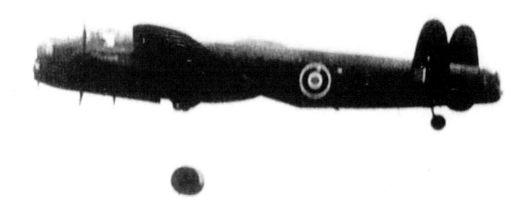

An Upkeep falls away from one of the Operation Chastise Lancasters – though this photograph almost certainly depicts a training flight, quite possibly at Reculver, involving a concrete-filled practice variant of the Upkeep. (HMP)

This drawing of Operation *Chastise* underway was created at the request of the Ministry of Information for propaganda purposes during the Second World War. (Martin Mace/HMP)

Success: Huge quantities of water pour through the breach in the Möhne Dam – an image which clearly shows the depth of water which was lost following the attack. As a result of this breach some 335 million tons of water flooded the West Ruhr valleys. In its path, this flood destroyed 125 factories, made some 3,000 hectares of arable land useless, demolished twenty-five bridges and badly damaged twenty-one more. (HMP)

Part of the main undercarriage leg of de Havilland Mosquito XX KB267 (coded AZ-E) – the aircraft in which Wing Commander Guy Penrose Gibson VC, DSO & Bar, DFC & Bar and Squadron Leader James "Jim" Warwick DFC were killed on 19 September 1944. (Courtesy of Anna Haworth)

Amongst the remains of KB267 exhibited at the excellent RAF Scampton Museum are these pieces of the Mosquito's fuselage markings, superimposed on a representative background. (Martin Mace/HMP)

The standard CWGC headstones marking the last resting places of Wing Commander Guy Penrose Gibson VC, DSO & Bar, DFC & Bar and Squadron Leader James "Jim" Warwick DFC in Steenbergen-en-Kruisland Roman Catholic Cemetery. The two headstones, the only Commonwealth 1939-1945 war casualties commemorated in this cemetery, are situated on the left side of the first avenue from the entrance. (via Martin Mace/HMP)

Much of the area around Gibson's crash site has been developed in the years since the war. The town of Steenbergen has since honoured Gibson and Warwick by naming streets after both of them – Gibsonstraat (seen here) and Warwickstraat. The roads are stated to meet on the exact location of the crash which is marked by a brick mosaic of the Union Flag. On the day that this photograph was taken, a chance arrival at the location by the photographer coincided with a fire in a nearby industrial unit. The smoke billowing into the sky may have looked much the same as on the night of 19/20 September 1944. (Courtesy of Anna Haworth)

The memorial to Gibson and the Dam Busters, made from the propeller of the de Havilland Mosquito in which he crashed, in the Dutch town of Steenbergen. (via Martin Mace/HMP)

Group Captain David Robertson, former Officer Commanding, No 617 Squadron, unveils a plaque in honour of Guy Gibson on the Porthleven Council Institute building at the harbourside, May 16 2012. On the right is Vic Strike, a distant relative of Guy Gibson's mother. (RAF St Mawgan)

Wing Commander Guy Gibson pictured sitting in a poppy field reading a book, 22 July 1943. (Imperial War Museum; TR1125)

A very distinguished wartime pilot would tell the story of how, as a post war group captain, he went to the Air Ministry to seek information about his promotion prospects. There an equally famous Second World War pilot, now in a staff job, drew the enquirer's attention to a list of then current group captains and very gently asked where the enquirer felt he ranked intellectually in that list. Having concluded that the answer was 'well down' the officer concerned shortly afterwards retired. Gibson did not lack intellect, but that is not the only quality required for higher rank.

Robert Owen commented,

'In some respects, if authority was trying to protect him, and prevent his return to operations, it might have been easier to have promoted him to group captain, thus further restricting his possibilities (and possibly his own expectations) for a return to ops.

'Since Gibson hankered after an operational role, and as long as the powers that be considered that he should not return to operations, the path that he followed appears to have been one of a narrow spectrum open to him. It was, perhaps, not the best, since placing him in an operational environment, yet denying him full participation (i.e. flying on ops) led to a seemingly inevitable result.'

Towards the end of July, Gibson's national status rose another notch. He was summoned to lunch, with his wife, at Chequers, the official country retreat for all Prime Ministers, set beautifully beneath the Chiltern Hills, near Aylesbury. The house and grounds had been presented for the use of the Prime Minister by Lord and Lady Lee of Fareham in 1921.

'Action this day' was a favourite Churchill expression. He tended to prefer men who responded to that injunction, rather than those who counselled a delay, however good their reasons might be. Gibson was in the right mould. At the same time as his Chequers visit, Churchill was corresponding about the merits of the controversial General Orde Wingate and considering his merits for higher office in the Far East. Wingate had some of the same characteristics as Gibson and was another person whom the Prime Minister would take off on tour with him.

After the lunch party of ten people, guests joined the Prime Minister in one of his favourite pastimes – watching films. By Eve Gibson's account she learned while walking round the rose garden with Mr Churchill that her husband would be going across the Atlantic. For Eve her visit to Chequers remained one of the highlights of her life. Later the same day, Gibson was in London and saw Air Chief Marshal Portal, the Chief of the Air Staff.

Gibson's next assignment was now being considered against a background of the constant British need to shore up relations with the United States, as well as the need to ensure that Canadians continued to believe that the sacrifices involved in their contribution of men to Bomber Command were having an impact and were appreciated.

In *Bomber Offensive*, published two years after the war, Arthur Harris underlined the point, writing, 'In January 1943, thirty-seven per cent of the pilots of Bomber Command belonged to the Dominion and Colonial Air Forces and of those sixty per cent were Canadian, forty per cent coming from other parts of the Empire – mainly from the Australian and New Zealand air forces.'

At the time of Operation Chastise, Churchill had been in the United States, arriving on the *Queen Mary*, staying at both the White House and what is now Camp David, the American equivalent of Chequers, and addressing Congress. During his speech there he had made much of the success of Chastise.

On 4 August 1943, Churchill sailed again in the *Queen Mary*, with Gibson as part of the considerable retinue accompanying him, which also included Mrs Churchill and their daughter Mary. The latter was given the post of her father's ADC and celebrated her twenty-first birthday while she was away.

The ship left from the Clyde, after many of those in the party had travelled in a special train from London. Churchill had averted plans for a meeting between Roosevelt and Stalin without him and was now to have another of his own series of meetings with the American President, in what became known as the first Quebec conference. It was codenamed Quadrant and a second conference in Quebec in 1944 would be Octagon. One of the decisions taken at the conference would be that the supreme commander for the landings in northern France, when they came in due course, would be American and not British.

Gibson enjoyed the whole experience though he was, theoretically, a very junior personage in a party which also included Portal, a great deal of other 'top brass' and government ministers. Both Gibson and Wingate were called on to meet Churchill privately, as well as to present to the combined chiefs of staff their experience of special operations. Gibson also addressed the entire assembled party on Operation Chastise.

While the Prime Minister was dealing with the great affairs of state and taking decisions on the course of the war, Gibson would spend not far short of four months in Canada and the United States, playing the part of Victoria Cross holding war hero, to the delight of many that he met.

An early engagement, on his birthday, 12 August, was to take a large press conference at which he demonstrated an ability, as he would on many further occasions, to say the right thing, telling the international press corps, 'RCAF fliers are just as good as RAF fliers. The RCAF, in my opinion, is just like the RAF. We fly under the same flag. We wear the same uniform and we fight the same enemy. We are very good pals too. Those who come over to us are jolly well trained. I don't know anything about their training. That's what I am going to try to find out.'

Sure enough, a week later Gibson visited an Air Observer School and officiated at a graduation ceremony, where flying badges were presented to men from a number of countries, including both Canada and Britain. Since early in the war Canada had played a major part in the British Commonwealth Air Training Plan through which large numbers of aircrew passed before heading to Britain, eventually to see action.

Those graduating had the opportunity to be congratulated by two VCs of the air. Also present was the Canadian First World War recipient, Air Vice Marshal Billy Bishop.

The pace after that might with some justice be described as relentless. In Canada places he visited included Banff, Montreal, Winnipeg, Moose Jaw, Calgary, Halifax, Ottawa and Vancouver and south of the border with the United States, Chicago, Washington DC, Los Angeles, Hollywood, San Francisco and Minneapolis.

At Bolling Field, near Washington, named after a senior American officer killed in the First World War, Gibson was presented with the American Legion of Merit, awarded for exceptionally meritorious conduct. The insignia was handed over by General Henry 'Hap' Arnold.

While in Canada, Gibson met Robert Young, younger brother of Melvin Young. Robert was about to qualify as a wireless operator. Gibson also met the mother of his Dams navigator, 'Terry' Taerum. Tragically, Taerum was killed in action a few days later.

At this time, the Assistant Air Attache in the British Embassy in Washington, coming towards the end of his posting, was Flight Lieutenant Roald Dahl, of Norwegian parentage. Dahl, already an author with many connections, had pushed the idea of a film to demonstrate to the American public the impact of the bombing of enemy targets. Howard Hawks, the top Hollywood film producer, director and screenwriter became involved. Gibson met both men, with the project turning into a film about the destruction of the dams.

A script was produced by Dahl, which had some florid touches and plenty of inaccuracies, though some of those could be accounted for by security considerations. Barnes Wallis for one took great exception to his depiction under the name of 'Professor Johnstone'.

The film was not made and a script from the same source, intended for Canadian radio, was not broadcast. What did eventually appear (in December 1943) was an article in the American magazine, *Atlantic Monthly*, purportedly written by Gibson, but certainly with chunks of Dahl's efforts included. It was called, "Cracking the Dams". This was regurgitated in the *Sunday Express*, an organ rather more visible to Gibson's peers and, in due course, he received some teasing. When Gibson came to write *Enemy Coast Ahead*, passages familiar to anyone who had read the *Atlantic Monthly* article were present again. Thus are versions of history created.

Roald Dahl had been working for Shell in Africa when war broke out. He volunteered for the RAF and flew Gladiators with No 80 Squadron in North Africa and was badly injured in a crash, the effects of which remained with him throughout his life. Dahl later saw action over Greece. He became a hugely successful writer. He was prone to exaggerating the extent of his RAF career and other matters. He died in 1990.

On 1 December 1943 Gibson returned to the UK, landing at Prestwick, Ayrshire from Montreal in a Liberator which was being ferried over to join the war effort. His trip had been a great success, as the fact that it was extended well beyond its original intended length indicates. He had responded to the brief he had been given.

On the question of reassuring Canada about the appreciation of its contribution, Gibson had entered the fray at a time when the situation was delicate. Entirely conscious that numerically they were making the largest provision of personnel and facilities for Bomber Command, the Canadian government had pressed previously for individual squadrons and a Canadian Group within the command. Prestige was not the only issue. The treatment of those suffering from 'lack of moral fibre', was one and so was the number of operations being flown by individuals. There was a Canadian view that it was a matter for the RCAF and not the RAF to rule on these things.

Arthur Harris was one of many who saw the value of an integrated force, rather than one split down national lines, with much future expansion being based on the RCAF. He also knew that the Royal Australian Air Force was pressing for its own group, though this wish was never fulfilled.

On squadrons and groups, the Canadian points were gradually conceded. Squadrons were given the designation 'Canadian' and No 6 Group, as a Canadian entity, first flew into action in January 1943. It was paid for by the Canadian government, apart from the pay and allowances of RAF and other personnel who served with it. The group's badge, approved in 1946, combined the Canadian maple leaf with the white rose of Yorkshire, which provided a considerable number of the group's bases.

When Gibson was across the Atlantic the arguments were still very much taking place. For example, with no consultation, the RCAF decided to grant home leave to aircrew who had completed one tour. The RAAF followed with a decision that aircrew would go home after one operational tour followed by one tour in an instructional capacity. There was another issue pushed by the Canadians on which Harris agreed though it was not implemented during the war. That was the concept that all pilots should be officers.

There were other political pressures at that time also based on national politics. The Polish Air Force was flying Wellingtons and the Poles wanted some Lancasters, while Harris was determined that it should not happen (they could have some Halifaxes if they liked) until all RAF, RCAF and other Dominion squadrons had received Lancasters. In the end, he lost that argument, which centred on the efficiency of the Polish squadrons.

The pressures in Canada and elsewhere were based on internal politics, the need to keep the voters happy. During his visit Gibson did an excellent job of telling Canadian voters how well Bomber Command was doing and how much the Canadian effort and sacrifice was appreciated.

Popular opinion was also a vital issue in the United States. In what he said there Gibson frequently made reference to his great dislike of the treatment of prisoners of war by the Japanese and his wish and that of his comrades to bomb the Japanese into submission. This attitude was no doubt genuine, but it also suited his masters. There was a need to quash a widely-held view in the United States that once the war in Europe had been won, British opinion would be resistant to the country's forces playing their full part in achieving a victory in the Far East.

So Gibson made an impact in the United States and Canada, but the trip, inevitably, had an impact on him. One of the changes was surprising in somebody with Gibson's opinions and background in middle class England. The American English that he had acquired while away, the use of which had impressed some of those he met, stayed with him on his return.

There was also a feeling amongst many with whom he came into contact that he had become more arrogant and self-centred. Some of the worst of the stories about Gibson's behaviour in daily life date from the nine and a half months of life left to him, following his return to Britain.

Having been constantly told that he was a hero, Gibson had, so it would seem, started to 'believe his own publicity'.

Fears that Gibson had disclosed too much about Chastise were raised and generally dismissed. The risk had most certainly been there. His briefing on such matters had been scant.

Now uppermost in Gibson's mind was the idea of a return to operations. At the earliest opportunity he travelled to Scampton, but found that No 617 Squadron had moved to Coningsby. Once there he was greeted by old friends including David Shannon. After Holden's death Mickey Martin had been temporary CO. Now the man in charge was Wing Commander Leonard Cheshire who, like Gibson, was somebody who preferred to be on operations. He had been commanding the bomber station at Marston Moor, but had dropped a rank to come to 617 Squadron.

Gibson, true to form, seems to have behaved almost as though he was still the CO. If he considered his successor's view of his arrival, it was a consideration that did not detain him. Cheshire himself claimed that he slipped away and allowed the squadron's old guard to resume their friendship with Gibson.

There was also a visit to No 5 Group, but there was no good news to be had there about what Gibson would regard as a suitable posting. He was to be regarded as 'non effective, sick' and would go to a post at the Air Ministry in London.

Go to the Air Ministry he did and, whatever other light duties he may have been given, this was the period when the draft of his book *Enemy Coast Ahead* was prepared, though it would not be published until 1946.

As with so much else about Guy Gibson, mystery abounds around the provenance of the book. Was it Gibson's idea? Did this man, not hailed at school or subsequently for his command of the English language really have such a book in him? If not, who did write it or help him write it? Why is the style uneven?

Richard Morris's detective work, including studying the original manuscript, left him with no doubt that Gibson had done the work himself, whoever might have intervened at different points.

For Morris the manuscript contained the kind of jokes, insubordinate comments, lack of tolerance for others, 'political incorrectness' in current parlance, passages to make his former English masters bury heads in hands – that was the authentic Guy Gibson. Eve Gibson provided plenty of evidence that her husband had undertaken the job and moved from a position of disliking it to enjoying it. She maintained this stance throughout her life, though there are indications that she may have intervened to improve some passages and improve the references to her.

The kind of phonetic misspellings that used to be a feature of office life everywhere occur in plenty of places, therefore it appears that Gibson dictated much of it at least into a dictaphone for later typing. He reacted on the page to the censor's comments and the comments of others who were shown passages.

Gibson liked to give the impression that he was ordered to write *Enemy Coast Ahead*. Maybe so, but Gibson had touched the edge of the literary world, for instance in his involvement with Roald Dahl and voices such as this must have added their opinion. 'You ought to write a book' is a theme that comes easily to the lips when in the presence of a person such as Gibson.

He was also somebody much involved with the Ministry of Information and had, in the previous few months, been at that organisation's service across the pond. Propaganda was a factor and, in this regard, it was fortunate that Gibson's views, as presented, often supported the Air Ministry line, for instance that the war would not be won by the bombing of German cities.

What did survive the censors and everyone else is still sometimes surprising. There is the account of the return of G for George from the dams. Gibson's published version includes:

Trevor asked a question – Trevor, who had fired nearly 12,000 rounds of ammunition in the past two hours. 'I am almost out of ammo,' he called, 'but I have got one or two incendiaries back here. Would you mind if Spam tells me when a village is coming up, so that I can drop one out? It might pay for Hoppy, Henry and Bill.'

I answered, 'Go ahead.'

How far then or later a passage like that was likely to improve the image of the RAF or the British war effort might be a subject for debate.

In the end, the key fact is that Gibson, whatever input there may have been from others, wrote a Second World War classic which has been selling and been quoted ever since.

Gibson began to move in another new world. He entered politics. Gibson's acquaintanceship with Winston Churchill had made the Prime Minister think that the young holder of the VC might be suitable material to become a Conservative MP. The same thought had occurred to the businessman of Canadian origin, Garfield Weston, who sat in Parliament for the Cheshire seat of Macclesfield and wanted to step down at the post war election to concentrate on his business interests.

The idea, for the moment, appealed to Gibson, and Weston continued to think that it was a good scheme. Next Gibson went north to visit the constituency, before placing himself before the local selection committee, who would have the final say.

Local selection committees can be irrational in all the parties. The colour of a potential candidate's socks has been known to matter more than opinions and ability to put them over.

Much of Cheshire is pretty flat, though nonetheless attractive, but on the eastern side of the county towards the boundary with Derbyshire, are the foothills of the Peak District. That is where Macclesfield was placed, a significant town, through which Bonnie Prince Charlie and his troops had passed when advancing south and again when they were retiring north in rather less good humour. Macclesfield was bordered by farming country, with the hills rising on one side.

Links to Gibson's world were tenuous. Silk was a major industry – today the town's bypass is called the Silk Road and there is more than one museum dedicated to the product. Macclesfield silk was used in the manufacture of parachutes. Nearby was the Avro factory and airfield at Woodford. On his first visit to Macclesfield Gibson visited a silk works and also the airfield, where Roy Chadwick, designer of the Lancaster, greeted him. Woodford assembled more than 4,000 Lancasters. Three years later Chadwick would die on the edge of the airfield in a flying accident.

Gibson also showed himself at Adlington Hall out in the countryside near the village of Prestbury. For centuries the hall has been the home of the Legh family. When Gibson walked through the door it was being used as a maternity hospital.

The climax of this 'press the flesh' visit to the Cheshire uplands was a public meeting, addressed by the former diplomat and civil servant, Lord Vansittart. Four years before the war Vansittart had trumpeted the threat posed by Germany. He had reached the heights of professions, being considered for the role of ambassador to the United States, before the post was given to Lord Halifax. Vansittart resigned from the civil service in 1941 and continued to thunder in public his condemnation of Germany. He would spend much time in the post war period expressing equal vehemence against the Soviet Union. In the view of Sir John Colville, a private secretary to Neville Chamberlain, Clement Attlee and (for much the longest time) Winston Churchill, Vansittart was, 'a man of striking intellectual ability, profound literary knowledge and poor judgement'.

Gibson sat on the platform, but did not speak. There were many who considered Vansittart's views extreme and the presence of the RAF wing commander and war hero sitting with him must have raised some eyebrows, beyond those of the constituency Labour Party, which quickly voiced its condemnation of Vansittart's opinions on the destruction of Germany.

Gibson's visit to Macclesfield attracted the attention of the press, as it was intended to do. The town was used to feting war celebrities. In 1940, Sergeant Eric Bann, a son of a well known local family, had flown Hurricanes in the Battle of Britain with No 238 Squadron. He was killed in action on 28

September when he baled out over the Isle of Wight and his parachute failed to open. He was buried in a family grave in Macclesfield.

In the months leading to his death Eric Bann, newly married, had maintained a flow of letters to his parents. When he was killed the *Macclesfield Courier* newspaper referred to him as 'Our local Cobber Kain' (a reference to a pilot much celebrated for his feats in the Battle of France) and in expressing sympathy to his family, remarked that, 'they can find comfort in the knowledge that their son died defending his home and the women and children of his land from the threat from the air.'

In a letter written on 16 September 1940 Bann had been raised to anti-German fury, describing how, 'yesterday the Yorkshire boy, Sergeant Pidd fell victim to these swines, machine gunning whilst coming down by parachute.' After seeing poor Pidd go, Bann vowed never to forgive the Hun.

At the time of Gibson's involvement in the affairs of Macclesfield, and for many years after, Eric Bann was a well-remembered part of the town's history. His brother Maurice served as ground crew on No 617 Squadron in Gibson's time as CO. The relationship was distant enough to leave Maurice Bann with no impression of Gibson.

For Gibson, his next appearance in public was on the now remarkably long-lived BBC radio programme, *Desert Island Discs*, first broadcast in 1942 and with many years still to run in the hands of its founder, Roy Plomley. Gibson's choices generally reflected experiences and phases of his life. The overture to *The Flying Dutchman* 'reminds me of the sea and I love the sea'; the *Royal Air Force March Past* by Sir (Henry) Walford Davies was on the list because, 'Every time I hear it, it never fails to send a shiver down my spine.'

Back in Cheshire, the Conservative selection committee had been discarding potential candidates, including Air Vice Marshal Donald Bennett who had set up the Pathfinder Force. A short list of five was arrived at, including Gibson, and the decisive meeting of the committee set for Saturday, 25 March. One surviving candidate was quickly eliminated and two votes taken on the other four, with Gibson emerging the winner. The speech he gave outside the meeting to the press had some polish and included a promise that one of his tasks, if elected to Parliament, would be to concern himself with the welfare of service personnel returning from the war.

Now it was for a general meeting of the Macclesfield Division Conservative and Unionist Association to endorse or reject the recommendation of its selection committee that Gibson should be the prospective National Conservative candidate for the constituency. This proved not to be a difficulty.

For Gibson, there was a course at the RAF Staff College to return to, though he did manage to travel to Cheshire on a further occasion to perform the duties of a prospective MP. He also had to ponder where his career was now heading. If, in due course, he was elected MP for Macclesfield, and that outcome could be reasonably predicted, then his RAF career would be at an end.

The doubts nagged for a long time. Eventually in late August a letter was despatched to the Macclesfield Conservatives announcing the resignation of the prospective candidate.

'The European war claims all my present time and energies and when it has been won I shall not be satisfied until I have played what part I can in bringing the Japanese war to a victorious conclusion,' he told them.

Gibson had been swept into Macclesfield on a tide that he had not created or initially sought to generate. However sincere he may have been when he accepted the nomination, he could not have thought through logically what the consequences would be.

Macclesfield maintained its liking of RAF connections. In the 1945 general election the division returned Air Commodore Arthur Harvey who, in 1937 had been the first commanding officer of No 615 (County of Surrey) Squadron of the Auxiliary Air Force. From 1938 Winston Churchill was the squadron's honorary air commodore and 615 became known as 'Churchill's Own'. Harvey represented Macclesfield, in the Conservative interest, until 1971, when he became Baron Harvey of Prestbury. He died in 1994.

One of the unsuccessful candidates for Macclesfield, Donald Bennett, would spend two months in 1945 as the Liberal Member of Parliament for Middlesbrough West.

With the launch of Operation Overlord, the much awaited and speculated about 'D-Day' on 6 June 1944, Gibson's passionate need to return to action had come right to the surface. He used his relationship with Arthur Harris and pleaded for the chance to return to playing a significant part in the war effort.

He was partly successful. The posting that came through was to what was now known as 55 Base at East Kirkby, where he would assist the base operations officer who performed a planning role, which Gibson might eventually take on for himself. The 'base' concept had been created in Bomber Command whereby a number of airfields would be grouped in one organisational unit.

This was still flying a desk, but it placed Gibson in the atmosphere of an operational bomber station, with the chance to grab any opportunities that might come to him to interpret his job description as requiring him to fly. East Kirkby was firmly in bomber territory, to the east of Coningsby. Today it is home to the Lincolnshire Aviation Heritage Centre. Spilsby came under East Kirkby at the time of Gibson's arrival, as did Strubby, though most of the activity at the latter involved Coastal Command and so was outside the remit of the East Kirkby operations officer.

Gibson was a moody spectator as the airmen of East Kirkby prosecuted the bomber war.

This was the period of the war when Bomber Command, for the time being, was not under the control of the Chief of the Air Staff. Rather (from 14 April to 14 September 1944) Arthur Harris reported to General Eisenhower at Supreme Headquarters Allied Expeditionary Force. There was a theoretical intermediary in Air Chief Marshal Tedder, the Deputy Supreme Commander, but Eisenhower and Harris got on well, as indeed Harris did with most of the American top brass. He often attended commanders-in-chief meetings.

This was a time when unfamiliar targets were being attacked as tactical support for the ground operations in northwest Europe combined with attempts to stifle the German programme of long range weapons; RAF operations given the code name Crossbow.

There were diversions. Gibson went with Squadron Leader Drew Wyness and his crew on a test flight and handled the controls. Wyness would soon move to No 617 Squadron and lose his life three months after his flight with Gibson. Hit by flak while attacking the Krebs Dam, the aircraft came down in the Rhine. It is believed that the crew survived the ditching but were murdered later that day. The date for the Gibson/Wyness flight has been recorded as 5 July, but there is contradictory evidence.

Mick Martin turned up in a Mosquito one day and also gave Gibson a trip. Martin was flying night intruder sorties with No 515 Squadron.

Gibson's logbook, by this stage in his career, is even more casually kept than ever. He did fly on an operation, though the details he gives are misleading and the No 630 Squadron ORB does not include his name. The logbook indicates that the target was at the village of Thiverny and that Squadron Leader Miller and crew were involved. Thiverny was attacked that day in an Operation Crossbow operation to a V1 storage site. Gibson reported success though others recorded that the operation was hampered by strong sunlight. Altogether, 132 Lancasters and twelve Mosquitos of Nos 5 and 8 Groups sought to destroy two flying bomb sites and one supply dump.

The previous night railway targets at Revigny and Aulnoye had been targeted by Nos 1, 3, 5 and 8 Groups and serious casualties suffered. These included four Lancasters from No 630 Squadron, though of the twenty-eight airmen involved in these losses, nine evaded and a further four survived as prisoners of war.

As things turned out Gibson's stay at East Kirkby was brief. It was not long before he was posted down the road to Coningsby and the headquarters of 54

Base. Here was somewhat more status and a feeling of being in the centre of things, a place that led the way and was the centre for No 5 Group's target marking activities. Gibson's new role as Base Air Staff Officer (BASO) did not, in theory, bring him any closer to flying, but it was an important position, with much freedom of action.

From this period of his life there are plenty of stories of Gibson becoming more bumptious and arrogant, with a 'don't you know who I am?' attitude. With old friends he appears to have been fine. Many to whom he was a new acquaintance did not find the experience of meeting him congenial.

Adding to his unrest was the growing feeling in many quarters that the war in Europe would soon be over. After the breakout from Normandy of Allied forces in late July, Paris was entered on 24 August, led, with an eye to public relations, by the French 2nd Armoured Division, headed by General Philipe Leclerc and Brussels was reached on the fifth anniversary of the British and French declaration of war.

History now knows that there was much hard fighting ahead, but as summer began to turn to autumn in 1944, it was possible to view the situation with considerable optimism. That is, until the failure of Operation Market Garden, launched on 17 September, the attempt to seize a series of bridges, cross the Rhine and finally take the German industrial heartland of the Ruhr.

Market Garden was an heroic failure. A number of VCs were awarded however and one recognised the RAF's participation. The posthumous award to Flight Lieutenant David Lord of No 271 Squadron came after, tasked on a re-supply mission, he had made two passes over the area of the fighting as his Army despatchers pushed out their load. The Dakota crashed with only one survivor. Both British and German troops watched in astonishment as this gallant act took place.

In August and early September Gibson grabbed what opportunities he could to see some action. He made a couple of flights on operations in Lockheed Lightnings which were then being evaluated for use by the No 617 Squadron controllers.

There was also a sortie in a Mosquito, accompanied by Wing Commander John Woodroffe, when Le Havre was the target. The purpose was to take cine film of what happened.

Still Gibson kept up the pressure for a full-blooded return to operations. There were more appeals, directly or indirectly, to both Harris and Cochrane. The latter at least recognised that one of the difficulties was the reality of how out of touch Gibson was. He was a vastly experienced bomber leader, yet he had been relatively inactive for over a year. In that time the bomber world had changed vastly.

The technology and the techniques had leapt forward and the hitting of tactical targets during the command's period under the control of SHAEF had increased confidence at all levels in the ability of the bombers to strike targets with a precision which was high compared with the earlier days of the war.

Gibson was not easy to teach, yet he needed teaching. He demonstrated the point on 2 September when he flew north in a Mosquito (a type on which he had little experience) and, to the amused interest of those present on the ground, needed three attempts to land at the small airfield at Scatsta, Shetland.

Desert Island Discs

Guy Gibson appeared on the radio programme *Desert Island Discs*, with the founder presenter, Roy Plomley, in a programme broadcast on Saturday 19 February, 1944.

His choice of music to take to the imaginary desert island was:

Warsaw Concerto by Richard Addinsell, performed by the London Sympnony Orchestra, soloist Louis Kentner.

Where or When (from *Babes in Arms*), Jack Hylton and his Orchestra.

A Thousand and One Nights Waltz, Johann Strauss II, performed by a symphony orchestra with Johann Strauss conducting.

The Flying Dutchman, Richard Wagner, Berlin State Opera Orchestra.

If I had My Way, Bing Crosby.

The Marines Hymn, Fred Waring and his Pennsylvanians.

Royal Air Force March Past, The Central Band of the Royal Air Force.

Ride of the Valkyries (from *Die Walkure*), Queen's Hall Orchestra.

Chapter 15

The Final Flight

There was much discussion and changing of plans at Bomber Command before the attacks for the night of 19/20 September were finalised. There was much to consider. The AOC-in-C wished to keep up the destruction of German cities. SHAEF still required attacks on targets of tactical value, the destruction of which would assist the Allied advance across Europe. Operation Market Garden was deeply in trouble and needed help. The delayed third airlift of troops to join the fighting at Arnhem and Nijmegen was taking place. The weather over Europe threatened to cause problems. Fog might well descend over eastern England as the bombers were returning.

Bremen was selected as a target for No 5 Group and then this was changed to the twin towns of Rheydt and Monchengladbach, just inside Germany. There would be red, green and yellow areas of attack. Red was the key target, the centre of Rheydt, and required to be controlled by a pilot experienced in the latest techniques. Plenty of such men were available. None of them was chosen. Instead, to the astonishment of many involved that night, the controller would be Gibson. Some participants were also disconcerted by the decision to have three marking points.

Three pilots from No 627 Squadron, operating Mosquitos, would be marker leaders. The highly experienced Squadron Leader Ronald Churcher would mark on red and would be Gibson's deputy controller.

Coningsby normally provided Mosquitos for No 5 Group controllers, but none proved to be serviceable. Late in the proceedings, No 627 Squadron at Woodhall Spa was asked to make an aircraft available and was told that the controller would collect it. There was also a change of personnel. The navigator originally allocated to accompany Gibson reported sick and Squadron Leader Jim Warwick, the Coningsby station navigation officer took his place. One account has Gibson walking into the mess and brusquely telling Warwick that his services were required.

Gibson and Warwick received a briefing from Squadron Leader Charles Owen who had been the controller on a previous attack on the area to be targeted that night. Gibson made it clear to Owen that he intended to select his own route home, ignoring the official instructions. Later, at Woodhall Spa, the atmosphere became charged as Gibson rejected the aircraft selected for him, giving no clear reason, and forced another crew to give up their Mosquito and take over the rejected aircraft. A few minutes before eight in the evening, Gibson and Warwick took off on what would prove to be their last flight.

Later returning crews would have different views of the success or otherwise of the organisation of the attack, perhaps a likely situation given the dispersed marking points. Red was a particular concern, with one of the issues being a problem with Churcher's aircraft. Eventually Gibson decided to mark himself, but found that his target indicators (TIs) did not release.

The delay increased the chance of collisions and the Luftwaffe night fighters were arriving and beginning to inflict casualties. Some aircraft assigned to red began to bomb on green. Gibson then accepted that situation and issued an order to bomb on the green markers.

Churcher, overcoming his problems, finally managed to place red TIs accurately and bombs began to fall on Rheydt.

Crews heard Gibson telling them to go home and it is believed that he remained over the target for some minutes, assessing results. That would be normal for a controller.

Around half an hour later, about 2230 hours, residents of the Dutch town of Steenbergen saw and heard an aircraft. Some felt it was in trouble. It was seen to circle in the area of the town. Two crew members were visible. There were flames and the aircraft crashed.

Guy Gibson and Jim Warwick died in that crash. They were buried side by side in Steenbergen.

In March 1945 the St Edward's School Chronicle carried the latest long list of old boys lost on active service. The names were in alphabetical order and first was Lieutenant (though the Commonwealth War Graves Commission gives him the rank of captain) Peter Robert Taylor Daniel, 4th Battalion The Buffs (Royal East Kent Regiment) who had died in 1943 and would be remembered on the Athens Memorial.

Guy Gibson came next and his death in action was described as an 'irreplaceable loss'.

There followed the words penned by Warden Kendall which had appeared in *The Times*.

'Others have spoken and will speak for many years to come of Guy Gibson's gift of leadership; I should like to add a more personal word as to his character. He was one of the most thorough and determined boys I have ever known, both at school and afterwards, and nothing could move him from his purpose of flying, neither his original rejection when at school by the RAF, owing to his short legs, nor the offer of ground jobs, nor a seat in Parliament during the war. His letter in answer to a line of congratulations after his dam bursting exploits ended: "PS – was awarded the VC yesterday." He came back quite unspoilt from a tour in America, and got back to flying as soon as possible afterwards. Once, when officially resting … he had to make a dangerous forced landing; a doctor drove up to help, and, finding him unhurt, took him back to the aerodrome. In the car he glanced at Guy and said: "It's a shame they make you fellows fly so young." Gibson appreciated the kind thought and the joke, but never said who he was.

'He shared to the full all the strength and the virility and modesty of English boys of all ranks, with their amazing good humour in trying conditions; he would not have wanted to claim more than this. One incident is worth recording. He was visiting his school after he had become famous and arrived just before dinner. The boys naturally asked him to speak, hoping to hear something of his action, so he was left alone with them. "What – am I to speak? Well, when I was a boy here Old Boys used to come down and say they never did any work. Don't believe them. I worked like hell!" That and a cheerful smile was all they got from him, but they understood.'

Trish Knight-Webb vividly recalled Guy's death. 'I do remember the telegram arriving bearing the news and the terrible silence in the house. In those days things like death were not discussed with children of my age (around eight) so what I picked up was mainly atmosphere.'

Guy Gibson's early and needless death added to the allure of his legend. It ensured that he will be remembered for his heroic and brilliant achievement over Germany in 1943, the memory undiluted by any later achievements or failure in a life of normal span. He was spared the frequent post war debate about the extent to which Operation Chastise had damaged the enemy war effort. That debate continues, though there should be none about the gallantry of the Dam Busters and the enormous impact they had on British morale and prestige.

Fatal Theories

Guy Gibson could have remained off operations, but died because he could not stay away from them. There are plenty of others who have had this compulsion for action in similar circumstances.

The story is well known of Douglas 'Tin Legs' Bader, newly released from Colditz, shocking an American officer by asking him where the nearest Spitfires were, so that Bader could have a final crack at the enemy.

Less well known in this regard is Eric Lock, a very high scoring Spitfire pilot in the Battle of Britain with No 41 Squadron.

Lock came from a Shropshire farming and quarrying family and joined the RAFVR in 1939 and was called up as war was about to be declared. He was commissioned before he went into action. Lock was very small and on his squadron became known as 'Sawn off', as well as 'Lockie'. On occasions he was 'Sawn off Lockie'.

In his book *Hornchurch Eagles*, Richard C. Smith wrote of Lock, 'He was basically a hunter; he was also a loner when it came to air fighting. Although he would take off with the squadron, once the enemy was sighted Lockie was gone and would not be seen again until he would land some time later with one or two enemy aircraft claimed destroyed.'

It has to be assumed from that that Lock's COs accepted his lack of teamwork because of his remarkable success against the enemy. By the end of 1940 he had been awarded the DSO, DFC and Bar. Like Guy Gibson he became a media celebrity.

On 17 November 1940 he was shot down and badly wounded by German fighters. He made a crash landing near the Suffolk airfield of Martlesham Heath and sat in his cockpit for two hours before being found by soldiers who carried him for two miles across dykes and ditches on a makeshift stretcher. As a result of his wounds Lock was in hospital for six months, part of the time spent at the Queen Victoria Hospital, East Grinstead, where he qualified as a Guinea Pig. He underwent fifteen operations.

Lock was back on operations again a few weeks after his release from hospital. After a refresher course, he joined No 611 (West Lancashire) Squadron as a flight commander. He arrived on the squadron in early July and failed to return from a 'rhubarb' (freelance fighter sortie seeking targets of opportunity) over France.

The squadron ORB says that Lock 'was last seen streaking down a road at the back of Boulogne, brassing off soldiers on bicycles and whooping over the R/T, "Ha ha look at the bastards running."'

The ORB goes on, 'It seems a ruddy awful waste to lose so great a pilot on so trivial an expedition.'

There are various theories as to how Lock lost his life and his body was never found, but that he was hit by anti-aircraft fire appears the most likely.

Eric Lock was a fighter pilot by trade and Guy Gibson a bomber pilot. They had different personalities. The similarities between two men who couldn't keep away from operations and were perhaps in action when they shouldn't have been are difficult to miss.

The compulsion that led Guy Gibson to his death is well established. However, the debate – and the research – goes on as to the circumstances of his death and it is highly likely that more evidence and revised ideas will emerge. The most ridiculous theory – though it retains currency amongst the chatter of the internet – is that Gibson was so unpopular that he was murdered through interference with the aircraft he flew on his last sortie.

Those who put forward the theory do not produce the evidence. In any case, the person who committed this fictional act would have needed a hatred strong enough to want to kill both Gibson and the much liked and amiable Warwick, as well as the genius (or was it the luck?) to be able to achieve damage (unnoticed and allowing take off and a long flight) to an aircraft only selected at the last moment.

The Friendly Fire Concept

That Guy Gibson was killed by his own side is a theory that has gained ground in recent years. It was articulated by James Cutler in an article in the respected magazine, *Britain at War*. Well aware of the other theories, the editor, Martin Mace, concluded that he should give this one an airing in the October 2011 issue.

Cutler explained that his research was inspired when he was working with Sir Peter Jackson on the re-make of the *Dam Busters* film. He was briefed to find and film interviews with everyone available who had known Guy Gibson.

His research led to the view that:

'In fact, there's a really glaring hole in the "pilot error" theory that no one seems to have spotted. On their own, the small outer wing fuel tanks on a Mosquito only gave the aircraft a range of about 270 miles. Yet the target that night – Mönchengladbach – was over 300 miles away, so clearly the switch to the main tanks would have to have been made on the way there. Indeed, Gibson crashed on the way back from the target long after the switch would have been made. The theory, first proposed by a Mosquito pilot and favoured by Richard Morris in his 1994 biography of Gibson, is, quite simply, impossible.

'My investigation began when an amateur historian put me in touch with the widow of a Lancaster gunner who had flown on Gibson's last raid and who had an astonishing story to tell. Eunice McCormack said that her husband, Bernard McCormack, a rear gunner with 61 Squadron, claimed that he had mistaken Gibson's Mosquito for a German Junkers Ju 88 night fighter and fired at it. This came to light at an air crew reunion in the 1980s when she heard her husband and his ex-comrades talking about how they had shot down none other than Guy Gibson – by mistake. At first it seemed like the tallest of tall stories – a hoax even – but it led me, via a log book and a secretly recorded confession, to long-lost official documents which, to my surprise, confirmed every detail of the widow's story.

'McCormack was secretly recorded by his wife explaining how he and the mid upper gunner had fired at an aircraft and later the intelligence officer had put to them the theory that it was Gibson they were firing at.'

There is a considerable number of reasons why this theory does not work. The reasons include:

The range of the Mosquito does not make the 'searching for the fuel cocks' theory impossible. There are, of course, other circumstances, including ignorance, in which a crew, not least one inexperienced on the type, might carry out such a search and overlook the prime need to fly the aircraft at the same time.

Gibson was an experienced night fighter pilot who would have a better idea than many that Lancaster gunners were likely to be spooked by the approach described.

Warwick was an experienced navigator. Becoming lost in the area he was in was not particularly likely. Following a slower aircraft with rear facing armament, with Gibson, a notoriously hard taskmaster, sitting beside him, would have been the last of last resorts.

The circumstances of the award of the DFC to the pilot of the Lancaster are said to be part of a cover up. The award of all decorations is something of a lottery. If the circumstances of this recognition had been an issue, it would have been simple to make no award or to write a citation stressing that this was a 'periodic' DFC, perhaps for gallant service over a complete tour.

Peter Mallender, the pilot, who lost his aircraft at the last moment to Gibson, has been recorded as giving his own views as follows, by the owner of a business he visited:

'One of my regular visitors was local resident, Peter Mallender. Peter was an experienced Mosquito pilot in No 627 Squadron at RAF Woodhall Spa. On 19 September 1944 he was in the officers' mess, when his squadron commander introduced him to Gibson, and his navigator Squadron Leader James Warwick. Mallender was told that Gibson was to use Mallender's regular aircraft Canadian-built KB267 for an operation that night. The CO said, "Yours is the best aircraft on the squadron, Mallender".

'Peter took the pair to the aircraft, having been told to brief them on the details of the aeroplane. Gibson explained (Peter said he was very haughty!) that they did not need a detailed briefing as they had flown a Mosquito together before. However Warwick had never been in a Canadian built one. Peter told me the fuel change-over cocks were in a different location to British Mosquitos and in an inquest with the CO, a day or so later, into what might have happened, Peter expressed his thought that Warwick couldn't find them and they had run out of fuel.

'After the war, and when he had retired Peter went to The Netherlands to see the grave, and he made enquiries about the event. He said none of the Dutch (he spoke to) had seen any aircraft nearby, or heard any gunfire, just a fast low-flying aircraft identified as a British intruder. Somebody told him they had seen a light moving around the cockpit. Peter then surmised that it probably was Warwick using a torch or hand-held light of some type, to find the fuel cocks, which were located behind the pilot's seat on Canadian Mosquitos.

'Peter's opinion was a sad end to a great pilot and his colleague, mostly due to his arrogance at not accepting the advice he was offered before he left Woodhall Spa.'

As with most incidents in life, the obvious causes should be dismissed before the exotic or bizarre are taken seriously. It is most likely that the cause of the death of Guy Gibson and Jim Warwick lies in a combination of circumstances allied to their inexperience on the type and their lack of time together as a team, perhaps exacerbated by aircraft malfunction and/or battle damage. It is highly likely that new evidence and revised ideas will emerge.

Chapter 16

The Film

If the publication of *Enemy Coast Ahead* and Paul Brickhill's book were starting points for the post war fame of the Dam Busters, then the film cemented that celebrity and ensured that the fame moved steadily into legend. The story concentrates on the search for a weapon to breach the German dams, the formation of No 617 Squadron and the action itself. The film closes immediately after the return to Scampton of the surviving aircraft. Nonetheless both the Brickhill and Gibson books were credited as the basis of what was produced.

For Brickhill, therefore, the title of his book meant that he was portraying the wartime story of a squadron. When the same title was used in the film it indicated an account of one operation carried out by that squadron.

It is perhaps worth noting that something that has changed over the years is the film's title. Released as *The Dam Busters*, it is now normally presented as *The Dambusters*. The same is true of *The Dam Busters March* by Eric Coates.

The rights to the Brickhill book had been bought by the Associated British Picture Corporation around three years before filming began. The late Professor John Ramsden commented that, even at that point, the intention was to provide a vehicle for Richard Todd, who was held on a long contract by the corporation. It is interesting, considering that Todd would become one of the stars epitomising the portrayal of British war heroes, that *The Dam Busters* would prove to be the first time that he would be seen going into action as an actor, rather than in real life.

The fact that an academic figure such as Professor Ramsden, Head of History at Queen Mary College, London, author of three of the six volumes of *History of the Conservative Party*, should consider it appropriate to write a book on *The Dam Busters* film is one more indication of the power of the story in the public mind.

Though the film makers set out determinedly to tell the true story of what had taken place, inevitably holes can be picked with the hindsight of sixty years. There are plenty of reasons for this. So much research has since been done on the events surrounding the breaching of the dams, some matters were still secret in the early 1950s, there was the tugging in different directions of the desire to tell a tale of heroism against the background of the debate already well under way about the rightness of the bomber offensive. Much attention was given to the account by Barnes Wallis of his part in promoting the dams as a target and producing a weapon capable of destroying the target. Details of that account have frequently been queried since.

As a result of the film, the legend of the Dam Busters includes the idea that the aircrew members who took part in the operation were carefully selected veterans. Some were veterans and some were carefully selected for their ability to contribute to the operation. Others were not veterans or were not specially chosen with the key objective in mind. Some came into neither category.

Creating the film was a long drawn out affair, as much as anything so that plenty of accurate detail could be included. A first full script was available for discussion in the late summer of 1952, a year and a half before filming began. Copies of the script were sent to many people involved in the real life story, producing the inevitable variation in views. Two people who witness a road accident rarely give the same account.

Ramsden gives an example, 'While Sir Arthur Harris complained that he had been made into an ogre, another veteran of Bomber Command thought he had been made, "far too human."' The result was that a studio insider re-wrote R.C. Sherriff's depiction of Harris.

Co-operation from the RAF had been secured at an early stage and this came to fruition in filming, using five Lancasters, skilfully flown – apparently 60ft in real life does not look like 60ft when filmed, so the aircraft had to fly lower. Filming was based at the RAF stations at Scampton and Hemswell.

Today re-enactors dressed as military officers can find themselves being saluted and possibly even occasionally encourage it, Ramsden pointed out that similar problems occurred while filming was taking place.

Having referred to landing Canberras ruining takes at Scampton and other ranks demanding their lunch venue back, he wrote, 'nor was it easy to tell who was who, so an order of the day went out, "Personnel will have noticed a good many queer characters about. Don't pay any attention to them. They're only actors."' Mistakes could take the opposite form. Charles Whitworth was heard to roar, 'You salute me. I'm not an actor.'

That the film was destined to be a success was indicated when it became necessary to hold two Royal Command performances in 1955 at the time of the twelfth anniversary of the raid. The venue was the Empire Cinema, Leicester Square. Outside, the names of Richard Todd and Michael Redgrave feature above the title and billed below it were, Ursula Jeans, Basil Sydney, Patrick Barr, Derek Farr and Ernest Clark.

The Cast (as listed at the time)

Members of No 617 Squadron
Wing Commander G.P. Gibson – Richard Todd
Flight Lieutenant R.D. Trevor-Roper – Brewster Mason
Flight Lieutenant R.E.G. Hutchison – Anthony Doonan
Flying Officer R.M. Spafford – Nigel Stock
Flight Lieutenant R.D. Taerum – Brian Nissen
Flight Sergeant J. Pulford – Robert Shaw
Pilot Officer G.R. Deering – Peter Assinder
Squadron Leader H.M. Young – Richard Leech
Squadron Leader H.E. Maudslay – Richard Thorp
Flight Lieutenant J.V. Hopgood – John Fraser
Flight Lieutenant W. Astell – David Morell
Flight Lieutenant H.B. Martin – Bill Kerr
Flight Lieutenant D.J.H. Maltby – George Baker
Flight Lieutenant D.J. Shannon – Ronald Wilson
Flight Lieutenant L.G. Knight – Denys Graham
Flight Lieutenant R.G. Hay – Basil Appleby
Flight Lieutenant J.F. Leggo – Tim Turner
Flight Sergeant G.E. Powell – Ewan Solon
Wing Commander Gibson's batman – Harold Goodwin

Other characters

Dr Barnes Wallis – Michael Redgrave
Mrs Wallis – Ursula Jeans
Wallis family doctor – Charles Carson
Dr David Pye – Stanley Van Beers
Dr W.H. Glanville – Colin Tapley
Committee members – Laidman Brown, Frederick Leister, Eric Messiter
Official, National Physical Laboratory – Raymond Huntley
Official, Ministry of Aircraft Production – Hugh Manning
Captain 'Mutt' Summers – Patrick Barr
RAF officer at trials – Anthony Shaw
Observers at trials – Hugh Moxey, Edwin Styles
Air Chief Marshal Sir Arthur Harris – Basil Sydney
Air Vice-Marshal the Hon Ralph Cochrane – Derek Farr
Farmer – Laurence Naismith
Group Signals Officer – Harold Siddons

BBC announcer – Frank Phillips
Uncredited actors included – Gerald Harper, Peter Arne, Richard Coleman, Arthur Howard, Lloyd Lamble, Edwin Richfield

Production team

Director – Michael Anderson
Director in charge of production – Robert Clark
Production Supervisor – W.A. Whittaker
Production Manager – Gordon C. Scott
Assistant Director – John Street
Continuity – Thelma Orr
Casting Directors – Robert Lennard and G. B. Walker
Screenplay – R.C. Sherriff
Director of Photography and Aerial Photography – Erwin Hillier
Special Effects Photography – Gilbert Taylor
Camera Operator – Norman Warwick
Special effects – George Blackwell
Editor – Richard Best
Art Director – Robert Jones
Make-up – Stuart Freeborn
Hairdresser – Hilda Winifred Fox
Music – Leighton Lucas; March by Eric Coates
Technical Adviser – Group Captain J.N.H. Whitworth

Many relative unknowns appeared in the film, partly because many of the parts in the film were for young men. There were few feminine touches. Actors portraying aircrew who had some fame already or went on to considerable careers included Robert Shaw, Nigel Stock, George Baker, Ewan Solon and Richard Leech, who recalled in later years that, when playing the part, he had no idea of 'Dinghy' Young's American connections, or the fact that he was sometimes, inaccurately, claimed to be American. These points rather tend to dismiss the claim occasionally made after the film's release that transatlantic accents had been included with a view to boosting box office returns in the United States.

Richard Thorp has starred in the soap *Emmerdale* for many years, as did Hugh Manning who died in 2004.

In contrast to those names mentioned in the preceding paragraph, some of the actors were 'unknown' and stayed that way. Peter Assinder, who played Deering, is not credited by the IMDb website with any film appearances after 1959. He died in 2008.

Chapter 17

Mrs Gibson

Evelyn Mary 'Eve' Moore was born in 1911, though when she met Guy Gibson she would give him the impression that she was several years younger than that. Eve grew up in comfortable circumstances in Penarth, near Cardiff in south Wales. Her father worked for a shipping company.

Showbusiness ambitions struck Eve early on. She could act and dance and that was the career she followed. Her parents wanted her to be a dance teacher, but overcame their disappointment and continued to support her.

Eve gained plenty of work although she was not a star. In December 1939 she met Guy Gibson. Different accounts give different precise dates of the first encounter and Eve and her future husband gave different versions of the exact circumstances. Coventry was the venue and Eve was part of the company of a revue called *Come out to Play*, whose cast included the much better known Jessie Matthews and her husband Sonnie Hale. Gibson was staying with his brother and sister in law.

However the actual meeting was contrived, Gibson was smitten by Eve on the stage and Eve when he met her. A relationship quickly developed, though Eve showed reluctance at first, hesitating in part because she considered her admirer very young and rather naive.

By Christmas time Gibson had discovered a reason to fly an aircraft to St Athan and had invited himself to the Moore family home. At this point he lost his mother who died on Christmas Eve of burns suffered in an accident at her London flat the previous day, though by this time, such an event does not appear to have had a great impact on him.

Over the following months Gibson found further excuses to watch Eve on stage.

On 21 November 1940 Gibson was allowed by Squadron Leader Widdows at No 29 Squadron to use a Blenheim to fly from Lincolnshire to Cardiff and on 23 November he and Eve were married in church in Penarth, followed by a reception at the Esplanade hotel. Some of those who were present reflected that Mr Moore had given his daughter a wedding that was almost up to peacetime standards. The *South Wales Echo* recorded the occasion under the headline, 'Penarth Actress Marries DFC Airman'.

Children were not part of the plan. Eve was unable to have children.

The wedding night was spent in a hotel at Chepstow, from which the couple could watch Bristol being bombed. Shortly afterwards Gibson returned to duty.

Gibson could be gauche in male company and he certainly could be in female company. He had a tendency to regard the provision of sexual gratification as a key role for women, something in which he was, of course not alone. In service life, women who were not officers or of officer class qualified for even less respect.

Smitten as he was with Eve, he quickly failed to meet the levels of attention and comfort that she expected. The accommodation he initially obtained for them in the Lincolnshire villages of Wellingore and then Navenby being cases in point.

Later, at West Malling, life would be happier and more comfortable, with the attractions of London not too far away. Later still, Eve worked for the Red Cross in Cardiff and so a separate life was developing.

Gibson continued to exhibit great attachment to Eve and could be a bore talking about her, but, while he was stationed at Coningsby, Eve acquired a flat in London, where she could enjoy the social life. Whatever attraction remained, the two were well apart.

It would appear that Eve was fed to the press by the Ministry of Information following Operation Chastise and she acquired some fame, through her husband's achievement, not her own. She was determined to stay in London, though she did support Gibson with her presence as he sought the Conservative Parliamentary nomination in Macclesfield.

On the day that Gibson took off on his last flight, Eve phoned him for a chat and interrupted his preparations.

The next day a telegram arrived at her London flat. It read, 'Regret to inform you Wing Commander Gibson reported missing on operational flight on the night of 19/20 September.'

With Margaret North, Gibson had pursued a very different relationship. She was the nurse whom he had supported as she tended the badly injured Gus Walker. He quickly asked her out, brushing aside the fact that she was only a corporal. They went to pubs and the cinema, with Gibson's mood varying between cheerful, philosophical and, on at least one occasion, distressed as he talked of his life and what the strains were of flying bombers to war.

There was talk of a life together after the war in a cottage by the sea. They thought of how they would furnish the cottage and what they might do there, though Eve was, of course a presence in their minds.

Quickly a further barrier was built when Margaret, knowing that there was little prospect of the dream life becoming a reality, married an NCO. It was not a happy marriage. Margaret and Gibson remained friends and in contact.

Eve Gibson died in 1988.

Appendix 1

Birth Of A Legend

The legend begins – the opening paragraphs of the front page report in *The Daily Telegraph*, dated 18 May 1943, followed by the result as it was seen at the time:

RAF BLOW UP THREE KEY DAMS IN GERMANY
DEVASTATION SWEEPS DOWN RUHR VALLEY
BRIDGES AND POWER PLANTS ENGULFED
ADVANCING FLOODS STILL SPREADING FAST

With one single blow the RAF has precipitated what may prove to be the greatest industrial disaster yet inflicted on Germany in this war. A force of Lancasters, loaded with mines and with crews specially trained for the task, early yesterday morning attacked and destroyed the great dams on the Möhne and Sorpe rivers, tributaries of the Ruhr, and also the dam on the Eder River.

Today walls of water sweeping down the Ruhr and Eder valleys are carrying everything before them.

The Air Ministry announced last night that a partial reconnaissance of the Ruhr Valley and the district near the Eder dam shows that the floods are spreading fast.

'The waters are sweeping down the Ruhr Valley,' it stated. 'Railways and road bridges are broken down. Hydro–electrical power stations are destroyed or damaged, a railway marshalling yard is under water.

'The floods from the breached Eder dam are already as great as the floods in the Ruhr Valley, but the country here is flatter and the water likely to spread over a greater area.'

GERMANS ADMIT HEAVY CASUALTIES
The German communiqué yesterday, admitting that two dams had been 'damaged' – it did not specify the area – said 'heavy casualties' were caused among the civilian population by the resulting flood.' That was as much as the people of Germany were allowed to know. There was no reference to the disaster in later news broadcasts from Berlin.

The pilots, on their return, reported seeing in the moonlight huge breaches in the dams with water bursting through. They saw a power station below the Möhne dam swept away in the flood and a 30ft high wall of water tumbling down the Eder valley.

Alongside was a photograph of Wing Commander Gibson under the heading, 'He drew the enemy's fire'.

AIR MINISTRY ACCOUNT

The full official account of the raid on the Dams in North-West Germany was given by the Air Ministry last night in the following statement:

'For many weeks picked Lancaster crews had been training for one operation. They worked in secrecy on a bomber station which, as far as possible, was cut off from any contact with the outside world.

'Only about half a dozen other men in the whole of Bomber Command knew what they were doing.

'In the early hours of yesterday morning, when the weather and light were exactly right, they carried out the operation. The purpose was to subject the whole of the Ruhr valley to almost as severe an ordeal as it has undergone by fire in the last three months, and do the same for another industrial area farther east.

'These picked men under the command of Wing Commander G.P. Gibson DSO and bar, DFC and bar, went out to attack three huge water barrage dams. Two of them were on the rivers Möhne and Sorpe, tributaries of the River Ruhr, and the other on the River Eder.

'The Lancaster crews knew how much depended on their success. The opportunity might never come again, and it was an opportunity, as they knew, of doing as much damage as could be done by thousands of tons of bombs dropped on many nights running.

'The Möhne and Sorpe dams control 70 per cent of the water catchment area of the Ruhr Basin. Before they were built, the Ruhr was always apt to run short of water in a dry season – the Sorpe reservoir alone takes two or three years to fill.

'If the reservoirs were suddenly emptied the floods that resulted could be as serious as the subsequent shortage of water: 134,000,000 tons of water would pour out from the Möhne reservoir alone.'

The Result

Extracted from RAF immediate interpretation report no K.1559, dated 18 May 1943.

This was prepared by RAF Medmenham where, from April 1941, an enormous amount of photo interpretation skill was brought together.

The photographs were taken by Spitfires of No 542 Squadron on 17 May. Three sorties were flown specified as D/578, D/581 and D/585.

Locality: The Möhne, Sorpe and Eder dams

Cover and quality

On sortie D/578 the Möhne valley barrage, the greater part of the storage lake and parts of the Ruhr valley as far as twenty miles downstream are covered on prints of large scale and excellent quality. The north end of the Sorpe lake with the dam and compensating basin is also covered. The sortie does not cover the Eder dam but portions of the lake, Bringhausen storage power station, the Affoldern flow power station and the flooded parts of the country for about six miles downstream are covered.

On sortie D/581 the upper part of the Möhne storage lake, part of the main lake and flooded areas 16 miles downstream from the Eder dam are covered on photographs of good scale and excellent quality.

On sortie D/585 about two miles of the Eder Valley near Affoldern are covered on photographs of large scale and good quality. The Eder Dam is not covered.

Period under review

These photographs were taken after the attack by aircraft of Bomber Command on the night of 16/17.5.43. No previous report of damage in this area has been issued.

Provisional statement of damage

Two of the dams are known to have been breached and the other damaged. Water is seen pouring through a great gap in the Möhne Dam and widespread damage has been caused by the rush of water down the valley. The villages are seen flooded, bridges swept away, power stations and water works isolated and railway communications disrupted.

Although the Eder Dam is not covered on these photographs there is evidence of damage caused by floods on a similar scale and over an even wider area than in the Möhne Valley.

The Sorpe Dam appears but slightly damaged.

The dams
i) The Möhne Valley Barrage
The dam is breached in the centre between the two valve houses. The breach at the crown of the dam measures about 230 feet narrowing to about 130 feet at its base. Water is seen pouring through into the compensating basin. Although the main pressure of the water at the time of photography has subsided, the water is still flowing through the gap.

The main power station at the foot of the dam has completely disappeared and must have been carried away by the first rush of water and masonry.

The water is seen rushing through the compensating basin and the northern embankment has been completely destroyed. The southern embankment is seen broken in several places, but the auxiliary power station remains standing.

The upstream lake is seen to be partly drained at the dam at 0900 hours and completely drained west of the Stockun embankment and sluice gate at 1045 hours. Water is still seen, however, east of this embankment.

ii) The Sorpe Dam
The dam has been damaged in the centre. The parapet on the upstream side of the road across the dam has been broken for a length of 200 feet. The downstream parapet is also damaged and water has run down to the compensating basin, either as the result of a splash or through seepage.

At the east end of the damage to the crown is a raised object about 40 feet in length and 25 feet wide blocking the road at a point where the seepage is most evident. The road is discoloured 200 feet each side of the damaged area. The level of the water in the lake appears unchanged.

The power station is not working at the time of photography but water appears to be running into the compensating basin through the by-pass tunnel.

iii) The Eder Dam
The dam itself is not covered on these sorties but the floods seen downstream and the partly drained lake upstream indicate beyond doubt that the dam has been breached.

Flood Damage
The Möhne Valley
In the neighbourhood of the dam part of the village of Guenne has been completely swept away. Between the dam and Nehein the water

appears to be more confined but in the flatter part of the Ruhr Valley west of Weckede floods have spread over a wide area and a number of farm buildings have been isolated. The whole village of Westick and the village of Dellwig are flooded.

At Froendenberg the damage is particularly severe. The embankments of the canal are mostly destroyed and the power station isolated. The railway bridge and the road bridge have been swept away and broken parts are seen downstream. The railway station and sidings are inundated and several passenger coaches have been swept off the tracks. A small factory is partly underwater.

At Langschede the bridge is partly submerged and the water works completely flooded. Between Nehein – Froendenberg and Nehein – Niederense the railway is in parts submerged and in parts washed away.

Floods are seen spreading towards Boesperde up the valley of the small river Hoenne.

The Eder Valley

At 0900 hours the generator house, the switch park and transformer enclosures of the Bringhausen storage power station were seen to be flooded. At 1630 hours most of the water had drained away but the switch and transformer park showed silting up and a portion of the north part washed away.

The embankment forming the north edge of the compensating basin between Henfurth and Affoldern at 0900 hours was seen destroyed at several points and the whole valley under water.

The village of Affoldern was partly submerged. The power station was flooded and the embankment destroyed. At 1630 hours many houses in the village were seen to have been demolished and the approaches to the bridge washed away.

The whole area between Wabern and Felsberg, about sixteen miles downstream from the Eder dam is seen to be completely under water. The railway station and sidings at Wabern are flooded and the embankment broken away. Isolated farmhouses and hamlets appear above the water but railways, roads and bridges have been completely submerged.

The floods are seen to have spread southwards as far as Uttershausen.

Appendix 2

Guy Gibson the Man

So what were the driving forces in Guy Gibson's complex personality? Teresa Bliss is an educational psychologist who graduated with an MSc from Cardiff University, followed by an M.Ed from Bristol University and a BA from the Open University. She has taught in primary and secondary schools and has headed units for children with learning, emotional, social and behavioural difficulties, as well as running training sessions for teachers, teaching assistants, parents, social services and other groups.

Her comments here are based on reading biographical material about Guy Gibson almost seventy years after his death. They are one expert's view from that inevitably limited perspective, but they perhaps offer some insights into some of the issues which moved Gibson from unexceptional child into a brilliantly high performing young adult.

'There are indications (in the material I have studied) of possible attachment difficulties with his mother. Mothers who abuse alcohol are often distant and emotionally unavailable to their children. A child born in India at that time would most likely have been raised by someone other than his mother who would have had social duties to perform. The relatively wealthy often left the rearing of their children to nannies, child rearing had low status and was often left to servants and boarding schools.

'Guy left India when he was only six years old and it is likely that the figure he would have attached to would have been a servant. This was probably emotionally traumatic for him. His parents are unlikely to have been sympathetic or to have filled the gap and at a very young age he would have needed to become emotionally self-sufficient. However what often happens is that there is a void which cannot easily be filled and continues into adulthood.

'Children with emotionally distant parents often believe that it is something inherent in them which makes them unlikeable or unloveable to their parents. They can spend the rest of their lives compensating, always looking for praise, validation and acceptance. That seems to be a theme in Guy's life.

'It is interesting that he married an actress who was older than him. For a woman to be six years older than her husband is a big age gap and unusual, particularly in those days. She seems to have been fairly glamorous. It is my hypothesis that she was a mother figure replacement. He married her just after his own mother's death. I guess his mother was fairly glamorous when compared with the servants and the young Guy would have looked for emotional nurturing from her and it wasn't forthcoming. Again children in these circumstances seek a replacement, even into adulthood.

'There is some very recent research (Rohner 2012) which indicates that the same parts of the brain are activated when people feel rejected as when they suffer physical pain, but unlike physical pain which we forget about, the psychological pain of rejection in childhood can cause an emotional pain that is relived and revisited throughout life. Furthermore an absent or emotionally distant mother or father can cause damage which lasts through well into adult life.

'The marriage was under strain in the period before Guy died. If his wife was able to give him the nurturing he craved it could have been a happy marriage. On the other hand people with Guy's background are often not good at sustaining relationships. This is partly because they are not good at reading others, they fail to be empathetic or sympathetic and fail to notice any sort of emotional distress in others; Guy was capable of being very dismissive of the feelings of others. Hence partners feel unloved and rejected. It is possibly why his mother took to drinking. His parents avoided the scandalous step of divorcing, they just lived apart which was what often happened in those days. Children from these sorts of families often crave attention and seek it at any cost, including getting into trouble. That didn't seem to be the way Guy went. One has to admire his focus and determination to achieve his goal of getting into the RAF.

'Guy's boastfulness would have been a cover for his deep feelings of inadequacy coming from emotionally distant parents during his childhood. Issues he had to contend with included:

• Distant and emotionally rejecting parents
• Lack of close family
• Small stature – this matters to pubescent boys in particular
• Not good at anything
• Poor social skills leading to a degree of rejection by peers

'The fact that Guy returned to visit his old school suggests that it is possible that he had some solace from schoolmasters. He would most likely have spent more time with some of them than with either of his parents. His schoolmasters gave him some of the emotional nurturing absent in his home life. A good relationship with an adult such as a teacher can be a significant factor in a young person's life and may just offer them enough validation to give them sufficient emotional resilience to carry on in the face of adversity.

'During his formative years Guy had no outstanding attributes that could set him apart from his peers and put him in a place where he could get the recognition he craved. Guy seemed to want acknowledgement from those with a high social status, he was prepared to buy friendship. Just as he was ignored and left out he visited that same pain on those who became subservient to him.

'The outstanding acts that became the legend of the Dam Busters quite possibly included behaviour which was both very brave but also vainglorious. That would account for the reports that he had aircrew who deeply respected him but also those who were afraid of him. It is likely that to impress others and gain the approval of superiors he may have put others in unnecessary jeopardy. I wonder what accounts of his behaviour would have been had the Dam Busters mission failed? His arrogant refusal of help with an unfamiliar plane on the last mission, quite possibly, led to not only his death but the death of his navigator.

'Having achieved the VC Guy possibly felt that he was "untouchable and invincible", the status of the VC is such that even those who disliked him and had left him out would have to acknowledge his bravery, for someone like Guy it would have been the sort of vindication and validation he had been seeking all his life. The story of his arrogant rejection of help (with the controls of the Mosquito before his last flight) is unsurprising.

'I wonder about the reports of a "happy go lucky streak". I would suggest that his pre-war flouting of the rules and doing stunts would be aimed at impressing others and seeking their approbation for being daring and a bit "naughty". In children we would call it inappropriate attention seeking. Obviously this would not have been expressed in this way then but that sort of behaviour is rather immature and childlike in wanting to impress others.

'When we start looking more intimately at heroes we frequently find flawed beings whose motivation is often not a selfless commitment to duty. Guy obviously had a very tough upbringing and he had to develop tactics to survive. As a child he wasn't good at much and he was small in stature so he compensated. The impact of distant parents may have left him with an emotional "black hole" which needed to be filled and the war gave him a platform to find ways of getting lots of approval and recognition, which he failed to receive from his parents.'

In a letter written to the author on 9 July 2012, Squadron Leader George 'Johnny' Johnson gave his thoughts on Gibson. In Operation Chastise he was Sergeant Johnson, the bomb aimer in Flight Lieutenant McCarthy's aircraft.

'I suppose that the most common question I am asked is. "What did I think of that particular gentleman (Gibson)?" I have to say that my opinion has to be retrospective because at the time I was a lowly sergeant and perhaps one of his lesser attributes was his inability to "come down" to lower ranks.

'He was a strict disciplinarian, somewhat bombastic and arrogant, but at that time he was one of, if not the most experienced bomber pilots in the command. Perhaps he had something to be bombastic about. You may have been told that on 106 Squadron he was known as the "arch bastard".

'However, when he came to form 617 Squadron I think he realised that he had got to get a lot more out of the crews in which case he seemed to calm down a little. He did everything he could for the squadron. He is reputed to have told the Air Ministry that he would stay in his office until they changed their minds about what they were refusing him. He did, and eventually they did.

'I think the true demonstration of leadership came on the actual attack on the Möhne Dam. He made the first attack and assessed the strength of the defences. As he called in each subsequent crew to attack he flew alongside them to attract some of the defences. To me that says, "You are doing this, I am doing it, we are doing it together." That to me is the essence of good leadership, always from the front.'

Flying Officer Edward Johnson (bomb aimer in Pilot Officer Knight's aircraft) recorded a rather different view, 'I had met Gibson previously at 106 Squadron, where he was the CO. He was very efficient, very straightforward and I think everybody liked him. He wasn't a bully or a show off, but he liked things to be done right and he also liked you to keep fit (sometimes a sore point) with runs round the aerodrome and so on. After a night out on the tiles these weren't always frightfully popular – but I think he was on the right lines.

'He was strict about work, but he was a great mixer – not so much during the working day but always at night – he could sup his ale with anyone.'

Richard Todd gave his assessment of Gibson from the point of view of the man who played him and therefore had to 'get under his skin'. These words were contained in a letter he wrote in 1995 to a thirteen-year-old schoolboy who had contacted him after deciding that Gibson was the 'famous person' on whom he would produce a school project.

'He was a young man of great physical and mental courage, allied to determination and stubbornness. He was a brilliant pilot but reckoned to be overshadowed in this respect by (his dams raid colleague) 'Mickey' Martin. He was a born leader of men but not entirely popular with those who served with him, since he was quite cold and calculating and inclined to be very "cocky".

'He was extremely ambitious both professionally and personally and yet very protective towards his subordinates. Had he survived the war he would have had a highly successful career in the RAF.'

Appendix 3

Harris and Gibson

Guy Gibson did not come suddenly to the notice of Arthur Harris before No 617 Squadron was formed. The 'relationship' went back some way. There had even been discussions on No 83 Squadron around the outbreak of war that Gibson might have become related to the then commander of No 5 Group. On 5 September 1939, Gibson's brother Alick married Ruth Harris. She was not related to the future leader of Bomber Command, but Richard Morris in his biography of Guy Gibson, says that his subject did nothing to dispel the rumours.

Much more importantly, Harris had noticed Gibson's keenness, early on in the war, when Harris was commanding No 5 Group. At the time that he nominated Gibson as the best of the bunch to go to the aid of Fighter Command in the battle at night, Harris had promised Gibson a top command when he returned to the Bomber Command fold.

So to Gibson Harris was not 'Cousin Arthur', though he did to some extent assume the guise of 'Uncle Arthur' in the effect he created rather than in any visibly avuncular behaviour. In March 1942 Harris wrote in a letter to Air Vice-Marshal John Slessor, then commanding No 5 Group, that Gibson, 'was without question the most full-out fighting pilot in the whole of 5 Group in the days when I had it.'

At this point Harris was a month into his post of Air Officer Commanding in Chief Bomber Command and was intent on the wholesale invigoration of the command. This was in the face of the perceived threat that its place in the war effort would be relegated following the damaging Butt report, which illustrated the extent to which the bombers were not finding their targets.

As a part of this process the AOC wanted more vigorous leadership of squadrons. If some good men had their feelings hurt, even suffered humiliation, in the process, so be it. That was far less a consideration than demonstrating to the War Cabinet, the Royal Navy, Coastal Command, the British public and the Americans, that Bomber Command could win the war and needed the men and the equipment to do it.

Now Slessor found that Gibson was being sent to him as part of the invigoration process.

Harris wrote, 'Since leaving bombers (Gibson) has done a 200 tour on night fighters... you will find him absolutely first class and as this is a two year old promise now in fulfilment, I am sure you will agree to its consummation.'

Harris had done his homework and had a target in mind. His preference was that Gibson should take command of No 207 Squadron, the first unit to fly the Avro Manchester into action and, at the time of the letter, in the process of converting to the Lancaster. The squadron's commanding officer was Wing Commander Charles Fothergill, 28 years old, who had been in the RAF since 1934.

The point was made pretty strongly. 'I understand that Fothergill who commands one of your Lancaster squadrons, though a good organizer, is not a fire eater and I am sure you will agree that these fine squadrons ought as far as possible to have the absolute pick. Gibson has only been a squadron leader a year, but I desire to give him wing commander rank and command of a Lancaster squadron as soon as he can convert.'

Even if Charles Fothergill lacked accomplishment as a fire eater, he had a distinguished RAF career. He had served in Iraq before the war, flying the Vickers Victoria and Vickers Valentia with No 70 Squadron. Returning to the UK, he served as an instructor with No 6 Flying Training School at Little Rissington, Gloucestershire, before moving the short distance to Filton to act as an instructor with No 501 (County of Gloucester) Squadron, which had been part of the Auxiliary Air Force, but as with the AAF had been embodied 'for the emergency'. Here he nurtured pilots who would fly in the Battle of Britain. Further instructing followed before Charles Fothergill went to No 97 Squadron and flew on operations in Manchesters. Command of No 207 Squadron was the next step.

After leaving 207 Fothergill spent most of the rest of hostilities as an instructor. He later, ironically, commanded No 617 Squadron (June 1945 to April 1946), as well as No 31 Squadron, soloed in a Meteor, was air attaché in Belgrade and retired from the RAF in 1960 as a group captain. During his time with No 617 he took the squadron on deployment to India. This did not constitute involvement in 'Tiger Force', as is sometimes claimed. Tiger Force had been formed from Bomber Command squadrons and was intended to be sent to the Pacific ahead of an invasion of Japan. The atomic bombs were dropped, Japan surrendered and Tiger Force was disbanded in September 1945.

John Slessor reacted to the direction he had been given by Harris, though for the time being Charles Fothergill remained in place at No 207 Squadron. Instead Slessor sent Gibson to No 106 Squadron. At this point the squadron was still flying Manchesters into action, but the Lancasters would soon arrive.

From now on Arthur Harris would play a major part in the development of Gibson's career, most obviously with his appointment to form and command No 617 Squadron, but also when it came to his journey across the Atlantic and in the decision regarding Gibson's final operation, though the precise nature of Harris's involvement there is difficult to pin down.

It is interesting though to note that in the much acclaimed biography of Harris, written by the late Air Commodore Henry Probert (first published in 2001) reference to Gibson is sparse. There are two entries in the index for him. One relates to his presence when Harris, as Air Officer Commanding, No 5 Group made a station visit. The other does make the point that Harris played a direct part in Operation Chastise and 'nominated' Gibson to lead it. The inference must be that Probert did not support the claim sometimes made that Gibson reached the point where he was able to influence Harris, and therefore his immediate subordinates, in the making of tactical decisions.

Harris wanted 'fire eaters' leading his command into action. He wished such men to be, in the language of the time, press on types, leaders from the front and Gibson clearly epitomised what Harris had in mind.

When *Enemy Coast Ahead* appeared Harris had written the introduction.

Here Harris stressed the author's, 'natural aptitude for leadership, his outstanding skill and his extraordinary valour,' which marked him early for command.

'He always had direct access to me,' wrote Harris, in the process of taking responsibility for the decision to allow the last fatal flight. He did not mention that towards the end of Gibson's life he had become, in the view of Harris, somewhat uppity and had made public pronouncements to the effect that the bombing of Germany was not the fundamental way in which the war would be won. His statements could have been interpreted as criticism of Harris, though that thought may not have occurred to Gibson.

Harris concluded his introduction to the book in ringing tones which seem at odds with how his personality is normally portrayed.

His glowing tribute to the man he had mentored read, 'If there is a Valhalla, Guy Gibson and his band of brothers will be found there at all the parties, seated far above the salt.'

In invoking the hall of the slain from Norse mythology, with occupants chosen by the god Odin, Harris deliberately left his readers with a picture of a great warrior, fallen in battle, yet living on with his comrades, eternally enjoying their honour and good fellowship.

Appendix 4

Gibson's Dog

Guy Gibson called his much-loved dog Nigger and the dog plays a small part in the story of the Dam Busters. That is historical fact and so cannot be changed.

Today the word is generally considered so offensive to black people that it is difficult to mention it, let alone have any discussion about it.

In the 1940s, in predominately white Britain, the situation was different. 'Nigger' was a not infrequent name for pets and much later than the 1940s items of clothing in shops and mail order catalogues would be described as 'nigger brown' in colour.

The edition of *Chamber's Twentieth Century Dictionary of the English Language* which appeared in 1926 gives 'black man' as the first meaning of 'nigger'. It is worth noting, without attaching much significance, that the word was recorded in the dictionary as being in use in Cornwall to denote a species of sea cucumber, a marine animal.

There is no evidence that it occurred to Guy Gibson that his choice of name for his dog might cause offence to anyone or that anyone ever put that thought to him.

So much has changed in the last seventy years and attitudes to the word 'nigger' are amongst those changes.

The inscription on the stone marking the spot where Nigger was buried at Scampton:

Nigger
The grave of a black Labrador dog. Mascot of 617 Squadron, owned by Wing Commander Guy Gibson VC, DSO, DFC. Nigger was killed by a car on the 16th May 1943. Buried at midnight as his owner was leading his squadron on the attack against the Möhne and Eder Dams.

Notes on Some People in the Gibson Story

Anderson, Michael Joseph (1920–) – Michael Anderson came from a theatrical family. He was considered rather an unknown when he was hired to direct *The Dam Busters*, but reservations about the level of his experience seem to have been quickly allayed. He went on to direct *1984* and *Around the World in Eighty Days*, for which he was nominated for an Academy Award and a Golden Globe.

The latter film attracted enormous publicity (though much more for the producer, Mike Todd than for Anderson). One reason for this exposure was the number of stars of the day who had cameo roles. Basil Sydney, who had appeared in *The Dam Busters* played a member of the Reform Club. Others to appear briefly included Frank Sinatra, Noel Coward, Buster Keaton, Marlene Dietrich, John Gielgud, Trevor Howard and Sir Cedric Hardwicke.

Shortly afterwards another major war film directed by Anderson came out in the shape of *Yangtse Incident*, the story of HMS *Amethyst* shelled and trapped on the Chinese river of the title in 1949.

Working in Hollywood, Anderson made science fiction films, including *Logan's Run*, which made much money and has achieved cult status. Richard Todd worked with Anderson again, starring as the maverick Lieutenant Commander John Kerans, who takes the British warship to safety. Other *Dam Busters* actors to appear were Richard Leech and Ewan Solon.

Brickhill, Paul Chester Jerome (1916–1991) – Brickhill, who was born in Melbourne and worked as a journalist with the *Sydney Sun*, served in the Royal Australian Air Force in the Second World War. He trained as a pilot in the UK and Canada and was posted to No 92 Squadron, RAF operating Spitfires in the Western Desert. He was shot down and captured on 17 March 1943.

After the war Brickhill became a foreign correspondent. Some of his wartime imprisonment had been at Stalag Luft III and, in 1950, his book *The Great Escape* was published, an account of the mass escape from that camp in 1944. Brickhill had been involved in the preparations for the escape, but suffered from claustrophobia and therefore declined to go into the tunnel which was the means of escape. As well as *The Dam Busters*, Brickhill wrote *Reach for the Sky*, the story of Douglas 'Tin Legs' Bader. He also wrote novels. Paul Brickhill's pen flowed less freely as he grew older and he had become somewhat reclusive by the time of his death.

Chadwick, Roy (1893–1947) – Roy Chadwick was born in Farnworth, near Manchester. His father was a mechanical engineer. The young Chadwick was fascinated by aircraft and demonstrated his passion by making models. He soon became part of the team built up by Alliott Verdon-Roe, a pioneer of British aviation and founder of A.V. Roe and Co Ltd.

Chadwick worked on a range of aircraft during the First World War and designs he was involved in later included the Avro Baby, a very early light aircraft, the Avian, used for record-breaking long distance flights and the Tutor, an important RAF trainer.

With war under way came the Manchester and Lancaster. He also created the Anson and later the York, Lincoln and Lancastrian emerged from his drawing board.

Chadwick, who was made CBE, was killed, aged 54, on 23 August 1947, flying as a passenger in an Avro Tudor, another of his designs, which crashed on a test flight. The aircraft took off from Woodford in Cheshire, where many Lancasters had been built, but crashed immediately. It was decided that the accident was caused by a mistake made in servicing and not noticed by the pilot.

Coates, Eric (1886–1957) – Coates was born Frank Harrison Coates in Hucknall, Nottinghamshire, but seems always to have been known as 'Eric'. He was a performer (particularly the viola), composer and conductor. He spent nine years as principal viola player under Sir Henry Wood in the Queen's Hall Orchestra, but was not entirely in accord with Sir Henry's methods, leading to his contract not being renewed.

As a composer, Coates's most well known work, apart from his contribution to *The Dam Busters*, was *By the Sleepy Lagoon*, which eventually became the theme tune for *Desert Island Discs*, though not until after Guy Gibson had appeared on the programme.

Coates was a gentle and modest man and suffered from poor health. He generally would not undertake film work, turning down an offer to go to Hollywood. He also declined an approach to write the score of *The Dam Busters*.

Geoffrey Self, biographer of Coates, recorded that Louis Levy of Associated British Pictures put pressure on him through Chappell's, the music publisher, stressing the national importance of the new film. It was suggested that if Coates would not do the score he could write a march which could be used as the basis of a score.

At this point accounts diverge, though most seem to agree that *The Dam Busters March* already existed, albeit not named as such, when Chappell's instigated a further approach to Coates. It is sometimes claimed that Coates had completed the march shortly before this approach or that he had written it some years previously for a film about the battle of El Alamein, a film which was never made.

Self wrote however, that the 'astonishing reply' from Coates to the latest request was, 'I think I finished it yesterday'. The ink score of the march indicated that it was completed on 14 June 1954. Rather than admit to the fact that it was proposed to use an existing work, Chappell's told Associated British Pictures that the march would be delivered in twelve days.

Geoffrey Self praised the creation highly, writing that, 'It is a superb march, universal in its popular appeal, with themes of inspired simplicity.' An Eric Coates Society was founded in 2008.

Kendall, Henry (1888–1963) – 'Warden' Kendall, as he became, was born in Liverpool on 11 November 1888. He was educated at Shrewsbury and took a degree (MA) in History at Pembroke College, Cambridge in 1911. For a few terms he taught at Rossall, the Lancashire public school, where only the headmaster could be married. One of his fellow masters was the future chronicler of the English countryside and broadcaster, S.P.B. Mais, who would be briefly and unhappily Professor of English at the RAF Cadet College, Cranwell.

Kendall returned to Shrewsbury as an assistant master in 1913. He was ordained in 1915 and served as a Royal Naval chaplain from that year until 1919 when he was made OBE. Once more Shrewsbury called him and he became a housemaster there.

In 1925 Kendall took the St Edward's Wardenship which had become available with his predecessor moving to Radley. He retained the post until 1954 (the longest tenure on record) and under him the school grew upwards and outwards with Kendall's personal drive, vision and considerable persuasive charm (not least with prospective donors) leading the way.

Chris Nathan, archivist at St Edward's, wrote that, 'The school was immediately reorganised in 1925 with the introduction of houses in place of tutorial sets. The school became his sole aim in life and he pursued its expansion in buildings and acreage with incredible zeal. School numbers doubled in his time from 240 to 480. He felt every Second World War casualty personally and in chapel read the list of those lost, often with tears streaming down his face. He oversaw the school until his retirement in 1954 and then continued his association as a governor from 1957 for six years. In 1963, the year of the school's centenary, he went abroad on a world tour at the school's behest to celebrate and 'spread the word' with Old Boys living overseas, and died on board ship en route for Vancouver, having already visited Southern Rhodesia, South Africa, Singapore, Australia and New Zealand.

'His life was the school but he also relished going to Mevagissey (in Cornwall) every summer to a cottage he owned there, together with a small sailing yacht moored nearby where parties of boys, old boys, governors and teaching colleagues were invited to enjoy the relaxed atmosphere. He never married. His love of books was legendary and after his death his bequest to the school library was voluminous, varied and valuable.

'His pronouncements on education, politics etc were widespread and lengthy and sometimes contradictory. His sermons were never intellectual, but often imaginative and original, yet always straight, simple and deeply felt. A strong disciplinarian believing in ample use of corporal punishment, as was common in his time, he was also a friendly and gentle man with an overwhelming love and protective care for all his charges.'

Sherriff, Robert Cedric (1896–1975) – R.C. Sherriff began his career working in London for Sun Insurance. He joined the 9th (Service) Battalion of the East Surrey Regiment, saw action at Vimy and Loos and was badly wounded at Ypres in 1917. He was awarded the MC.

After the war he returned to the world of insurance and began writing plays as a means of raising funds for the Kingston (Surrey) Rowing Club of which he was a member. The turning point in Sherriff's career came in December 1928 when his play *Journey's End* was staged at the Apollo Theatre, later moving to the Savoy Theatre for a long run. The actors in the early days included Laurence Olivier.

This story of doomed British soldiers in the trenches at St Quentin, as the German spring offensive of 1918 approaches, was inspired by his own wartime letters home. It shot Sherriff to fame, gave him financial independence and has continued to be produced ever since. As recently as 2011 the play reappeared in the West End.

Subsequently Sherriff's progress as a playwright was sketchy. Following the success of *Journey's End*, Sherriff became what would now be called a mature student at New College, Oxford, reading history. He put this course on hold and then abandoned it when he was invited to work as a scriptwriter in Hollywood. He was also a novelist and wrote an autobiography, *No Leading Lady*, which appeared in 1968.

Summers, Joseph (1904–1954) – Frequently known in later years as 'Mutt' (apparently from his habit of relieving himself by aircraft he was about to fly because he believed full bladders could be fatal in an accident), Joseph Summers was born in Hull. He joined the RAF on a short service commission and served with No 29 Squadron.

Summers proved to be an outstanding pilot and it took only six months for him to be posted to the Aircraft and Armament Experimental Establishment at Martlesham Heath, Suffolk. He tested a range of aircraft and showed further great skill in rescuing dangerous situations. From 1929 he was chief test pilot for Vickers at Weybridge and for a time held the same position with Supermarine after Vickers had acquired that company. On 6 March 1936 he made the first flight in the prototype of the Spitfire.

Summers eventually retired after a remarkably distinguished testing career in 1951. He had been made OBE in 1946 and was advanced to CBE in 1953. His early death occurred through illness.

His brother, Wing Commander Maurice Summers, was also a test pilot. On 1 February 1945 he and the other crew member were forced to take to their parachutes when a Vickers Warwick became uncontrollable, after taking off from Weybridge for investigation of rudder problems from which the type suffered. They survived, but two women were killed when the Warwick fell on houses in Ruxley Lane, West Ewell, Surrey.

Todd, Richard (1919–2009) – He was born Richard Andrew Palethorpe-Todd in Ireland and was educated at Shrewsbury School. His involvement with acting before the Second World War included appearing as an extra in the film *A Yank at Oxford*.

During the war Todd served with the King's Own Yorkshire Light Infantry and with 7th (Light Infantry) Parachute Battalion. While with the latter he saw action at Pegasus Bridge on D-Day. He would later appear in depictions of that event in both the films, *D-Day, The Sixth of June* and *The Longest Day*. On neither occasion did he play himself.

In the post war world he was also prominent in *The Hasty Heart* in London and on Broadway, as well as the film version. Other films in which he was a star included *Yangtse Incident* and *Operation Crossbow*.

Todd was appointed OBE. His obituary in *The Daily Telegraph* described him as, 'handsome, blue-eyed and with an erect military bearing.' He was also extremely approachable and willing to help those doing research.

Wallis, Sir Barnes Neville (1887–1979) – Born in Derbyshire, the son of a general practitioner, Barnes Wallis attended Haberdashers' Aske's Hatcham

Boys' School in south London and subsequently Christ's Hospital in Sussex. In 1904 he took up indentures with the Thames Engineering Works, moving four years later to the J.S. White Company at Cowes, Isle of Wight, establishing himself quickly in the drawing office.

Here he met H.B. Pratt, who had moved from Vickers. In 1913 Pratt, an airship specialist, returned to Vickers as Chief Designer, Airships, with Wallis joining him in a senior capacity.

Having been laid off in 1921, Wallis took an external degree in engineering at London University. After teaching in Switzerland, he returned to Vickers and became chief designer of the Airship Guarantee Company, tasked with creating the R100. Later Wallis became a senior figure in a complicated aircraft design establishment at Vickers. His designs, with R.K. Pierson, included the Wellington bomber, one of the aircraft to incorporate the Wallis method of geodetic construction.

The large bombs, including the Tallboy, designed by Wallis played an important part in Bomber Command operations in the latter part of the war.

Wallis remained at Vickers long after the war, a driven man, often infuriated by senior management and civil servants and sometimes having the same kind of effect on them.

Appendix 6

The Squadrons and the Airfields

These are the squadrons with which Guy Gibson served and the aircraft and airfields with which he was particularly associated.

No 83 Squadron

No 83 Squadron of the Royal Flying Corps was formed at Montrose on 7 January 1917. Although the squadron moved south within a few days, links with Scotland remained strong, so that when the squadron badge was granted by King George VI in 1938 it featured a red deer antler. The six points of the antler commemorate an occasion in the First World War when six DFCs were earned by the squadron in one operation.

In March 1917 the squadron moved to St Omer in France and remained at various airfields on the continent, carrying out night bombing and reconnaissance operations, until the end of the fighting. It was equipped with the FE2b two seater 'pusher' biplane. Back in the UK, disbandment of the squadron occurred at the end of 1919.

As the threat of war increased in the mid 1930s, 83 Squadron became one of the squadrons from the Great War to be reformed, this taking place at Turnhouse in August 1936.

Following Guy Gibson's period of service, No 83 converted from Hampdens to Avro Manchesters in December 1941 and then to Lancasters in the following spring. With this type the squadron would operate for the rest of hostilities. It moved to Wyton in the late summer of 1942 and to Coningsby in April 1944. This latter move took the squadron out of the Pathfinder Force, as it became the marking squadron in No 5 Group. The Lancaster development, the Lincoln arrived in 1946. For a time in 1956 and 1957 the squadron was disbanded, before receiving Vulcans until a further disbandment in 1969.

No 29 Squadron

The squadron was formed at Gosport in November 1915. Later in the First World War it served in France, flying a number of different types of aircraft on fighter, ground attack and escort missions. After a short spell in Germany the squadron returned to the UK and disbanded at the close of 1919.

No 29 Squadron was reformed at Duxford in 1923 and flew successively, Snipes, Grebes, Siskins and Bulldogs, before re-equipping with Demons and moving to Egypt in 1935. The squadron operated Gordons for a time and then received Demons fitted with gun turrets. Debden became a new home in November 1937 and Blenheims were taken on charge from December 1938.

Following Guy Gibson's service, 29 Squadron operated from a number of UK airfields, including a further spell at West Malling. The Mosquito became the squadron's aircraft in 1943 and this continued, through various updates until the jet age was entered with Meteors at Tangmere in the summer of 1951. Javelins and Lightnings were also flown before disbandment in 1974. Further service with Phantoms (including a detachment to the Falklands immediately after the 1982 war with Argentina) and Tornados occurred between 1975 and 1998. Following the Iraqi invasion of Kuwait, the squadron flew throughout Operation Desert Storm in the air defence role.

The squadron was reformed in 2003, now No 29(R) Squadron, as the Typhoon Operational Conversion Unit, being 'stood up' for operational service in 2005. In the summer of 2012, No 29 was still flying Typhoons, from Coningsby.

The 29 Squadron badge shows an eagle attacking a buzzard.

No 106 Squadron

Formed at Spittlegate, close to Grantham, on 23 September 1917, No 106 Squadron quickly moved to Andover in Hampshire. From May 1918 the squadron was based in Ireland, in an Army co-operation role, initially flying the RE8 two seater biplane. Disbandment took place in 1919 and 106 was reformed at Abingdon as a bomber squadron in 1938. Hawker Hinds were quickly replaced with Fairey Battles, then there was a spell with Ansons, before Hampdens arrived in May 1939.

From May 1942, No 106 flew Lancasters, moving from Coningsby to Syerston four months later and Metheringham in November 1943.

The RAF website credits the squadron with operating on 496 nights during the Second World War, flying 5,834 sorties, losing 187 aircraft and being credited with twenty enemy aircraft destroyed, three probably destroyed and twenty-nine damaged.

There were 267 decorations for squadron personnel for actions in the Second World War, including a Victoria Cross gazetted on 26 October 1945 for Warrant Officer (sergeant at the time of his action) Norman Jackson, a flight engineer on an operation to Schweinfurt on 26 April 1944. After his Lancaster had been attacked by a night fighter, Jackson climbed outside the aircraft in an attempt to extinguish the fire which had broken out. He was burned, and wounded in a further attack by the fighter. He descended by his damaged parachute, broke an ankle on landing and was later stoned by civilians.

No 106 Squadron was disbanded in February 1946. Between 1959 and 1963 the squadron was revived and deployed Thor ballistic missiles.

No 617 Squadron

After Guy Gibson's departure the squadron continued to be used for precision operations and was not included in the Bomber Command 'Main Force'.

Flying from Coningsby, on 15/16 September 1943, a costly attack was mounted against the Dortmund-Ems Canal. This was followed by attacks on the Antheor viaduct on the border between France and Italy.

Led by Wing Commander Leonard Cheshire, the squadron achieved great success when making pinpoint attacks on factories in enemy territory during early 1944. From January 1944, No 617 was based at Woodhall Spa.

A key contribution was made to the success of the Allied landings in Normandy on 6 June 1944, when 617 flew Operation Taxable, which involved dropping bundles of 'window' during precision flying over the English Channel as part of a plan to simulate an invasion fleet approaching the Pas de Calais rather than Normandy.

Shortly afterwards, the first 12,000lb Tallboy bombs were dropped on the Saumur railway tunnel in northern France, an operation aimed at disrupting German reinforcements and supplies to resist the advancing Allies.

Later in the year, led by Wing Commander 'Willie' Tait, the squadron took its Lancasters to Russia for an attack on the German capital ship *Tirpitz*. In the second of two further attacks, with No 617 operating with No 9 Squadron, the ship was capsized. There were additional attacks on dams, including the breaching of the Kembs dam.

On 14 March 1945 a Lancaster of No 617, flown by Squadron Leader 'Jock' Calder, dropped the first 22,000lb 'Grand Slam' bomb used in action; the target was the Bielefeld railway viaduct in North Rhine-Westphalia.

The last Second World War operation by the squadron was an attack on Hitler's mountain lair – 'the Eagle's Nest' – at Berchtesgaden.

In the post-war era 617 Squadron received the Avro Lincoln in 1946 and the Canberra in 1952. Between 1955 and 1958 the squadron did not exist, but it was then reformed at Scampton and given Avro Vulcans as part of the V

Bomber force. After another brief disbandment, effectively covering the year 1982, the squadron appeared again at Marham and received the Tornado. In 2012 , No 617 was at Lossiemouth with the Tornado GR4.

For a squadron founded at a relatively late date, No 617 has enjoyed considerable immunity from all the cutbacks and slashings suffered by the RAF since the Second World War. This is especially worthy of note because the principles of allocating number plates to squadrons, established in 1919, laid much stress on the 'seniority' of squadrons and this has been a major factor in decisions ever since. In post Second World War allocations of number plates, merit and achievement were considered, including participation in the Battle of Britain. No 617 Squadron's outstanding operational record was noted at that point.

In the 1950s Nos 120 and 617 Squadrons were awarded their standards, much earlier than would normally have been the case. This was intended to mark the exceptional wartime accomplishments of both squadrons and, through many revisions to number plate decision-making since, this has, in the main, ensured No 617's continuing existence.

With the modern RAF the history of 617 Squadron continues to resonate. Robert Owen commented, 'The squadron is extremely aware and proud of its history, as are most, if not all squadrons. Certainly No 617 has a cachet, and those who serve on the squadron are very much aware of this. In keeping with the RAF's ethos, service and unit heritage are keenly promoted and the squadron has a recently refurbished, extended history room to record and promote its history to serving members and visitors alike. From my own experience, having strong links with those given the secondary duty of Squadron History Officer, they relish the role and execute it with great enthusiasm and pride.'

Battle Honours for No 617 Squadron
Fortress Europe 1943–1945*, The Dams*, Biscay Ports 1944*, France and Germany 1944–1945*, Normandy 1944*, *Tirpitz**, Channel and North Sea 1944–1945*, German Ports 1945*, Gulf 1991, Iraq 2003*.

(Honours marked with an asterisk may be emblazoned on the Squadron Standard.)

Guy Gibson's Principal Aircraft

de Havilland Tiger Moth – From the 1930s to the early 1950s the Tiger Moth biplane was an RAF basic trainer. Royal Navy use continued for considerably longer. As a military aircraft the 'Tiger' spread through the

Commonwealth and elsewhere. Its civilian uses, continuing to this day, have been extremely varied. Had a German invasion taken place in 1940, Tiger Moths converted to be light bombers would have gone into action over the landing beaches.

Hawker Audax – Derived from the Hawker Hart, the Audax was developed initially for army co-operation duties and served in the role with the RAF until being displaced by the Lysander. As the Lysanders arrived, so the Audax became an aircraft for communications and advanced training. The Audax continued in use during the Second World War, notably in overseas theatres. In desperate circumstances the type flew into action as a fighter against the Japanese.

Hawker Hind – A light bomber, developed from the Hawker Hart. It thus came within the family of military aircraft developed by Hawker in the 1920s and 1930s, under the design auspices of Sydney Camm. The Hind largely left front line RAF service in the late 30s, with the arrival of the Fairey Battle and Bristol Blenheim, but continued into the Second World War, briefly as an Army co-operation aircraft, for longer as a trainer. Having been sold to a number of overseas air forces, the Hind did see wartime action as a bomber, for example, in the hands of the South African Air Force against Italian forces in Kenya.

Handley Page Hampden – Designed as a twin-engined day bomber, the Hampden entered RAF operational service in September 1938. A year later the type's inadequacy against German fighters in daylight became all too clear. Hampden crews continued to fly gallantly, mainly at night, against the enemy until 1942. The Hampden's operational career was extended by its use in Coastal Command as a torpedo bomber and for maritime reconnaissance.

Bristol Beaufighter – Developed in a hurry from the Beaufort and Blenheim designs, to meet the need for a fighter capable of being used in night fighter and long range escort roles, the Beaufighter first flew in 1939 and entered squadron service in 1940. Later in the war, the Beaufighter became associated in many minds with anti-shipping strikes. The last of the type was withdrawn from RAF service in 1960. Later uses for Beaufighters included as target tugs.

Avro Manchester – Perhaps it is difficult to believe now that Avro developed the Manchester to meet the same Air Ministry specification (P.13/36) for which Handley Page produced the Hampden. With two Rolls Royce Vulture engines the Manchester was underpowered and a significant number were lost in crashes. Less than 200 flew operationally in Bomber Command. Eventually a Manchester was fitted with four Rolls Royce Merlin engines, with the wingspan increased. The Lancaster was born.

A pilot who experienced the problems of the Manchester was Sergeant Les Syrett, who flew eighteen operations on them with No 207 Squadron. His first trip was to Brest in February 1941, as second pilot, but when the pilot was wounded Syrett took over the controls, completed the bombing run and brought the aircraft back. He received an immediate DFM.

On 21 June 1941 Sergeant Syrett took off from Waddington on an air test. Almost immediately both engines cut out and the Manchester plunged into a field. Syrett survived, despite injuries that included a broken neck and back and became a member of The Guinea Pig Club. With him in the aircraft were Squadron Leader C.J.F. Kydd who was killed and Flight Sergeant J.W. Arnott, who died of his injuries a month later.

Avro Lancaster – The most famous and distinguished RAF bomber of the Second World War. Usually it is regarded as a four-engined version of the Manchester, though that was not the only difference between them. When the Air Ministry authorised the project in 1940 it stressed that as many Manchester components as possible should be used.

The first flight of a prototype took place on 9 January 1941 and with success clearly in the offing, a considerable number of further test flights took place. A new tail unit was designed before the first flight of a production model on 13 May 1941. In June Avro received a contract to produce 454 Lancaster Mk 1s, with four Merlin XX engines and there was a requirement to manufacture two prototype Lancaster Mk IIs with Bristol Hercules VI engines.

On 24 December 1941 No 44 Squadron, based at Waddington, Lincolnshire became the first squadron in Bomber Command to receive Lancasters. The first Lancaster operation occurred on 3 March 1942 when four of the type from No 44 Squadron laid mines in the Heligoland Bight between the mouth of the River Elbe and the Heligoland Islands.

Over 7,000 Lancasters were built and fifty-seven Bomber Command squadrons were equipped with them during the Second World War. Uses of the Lancaster following the war included in-flight re-fuelling (in which role it participated in the Berlin Air Lift) and as a freighter by British South American Airways.

In 1943 a Lancaster IV was planned, but this was developed into the Type 694 Lincoln which, as a result of some delays and the Japanese surrender, did not achieve operational service in the Second World War.

de Havilland Mosquito – Eventually known as 'The Wooden Wonder', the Mosquito developed from a pre-war unofficial project by de Havilland. Initially, the Air Ministry failed to see the potential in the idea.

Eventually an order was placed in March 1940, but even then progress was slow with other requirements being given priority. The first flight of a Mosquito took place on 25 November 1940. By this time some in authority were beginning to understand the advantages of the aircraft, including its ability as a bomber which could manoeuvre like a fighter.

The first variety of the Mosquito to enter operational service was for photo-reconnaissance, with bombers following for No 2 Group, the first going to No 105 Squadron at Swanton Morley, Norfolk. They went into action for the first time as a follow up to the thousand bomber attack on Cologne at the end of May 1942.

The Mosquito carried a crew of two who perhaps needed to be slim to escape in a hurry through the hatch in the floor. Comparison was made with a Victorian child acting as a chimney sweep. The wooden construction raised many eyebrows, but the aircraft was still able to survive considerable punishment.

Airfields

Yatesbury

Teaching was a long tradition at Yatesbury. The Royal Flying Corps and then the RAF carried out training there from 1916 to 1919. As the First World War ended, Yatesbury also became a place where squadrons disbanded. Early in 1920 the station closed and farming took over again.

As with so many airfield sites, a fresh call to serve came about in the mid 1930s. From 1936 the Bristol Flying School returned Yatesbury to its previous function, training pilots for the RAF. This activity moved elsewhere with the outbreak of war. Since 1938 the training of wireless operators for airborne service had been a further function of Yatesbury and this was developed during the war, so that by its end over 50,000 men had passed out in this trade according to the RAF Yatesbury Association.

Some flying training returned in peacetime and, during the Cold War, fitters, mechanics and radar operators were instructed. From 1954 to 1958 the old flying school was used as the headquarters of No 27 Group, which also had a training role, and was known as RAF Cherhill.

The RAF departed from Yatesbury in 1969, though derelict buildings remain. Plans to create housing and commercial activity on the site have not reached fruition.

Netheravon

Even before the First World War there was flying at Netheravon, on the River Avon and close to Amesbury in Wiltshire. Watchers then would have seen balloons, but the Royal Flying Corps based aircraft there during the war.

For a time in the 1939–1945 war, No 296 Squadron, the former Glider Exercise Unit, was stationed at Netheravon, still carrying out glider training, flying Hawker Harts and then Armstrong Whitworth Whitleys.

Sutton Bridge

Sutton Bridge airfield was a place of which geographical description is difficult. In *Lincolnshire Airfields in the Second World War*, Patrick Otter wrote, 'The airfield straddled one of those geographic points where three English counties converged. Aircraft actually landed in Norfolk, but were serviced in Lincolnshire, while some of the men stationed there lived in Cambridgeshire. The station headquarters, however, was in Lincolnshire and therefore falls within the purview of this book.'

Personnel travelling to and from the station experienced more split personality nearby. The A17 road and the Midland and Great Northern railway line shared a bridge to cross the River Nene.

Operations at the airfield site began in the mid 1920s, with summer camps for both RAF and Naval fighter squadrons. In the next decade the airfield was formally established, hosting No 3 Armament Training School.

On 2 September 1939, the Armament Training School moved out and for a time Sutton Bridge was one of those places where recruits received their initiation into RAF life. Then it was a short-lived operational fighter airfield in No 12 Group and hosting Nos 264 and 266 Squadrons.

In March 1940, No 6 Operational Training Unit came into being at Sutton Bridge, having previously been the No 11 Group Fighter Pool, based at St Athan in south Wales. So it was that many of the Hurricane pilots who would fly in the Battle of Britain learned some of their skills where three eastern counties converged. A decoy site was established at Terrington Marshes to deflect German bombing.

Eventually the OTU was renumbered and then transferred to Scotland. A gunnery school produced air gunners for both bomber and fighter commands. Further training took place, but flying ended at Sutton Bridge in 1946. The last RAF activity at the former airfield was in 1958.

A memorial, featuring a propeller blade was placed beside the bridge over the River Nene. The bridge still carries road traffic, but the railway line closed in 1959.

Turnhouse

A Royal Flying Corps base at Turnhouse on the outskirts of Edinburgh was established in 1915. Between the wars the airfield was particularly associated with No 603 (City of Edinburgh) Squadron of the Auxiliary Air Force. The squadron was founded at Turnhouse on 14 October 1925 and also had a town headquarters in Learmouth Terrace, Edinburgh. On the outbreak of the Second World War, the airfield became part of Fighter Command.

Commercial services from Turnhouse began after the war, with military ownership remaining in place for a good many years. Now Turnhouse is Edinburgh Airport, with major expansion plans.

Scampton

Scampton, a few miles north west of Lincoln, was a landing field for the Royal Flying Corps in the First World War, when it was first known as Brattleby, until 1917 when it took the name of Scampton, another nearby village. After closure in 1919, RAF Scampton reopened in 1936 as part of the RAF expansion scheme. The station was mothballed for a period in the 1990s, but is now the home of the Red Arrows, the Royal Air Force Aerobatic Team, as well as a museum featuring much material associated with Guy Gibson and No 617 Squadron.

Above the museum is the office used by Gibson when commanding No 617. It was refurbished in 2012 and is laid out as it would have been in Gibson's time, though the furniture and other artefacts, such as a pipe, are not original.

Lossiemouth

The construction of RAF Lossiemouth took place during 1938 and 1939. The initial unit occupying that station was No 15 Flying Training School. From April 1940 Lossiemouth was in the possession of Bomber Command and became home to No 20 Operational Training Unit. On occasions the station was a convenient starting point for operations, including one of the attacks on the *Tirpitz* in 1944.

At the end of the Second World War the station had a brief spell in Coastal Command before joining the Royal Navy in 1946. At this point the base was HMS *Fulmar*, RNAS Lossiemouth. Pilots were given basic training and then, from nearby Milltown, practised landings on the aircraft carrier, HMS *Theseus*, stationed in the Moray Firth. The students then moved to the other end of the British Isles, to continue their progression at RNAS Culdrose, near Helston, in the west of Cornwall.

In September 1972 Lossiemouth returned to the RAF. In the years that followed residents included No 202 Squadron with helicopters, the Jaguar conversion team, No 8 Squadron with Shackletons and No 48 Squadron, RAF Regiment, operating Rapier surface to air missiles.

The station received the Freedom of Moray in 1992. In the following year No 12 Squadron, based at Lossiemouth, exchanged its Bucaneers for Tornados. In 1994 No 617 Squadron brought its Tornados to the station from RAF Marham in Norfolk.

Today the RAF describes Lossiemouth as its 'largest and busiest fast jet base'. In 2012 the station was home to Nos 12, 617 and XV (R) Squadrons, 5 Force Protection Wing Headquarters comprising Nos 51 Squadron RAF Regiment and 2622 (Highland) Squadron Royal Auxiliary Air Force Regiment and the search and rescue helicopters of D Flight, No 202 Squadron.

The continuing emotive power of the name of No 617 Squadron was illustrated in July 2012 by the RAF's own proud description of the squadron's return to Lossiemouth:

'617 SQUADRON, "The Dambusters", made an emotional return to RAF Lossiemouth last night following a successful, four month, operational deployment in Afghanistan.

'Around 130 personnel consisting of ground and air crews touched down to a very welcome cool Scottish evening and were met by the RAF Lossiemouth Station Commander, Group Captain Ian Gale. He praised their excellent achievements in theatre as Pipe Major Barry Ashby added some traditional accompaniment to the homecoming proceedings. It was a difficult time for the families and friends of the returning heroes who watched the aircraft land a few hundred metres away, but had a further short wait until the coaches carrying their loved ones arrived at their location. However, as the first returning men and women appeared between two Tornado GR4 aircraft, parked nose to nose to form an impressive gateway, the many expectant children, closely followed by wives, husbands, girlfriends, boyfriends and parents all rushed forward to meet and embrace them.

'It was a highly emotional reunion with many tears of happiness being shed – even the media present were moved by the occasion. Sergeant Kieren Brenchley (41) from Elgin who had missed both his wife's 30th and son's fifth birthdays said, as he hugged Claire, Oliver and daughter Katie: "I'm delighted to be home, really pleased."'

West Malling

There was a landing ground on the site of West Malling during the First World War, which was operated privately later. For a time it was known as Kingshill, a nearby district, and it was the base for the Maidstone School of Flying. The name, West Malling airfield, was applied and then Maidstone Airport. Shows and displays were held. The RAF moved in in 1940, while construction work was still going on and West Malling played a limited part in the Battle of Britain. The Defiants of No 141 Squadron were based there briefly, but were withdrawn to Prestwick in Scotland after suffering heavy casualties.

West Malling ceased to be an operational RAF airfield in 1969, having been a US naval air station for a time. Civilian air displays were held until the 1980s.

Coningsby

Coningsby was not opened until 1940 and No 106 Squadron, then flying Hampdens, was the first squadron to take up residence, in February 1941, to be joined by No 97 Squadron in the following month, No 97 arriving shortly after it had received its first Manchesters. Later in the war Coningsby would be associated with Nos 617 and 61 Squadrons. In the peacetime era, Mosquitos, Washingtons, Canberras and Vulcans were to be found at Coningsby and the station was designated to be a home to the TSR-2, cancelled in 1965 after bitter political and inter-service dispute.

More recently, the Phantom, Tornado and Jaguar have all added to Coningsby's history. For many years, the Battle of Britain Memorial Flight and its visitor centre have attracted aviation enthusiasts to the station. One of the stars of the Flight is Lancaster PA474, which was named City of Lincoln in the 1970s, but has recently gone under other guises.

Woodhall Spa

The airfield was a little south of the village of Woodhall Spa, in an area packed with wartime bomber bases. It was built in 1941 as a satellite of Coningsby and with concrete runways. As well as No 617 Squadron, the squadrons especially associated with Woodhall Spa were Nos 97, 619 and 627. However, the first use was by Hampdens of No 106 Squadron, when the grass at Coningsby became waterlogged. From the beginning of 1944 Woodhall Spa was a sub station of No 54 base, which took in Coningsby and Metheringham as well.

Following the victory in Europe it was used in the preparation of the planned Tiger Force to go to the Far East. Bombs were later stored on the site and for a time it was a base for Bloodhound missiles. The RAF continues to hold part of the site, for storage and servicing. Another area is now the Thorpe Camp Visitor Centre set up 'to commemorate those who fought for freedom in World War Two based in Lincolnshire'.

In the centre of the village of Woodhall Spa is the imposing Dambusters Memorial, standing in Royal Square where the Royal Hydropathic Hotel and Winter Gardens were located until they were bombed in 1943.

Appendix 7

The Crews and the Decorations

The men who set off for the dams

First Wave

AJ-G

Pilot: Wing Commander G.P. Gibson DSO (and bar), DFC (and bar)
Flight Engineer: Sergeant J. Pulford
Navigator: Pilot Officer H.T. Taerum, RCAF
Wireless Operator: Flight Lieutenant R.E.G. Hutchison DFC
Bomb Aimer: Pilot Officer F.M. Spafford DFM, RAAF
Front Gunner: Flight Sergeant G.A. Deering, RCAF
Rear Gunner: Flight Lieutenant R.D. Trevor-Roper DFM

AJ-M

Pilot: Flight Lieutenant J.V. Hopgood DFC (and bar)
Flight Engineer: Sergeant C. Brennan
Navigator: Flying Officer K. Earnshaw, RCAF
Wireless Operator: Sergeant J.W. Minchin
Bomb Aimer: Pilot Officer J.W. Fraser, RCAF
Front Gunner: Pilot Officer G.H.F.G. Gregory DFM
Rear Gunner: Pilot Officer A.F. Burcher DFM, RAAF

AJ-P

Pilot: Flight Lieutenant H.B. Martin DFC
Flight Engineer: Pilot Officer I. Whittaker
Navigator: Flight Lieutenant J.F. Leggo DFC, RAAF
Wireless Operator: Flying Officer L. Chambers, RNZAF
Bomb Aimer: Flight Lieutenant R.C. Hay DFC, RAAF
Front Gunner: Pilot Officer B.T. Foxlee DFM, RAAF
Rear Gunner: Flight Sergeant T.D. Simpson, RAAF

AJ-A

Pilot: Squadron Leader H.M. Young DFC (and bar)
Flight Engineer: Sergeant D.T. Horsfall

Navigator: Flight Sergeant C.W. Roberts
Wireless Operator: Sergeant L.W. Nichols
Bomb Aimer: Flying Officer V.S. MacCausland, RCAF
Front Gunner: Sergeant G.A. Yeo
Rear Gunner: Sergeant W. Ibbotson

AJ-J
Pilot: Flight Lieutenant D.J.H. Maltby DFC
Flight Engineer: Sergeant W. Hatton
Navigator: Sergeant V. Nicholson
Wireless Operator: Sergeant A.J.B. Stone
Bomb Aimer: Pilot Officer J. Fort
Front Gunner: Sergeant V. Hill
Rear Gunner: Sergeant H.T. Simmonds

AJ-L
Pilot: Flight Lieutenant D.J. Shannon DFC, RAAF
Flight Engineer: Sergeant R.J. Henderson
Navigator: Flying Officer D.R. Walker DFC, RCAF
Wireless Operator: Flying Officer B. Goodale DFC
Bomb Aimer: Flight Sergeant L.J. Sumpter
Front Gunner: Sergeant B. Jagger
Rear Gunner: Flying Officer J. Buckley

AJ-Z
Pilot: Squadron Leader H.E. Maudslay DFC
Flight Engineer: Sergeant J. Marriott DFM
Navigator: Flying Officer R.A. Urquhart DFC, RCAF
Wireless Operator: Warrant Officer A.P. Cottam, RCAF
Bomb Aimer: Pilot Officer M.J.D. Fuller
Front Gunner: Flying Officer W.J. Tytherleigh DFC
Rear Gunner: Sergeant N.R. Burrows

AJ-B
Pilot: Flight Lieutenant W. Astell DFC
Flight Engineer: Sergeant J. Kinnear
Navigator: Pilot Officer F.A. Wile, RCAF
Wireless Operator: Warrant Officer A.A. Garshowitz, RCAF
Bomb Aimer: Flying Officer D. Hopkinson
Front Gunner: Flight Sergeant F.A. Garbas, RCAF
Rear Gunner: Sergeant R. Bolitho

AJ-N
Pilot: Pilot Officer L.G. Knight, RAAF
Flight Engineer: Sergeant R.E. Grayston
Navigator: Flying Officer H.S. Hobday
Wireless Operator: Flight Sergeant R.G.T. Kellow, RAAF
Bomb Aimer: Flying Officer E.C. Johnson
Front Gunner: Sergeant F.E. Sutherland, RCAF
Rear Gunner: Sergeant H.E. O'Brien, RCAF

Second Wave
AJ-E
Pilot: Flight Lieutenant R.N.G. Barlow DFC, RAAF
Flight Engineer: Pilot Officer S.L. Whillis
Navigator: Flying Officer P.S. Burgess
Wireless Operator: Flying Officer C.R. Williams DFC, RAAF
Bomb Aimer: Pilot Officer A. Gillespie, DFM
Front Gunner: Flying Officer H.S. Glinz, RCAF
Rear Gunner: Sergeant J.R.G. Liddell

AJ-W
Pilot: Flight Lieutenant J.L. Munro, RNZAF
Flight Engineer: Sergeant F.E. Appleby
Navigator: Flying Officer F.G. Rumbles
Wireless Operator: Warrant Officer P.E. Pigeon, RCAF
Bomb Aimer: Sergeant J.H. Clay
Front Gunner: Sergeant W.Howarth
Rear Gunner: Flight Sergeant H.A. Weeks, RCAF

AJ-K
Pilot: Pilot Officer V.W. Byers, RCAF
Flight Engineer: Sergeant A.J. Taylor
Navigator: Flying Officer J.H. Warner
Wireless Operator: Sergeant J. Wilkinson
Bomb Aimer: Pilot Officer A.N. Whittaker
Front Gunner: Sergeant C. McA. Jarvie
Rear Gunner: Flight Sergeant J. McDowell, RCAF

AJ-H
Pilot: Pilot Officer G. Rice
Flight Engineer: Sergeant E.C. Smith
Navigator: Flying Officer R. MacFarlane

Wireless Operator: Warrant Officer C.B. Gowrie, RCAF
Bomb Aimer: Warrant Officer J.W. Thrasher, RCAF
Front Gunner: Sergeant T.W. Maynard
Rear Gunner: Sergeant S. Burns

AJ-T
Pilot: Flight Lieutenant J.C. McCarthy DFC, RCAF
Flight Engineer: Sergeant W.G. Radcliffe
Navigator: Flight Sergeant D.A. MacLean, RCAF
Wireless Operator: Flight Sergeant L. Eaton
Bomb Aimer: Sergeant G.L. Johnson
Front Gunner: Sergeant R. Batson
Rear Gunner: Flying Officer D. Rodger, RCAF

Third Wave
AJ-C
Pilot: Pilot Officer W.H.T. Ottley DFC
Flight Engineer: Sergeant R. Marsden
Navigator: Flying Officer J.K. Barrett DFC
Wireless Operator: Sergeant J. Guterman DFM
Bomb Aimer: Flight Sergeant T.B. Johnston
Front Gunner: Sergeant H.J. Strange
Rear Gunner: Sergeant F. Tees

AJ-S
Pilot: Pilot Officer L.J. Burpee DFM, RCAF
Flight Engineer: Sergeant G. Pegler
Navigator: Sergeant T. Jaye
Wireless Operator: Pilot Officer L.G. Weller
Bomb Aimer: Flight Sergeant J.L. Arthur, RCAF
Front Gunner: Sergeant W.C.A. Long
Rear Gunner: Warrant Officer J.G. Brady, RCAF

AJ-F
Pilot: Flight Sergeant K.W. Brown, RCAF
Flight Engineer: Sergeant H.B. Feneron
Navigator: Sergeant D.P. Heal
Wireless Operator: Sergeant H.J. Hewstone
Bomb Aimer: Sergeant S. Oancia, RCAF
Front Gunner: Sergeant D. Allatson
Rear Gunner: Flight Sergeant G.S. McDonald, RCAF

AJ-O
Pilot: Flight Sergeant W.C. Townsend DFM
Flight Engineer: Sergeant D.J.D. Powell
Navigator: Pilot Officer C.L. Howard, RAAF
Wireless Operator: Flight Sergeant G.A. Chalmers
Bomb Aimer: Sergeant C.E. Franklin DFM
Front Gunner: Sergeant D.E. Webb
Rear Gunner: Sergeant R. Wilkinson

AJ-Y
Pilot: Flight Sergeant C.T. Anderson
Flight Engineer: Sergeant R.C. Paterson
Navigator: Sergeant J.P. Nugent
Wireless Operator: Sergeant W.D. Bickle
Bomb Aimer: Sergeant G.J. Green
Front Gunner: Sergeant E. Ewan
Rear Gunner: Sergeant A.W. Buck
In the cases of aircraft A, Z, B, E, K and S, there were no survivors and the
positions of the two gunners are based on the best available evidence.

The thirty-four 'immediate' awards made to aircrew who participated in the
attack on the Dams

Victoria Cross
Wing Commander G.P. Gibson DSO (and bar), DFC (and bar)

Distinguished Service Order
Flight Lieutenant J.C. McCarthy DFC
Flight Lieutenant D.J.H. Maltby DFC
Flight Lieutenant H.B. Martin DFC
Flight Lieutenant D.J. Shannon DFC
Pilot Officer L.G. Knight

Conspicuous Gallantry Medal
Flight Sergeant K.W. Brown
Flight Sergeant W.C. Townsend DFM

Bar to Distinguished Flying Cross
Flight Lieutenant R.C. Hay DFC
Flight Lieutenant R.E.G. Hutchison DFC

Flight Lieutenant J.F. Leggo DFC
Flying Officer D.R. Walker DFC

Distinguished Flying Cross
Flight Lieutenant R.D. Trevor-Roper DFM
Flying Officer J. Buckley
Flying Officer L. Chambers
Flying Officer H.S. Hobday
Flying Officer E.C. Johnson
Pilot Officer G.A. Deering
Pilot Officer J. Fort
Pilot Officer C.L. Howard
Pilot Officer F.M. Spafford DFM
Pilot Officer H.T. Taerum

Bar to Distinguished Flying Medal
Sergeant C.E. Franklin DFM

Distinguished Flying Medal
Flight Sergeant G.A. Chalmers
Flight Sergeant D.A. MacLean
Flight Sergeant T.D. Simpson
Flight Sergeant L.J. Sumpter
Sergeant D.P. Heal
Sergeant G.L. Johnson
Sergeant V. Nicholson
Sergeant S. Oancia
Sergeant J. Pulford
Sergeant D.E. Webb
Sergeant R. Wilkinson

Appendix 8

Some Memorials

There is a memorial stone at the Derwent dam which was unveiled on 2 October 1986 by David Shannon.

Under the badge of No 617 Squadron it reads:

'This stone was erected by public subscription to the gallant men of 617 Dambuster Sqd RAF who successfully breached the dams of Western Germany in World War II using the bouncing bomb devised by Dr Barnes Wallis.

'Derwent Dam was chosen because of it's (*sic*) close resemblance to the German dams for intensive low level practice and bomb aiming techniques.

'They paid for our freedom.'

Two memorials in the vicinity of the German dams
Durch den feindlichen. Fliegerangriff auf die Moehne-Talsperre am 17 Mai 1943 fielen der Hochwasser-Katastrophe in der Stadt Neheim-Husten zum Opfer:

(Names)
In Ehrfurcht Beugen Wir Uns vor der Grosse ihres Opfers fur Gross-Deutschland.
Ihr Gedenken wird ewig in uns fortleben. Ihren Hinterbliebenen aber wendet sich unsere Teilnahme und Hilfe zu.
Der gauleiter des Gaues Westfalen – Sud
Albert Hoffman, Gaulieter-Stellvertreter

This translates as:
Due to the hostile flight-attack on the Moehne Dam on the 17 May 1943 the following fell victim to the flood-disaster in the town of Neheim-Huesten:

(Names)
In reverence we bow to their ultimate sacrifice to greater Germany. The memory of them will eternally live on in us. But to those left behind we send our condolences and our help.
Albert Hoffmann, vice-Gauleiter

Dem britischen Terrorangriff auf die Moehnetalsperre fielen nach abschliessenden Feststellungen weiter zum Opfer.

(Names)
Sie starben für ihre Heimat und damit, wie die Gefallenen an allen fronten, für Gross-Deutschland. Wir beugen uns vor der Grosse ihre Opfers, das uns verpflichtet, dem Hass und dem Vernichtungswillen der Feinde zu trotzen und in umerschutterlicher Widerstands-kraft zu kampfen und zu arbeiten für den Sieg.
   Bochum 7 Juli 1943
   Der Gauleiter und Reichsverteidigunskommissar
   Albert Hoffman.

This translates as:
   After final consideration, the following also fell victim to the British terror attack on the Moehne-Dam. They died for their country and therefore, like the fallen on all fronts, for Greater Germany. We bow to their ultimate sacrifice, which obliges us, to defy the hatred and will of annihilation of our enemies and in unshakable power of resistance to fight and work for victory. Bochum, 07 Juli 1943.
   Der Gauleiter und Reichsverteidigungskommissar
   Albert Hoffmann
   (A Gauleiter was the head of a Nazi administrative district.)

Appendix 9

Citations for Guy Gibson's Decorations

Distinguished Flying Cross, 9 July 1940

For gallantry and devotion to duty during air operations.

Bar to Distinguished Flying Cross, 16 September 1941

This officer continues to show the utmost courage and devotion to duty. Since joining his present unit, Squadron Leader Gibson has destroyed three and damaged a fourth enemy aircraft. His skill was notably demonstrated when, one night in July of 1941, he intercepted and destroyed a Heinkel 111.

The Distinguished Flying Cross came into being as a result of a Royal Warrant of 3 June 1918, shortly after the establishment of the RAF. It was considered the equivalent of the Navy's Distinguished Service Cross and the Army's Military Cross and was awarded to officers and warrant officers of the RAF who displayed valour, courage or devotion to duty, 'whilst flying in active operations against the enemy'. The equivalent award for other ranks was the Distinguished Flying Medal.

Major changes to the system of awards were made in 1993, instigated by the then Prime Minister, John Major. In those changes, the DFM was abolished and the DFC is now available to all RAF ranks flying against an enemy.

Distinguished Service Order, 20 November 1942

Since being awarded a bar to his DFC this officer has completed many sorties including leading a daylight raid on Danzig and an attack on Gdynia. In the recent attack on Le Creusot, Wing Commander Gibson bombed and machine gunned the transformer station nearby from five hundred feet. On 22 October 1942 he participated in the attack on Genoa and two days later he led his squadron in a daylight sortie against Milan. On both occasions Wing Commander Gibson flew with great distinction. He is a most skilful and courageous leader whose keenness has set a most inspiring example.

Bar to Distinguished Service Order, 2 April 1943

This officer has an outstanding operational record, having completed 172 sorties. He has always displayed the greatest keenness and in the past two months has taken part in six attacks against well defended targets, including Berlin.

In March 1943 he captained an aircraft detailed to attack Stuttgart. On the outward flight engine trouble developed but he flew on to his objective and bombed it from a low level. This is typical of the outstanding determination to make every sortie a success.

By his skilful leadership and contempt for danger he has set an example which has inspired the squadron he commands.

The Distinguished Service Order had been instituted in 1886 and did, as its name suggests involve admission to an order. At its institution and in the Second World War, it was only available to officers in the Royal Navy and Army and, from 1918, in the RAF too. As a gallantry award it ranked immediately below the Victoria Cross. In the earlier years the DSO was sometimes awarded for distinguished service that did not involve coming under enemy fire.

In the changes of 1993 the DSO became reserved for outstanding leadership and service on military operations, ceasing to be an option to recognise gallantry rather than leadership.

In the first years of the Second World War there was no equivalent decoration to the DSO for RAF other ranks. On 10 November 1942 the Conspicuous Gallantry Medal (Air), became available for RAF and Army other ranks who performed gallant deeds of sufficient quality, 'whilst flying in active operations against the enemy.' It was thus possible for two NCO pilots on Operation Chastise to receive the decoration. Previous to November 1942 the CGM had been purely a Royal Navy award.

In 1993 the CGM was abolished and the Conspicuous Gallantry Cross was instituted to recognise gallantry 'at the second level', i.e., acts considered not quite of VC standard, by all ranks of all services.

Victoria Cross, 28 May 1943

This officer served as a night bomber pilot at the beginning of the war and quickly established a reputation as an outstanding operational pilot.

In addition to taking the fullest possible share in all normal operations, he made single-handed attacks during his 'rest' nights on such highly defended objectives as the German battleship *Tirpitz*, then completing in Wilhelmshaven.

When his tour of operational duty was concluded, he asked for a further operational posting and went to a night fighter unit instead of being posted for instructional duties. In the course of his second operational tour, he destroyed at least three operational bombers and contributed much to the raising and development of new night fighter formations.

After a short period in a training unit, he again volunteered for operational duties and returned to night bombers. Both as an operational pilot and as a leader of his squadron, he achieved outstandingly successful results and his personal courage knew no bounds. Berlin, Cologne, Danzig, Gdynia, Genoa, Le Creusot, Milan, Nuremberg and Stuttgart were among the targets he attacked by day and by night.

On the conclusion of his third operational tour, Wing Commander Gibson pressed strongly to be allowed to remain on operations and he was selected to command a squadron then forming for special tasks. Under his inspiring leadership, this squadron has now executed one of the most devastating attacks of the war – the breaching of the Möhne and Eder dams.

The task was fraught with danger and difficulty. Wing Commander Gibson personally made the initial attack on the Möhne dam. Descending to within a few feet of the water and taking the full brunt of the anti-aircraft defences, he launched his projectiles with great accuracy. Afterwards he circled very low for thirty minutes, drawing the enemy fire on himself in order to leave as free a run as possible to the following aircraft which were attacking the dam in turn.

Wing Commander Gibson then led the remainder of his force to the Eder dam where, with complete disregard for his own safety, he repeated his tactics and once more drew on himself the enemy fire so that the attack could be successfully developed.

Wing Commander Gibson has completed over 170 sorties, involving more than 600 hours of operational flying. Throughout his operational career, prolonged exceptionally at his own request, he has shown leadership, determination and valour of the highest order.

On 29 January 1856 at Buckingham Palace, Queen Victoria signed the warrant that brought into being the Victoria Cross. This warrant stated that, 'It is ordained that the Cross shall only be awarded to those Officers or Men who have served Us in the presence of the enemy and shall then have performed some signal act of valour or devotion to their country.'

Though subsequent warrants have changed the conditions for the award of the VC, as has practice and precedent, the VC remains the highest British award for military heroism. There were nineteen awards to airmen during the First World War. During the Second World War it was awarded to thirty-two aircrew. At that time, the VC and a Mention in Despatches were the only posthumous awards allowed under King's Regulations.

Bibliography

Books and other sources consulted during the preparation of this work include:

Arthur, Max. *Dambusters.* Virgin Books, 2008
Balme, Elsie. *Seagull Morning.* Tabb House, 1990
Bowyer, Chaz. *For Valour, the Air VCs.* Grub Street, 1992
Braddon, Russell. *Cheshire VC.* The Companion Book Club edition, undated
Brickhill, Paul. *The Dam Busters.* Pan Books edition, 1954
Brooks, Robin J. *Kent Airfields in the Second World War.* Countryside Books, 1998
Carlson, Mark. *Flying on Film.* Bear Manor Media, 2012
Chorley, W. R. *Bomber Command Losses.* Midland Counties Publications, six volumes from 1992
Colville, John. *The Fringes of Power – Downing Street Diaries 1939–1953.* Hodder and Stoughton, 1985
Cooper, Alan. *Beyond the Dams to the Tirpitz.* William Kimber, 1983
Cornwell, Peter D. *The Battle of France Then and Now.* Battle of Britain International, 2007
Crook, M.J. *The Evolution of the Victoria Cross.* Midas Books, 1975
Davidson, Rev Thomas (edited by). *Chambers Twentieth Century Dictionary.* W. & R. Chambers, 1926
Dimbleby, Jonathan. *Richard Dimbleby.* Hodder and Stoughton, 1975
Divine, A.D. DSM. *Dunkirk.* Faber and Faber, 1945
Euler, Helmuth. *Wasserkreig.* Foto-Studio Euler, 1992
Falconer, Jonathan. *Filming the Dam Busters.* Sutton Publishing, 2005
Falconer, Jonathan. *The Dam Busters Story.* Sutton Publishing, 2007
Fareham, John. *Guy Gibson VC.* Bretwalda Books, 2012
Foster, Charles. *Breaking the Dams.* Pen and Sword Aviation, 2008
Franks, Norman R. *Fighter Command Losses of the Second World War, volume 1 1939–1941.* Midland Publishing, 1997

Gibson, Guy. *Enemy Coast Ahead*. Michael Joseph, 1946 (and subsequent editions)

Hallam, Vic. *Lest We Forget*. Self published, two editions, undated

Harris, Marshal of the Royal Air Force Sir Arthur. *Bomber Offensive*. Pen and Sword Military Classics edition, 2005

Harvey, David. *Monuments to Courage, vol ll*. Kevin and Kay Patience, 1999

Hastings, Max. *Bomber Command*. Michael Joseph, 1979

Holland, James. *Dam Busters*. Bantam Press, 2012

Humphries, Harry. *Living with Heroes*. The Erskine Press, 2008

Hunt, Leslie. *Twelve Squadrons*. Crecy Books, 1992

Jefford, Wing Commander C.G. *RAF Squadrons*. Airlife, 1998

Jenkins, Roy. *Churchill*. Macmillan, 2001

Kellow Bob (edited by Peter Carlyle-Gordge). *Paths to Freedom*. Kellow Corporation, 1992

Lyall, Gavin. *Freedom's Battle. Vol 2, The War in the Air, 1939–1945*. Hutchinson, 1968

Middlebrook, Martin and Everitt, C. *The Bomber Command War Diaries: An Operational Record Book, 1939–1945*, Viking, 1985

Monday, David. *British Aircraft of World War ll*. Chancellor Press, 1994

Morpungo, J.E. *Barnes Wallis*. Longman, 1972

Morris, Richard, with Owen, Robert (edited by). *Breaching the German Dams*. Newsdesk Communications with RAF Museum, 2008

Morris, Richard. *Guy Gibson*. Penguin Group, 1994

Neilland, Robin. *The Bomber War*. John Murray, 2001

Orange, Vincent. *Dowding of Fighter Command*. Grub Street, 2008

Ottaway, Susan. *Guy Gibson, The Glorious Dambuster*. Speedman Press, 2009

Otter, Patrick. *Lincolnshire Airfields of the Second World War*. Countryside Books, 1996

Probert, Air Commodore Henry. *Bomber Harris, His Life and Times*. Greenhill Books, 2003

Probert, Air Commodore Henry. *High Commanders of the Royal Air Force*. HMSO, 1991

Ramsden, John. *The Dam Busters*. I B Tauris, 2003

Ramsey, Winston G. (edited by). *The Blitz Then and Now*. Battle of Britain Prints International, 1988

Ray, John. *The Battle of Britain: New Perspectives*. Arms and Armour Press, 1994

Ray, John. *The Night Blitz, 1940–1941*. Arms and Armour, 1996

Rennison, John. *The Digby Diary*. Aspect Publishing, 2003

Ryan, Cornelius. *A Bridge Too Far.* Coronet, 1975

Self, Geoffrey. *In Town Tonight.* Thames Publishing, 1986

Shortland, Jim. *The Story of the Dams Raid.* Lincolnshire's Lancaster Association, 1993

Smith, Richard C. *Hornchurch Eagles.* Grub Street, 2002

Sweetman, John. *Operation Chastise.* Jane's. 1982

Sweetman, John. *The Dambusters Raid.* Arms and Armour, 1990

Thompson, W.R. *Lancaster to Berlin.* Goodall, 1985

Thorning, Arthur G. *The Dam Buster who Cracked the Dam.* Pen and Sword Aviation, 2008

Van den Driesschen Jan, with Eve Gibson. *We Will Remember Them.* The Erskine Press, 2004

Ward, Chris and Wachtel Andreas. *Dambuster Crash Sites.* Pen and Sword, 2007

Webster, Sir Charles and Frankland, Noble. *The Strategic Air Offensive Against Germany (four volumes).* HMSO, 1961

Wynn, Kenneth G. *Men of the Battle of Britain.* Battle of Britain Memorial Trust, new edition, due to be published

Yates, Harry, DFC. *Luck and a Lancaster.* Airlife, 1999

(no author credited) *Cometh the Hour - Cometh the School.* St Edward's School Society, 2004

Newspapers and periodicals, including the *Daily Express, Daily Mail, Daily Telegraph, The Times, The Guardian, Sunday Express, Kent Messenger, Glasgow Herald, Macclesfield Courier, Sydney Morning Herald, Montreal Daily Star, Los Angeles Times, Royal Air Force Historical Society Journal, Britain at War, War & Society, Journal of Strategic Studies, Flight, Everyone's War.*

Logbooks of Wing Commander G.P. Gibson and Flying Officer J. Buckley

DVD, *Guy Gibson VC & the Porthleven he Loved,* produced by Vic Strike

www.bbc.co.uk

www.cwgc.org

www.oxforddnb.com

Fry, Eric, 'Spafford, Frederick Michael (1918–1943)', Australian Dictionary of Biography, National Centre of Biography, Australian National University, www.adb..anu.edu.au.

www.bombercommandmuseum.ca

www.rafyatesbury.webs.com

www.epsomandewellhistoryexplorer.org.uk

www.victorianweb.org

Index

Anderson, Flight Sergeant, C.T., 82, 83, 85, 86, 87, 104, 109–11, 177
Astell, Flight Lieutenant, W., 85–86, 88, 97, 100, 137, 174
Augsburg, 55, 66
Avro Lancaster, vii, xi, 53–56, 58–60, 62–64, 66, 68–69, 73–74, 81, 82, 84, 88–89, 93–101, 110, 112, 119, 122, 125, 132–33, 136, 142–43, 153, 157, 162–64, 167, 172
Avro Manchester, 53, 55, 57, 74, 85, 153, 157, 162, 166–67, 172

Bader, Group Captain, Sir Douglas Robert Steuart, 5, 131, 157
Bagot-Gray, Pilot Officer, Douglas Leslie Parnell, 11–12
Baily, Pilot Officer, Philip Herbert, 11–12
Baldwin, Air Vice Marshal, J.E.A., 55
Banks, Sergeant, Arthur, 5
Barlow, Flight Lieutenant, R.N.G., 85–86, 90, 95, 101, 175
Battle of Britain, x, xi, 10, 29–32, 36–39, 43, 48, 87, 122, 131, 153, 165, 169, 172
Berlin, 33–35, 70–71, 73, 84, 90,
Bremen, 55, 58, 128
Bridgman, Squadron Leader, Anthony, 14, 34
Bristol Beaufighter, 38, 40–41, 44, 46–47, 48–50, 166
Bristol Blenheim, x, xi, 18, 38–40, 42, 44, 57, 139, 163, 166
Brown, Flight Sergeant, K.W., 86, 103–4, 176, 177
Burpee, Pilot Officer, L.J., 86, 103, 176
Byers, Pilot Officer, V.W., 86, 101–2, 175

Canada, 5, 70, 116–18, 119, 156
Chamberlain, Arthur Neville, British Prime Minister, 17–18, 25, 122
Cheshire, Group Captain, Geoffrey Leonard, VC, 74, 120, 164

Chesil Beach, 79
Churcher, Squadron Leader, Ronald, 128–29
Churchill, Winston, British Prime Minister, 25, 30–31, 37, 67, 79, 91, 114–16, 121–22, 124
Clarke, Arthur C, 43
Coastal Command, x, 21, 32, 56, 77, 125, 152, 166, 170
Cochrane, Air Chief Marshal, the Hon Ralph, 72, 74–75, 88, 91, 94, 98, 126, 137
Colbeck-Welch, Wing Commander, Edward, 50–51
Cologne, 55, 58–59, 64, 72, 168, 183
Cornwall, 1, 4–5, 29
Coryton, Air Chief Marshal, William Alec, 59–61, 66, 72
Cunningham, Group Captain, John, 49

Danzig, 59, 74, 181, 183
de Havilland Mosquito, 69, 81, 125–29, 132–34, 149, 163, 168, 172
de Havilland Tiger Moth, 165–66
Denmark, 23–24, 27
Desert Island Discs, 123, 127
Dimbleby, Richard, 70–71
Dortmund-Ems Canal, 29, 32, 164
Douglas, Marshal of the Royal Air Force, William Sholto, 37–38, 77
Dowding, Air Chief Marshal, Hugh Caswall Tremenheere, 21, 37–38
Dusseldorf, 55, 59, 61

Eder Dam, 79, 94, 99–104, 142–46, 155, 18
Emmett, Group Captain, E.C., 18
Essen, 55, 58, 59, 62, 69–70, 73, 150, 180
Evill, Air Chief Marshal, Douglas, 91

Fleet Air Arm, x, 32, 61
Folkestone, 4–5
Fothergill, Wing Commander, Charles, 153

Gdynia, 61, 183
Genoa, 66–67, 181, 183
Germany, vii, x, 9, 17–18, 22, 31, 34, 55–57,
    59, 63, 66–67, 70, 76–78, 88, 92, 93, 99,
    101, 122, 128, 130, 142–43, 154, 163, 165,
    179–80
Gneisenau, 61–62

Hamburg, 26, 56
Handley Page Halifax, xii, 62, 65, 119,
Handley Page Hampden, x, 14–15, 17, 19,
    21, 23–24, 28–29, 33–34, 36, 53, 62, 78,
    162, 163, 166, 172
Hannah, Sergeant, John, VC, 33
Harris, Marshal of the Royal Air Force,
    Arthur Travers, vii, xi, 20, 22–23, 37–38,
    51, 53–57, 60, 62, 66–67, 71–72, 74, 81,
    89, 91, 98–99, 100, 102, 104–5, 114, 116,
    118–19, 124–26, 136–37, 152–54, 157
Hawker Audax, 11–12, 166
Hawker Hind, 11, 13, 14, 163, 166
Harvey, Air Commodore, Sir A.V, MP, 124
Highball Bomb, 81, 91
Hopgood, Flight Lieutenant, J.V., 58, 66,
    85, 87–88, 93–98, 105, 108–9, 137, 173
Hovey, Sergeant, W.E., 4
Hutchison, Flight Lieutenant, R.E.G., 59, 83

India, 2–3, 5, 60, 85, 147, 153

James, Sergeant, Richard, 43–44, 46–47,
    49–51
Kiel, Germany, x, 19, 28, 55, 88,
Knight, Flight Lieutenant, L.G., 96, 100,
    137, 150, 175, 177

Le Creusot, 65, 181
Le Havre, 126
Learoyd, Squadron Leader, R.A.B., VC,
    29–30
Leigh-Mallory, Air Chief Marshal, Sir
    Trafford, 47
Lincolnshire, vii, 7, 11, 15, 17, 38, 41–42,
    45, 48, 54, 105, 124, 139, 140, 167, 169,
    172
Lister Dam, 102–3
Lock, Flight Lieutenant, Eric Stanley, 131
Lockheed Lightning, 126
Lübeck, 55
Ludlow-Hewitt, Air Chief Marshal, Sir
    Edgar Rainey, 22, 36

Luftwaffe, 20, 25, 27, 30, 33, 36–37, 40–42,
    46, 110, 129

Mallender, Squadron Leader, Peter,
    133–34
Maltby, Flight Lieutenant, D.J.H., 93,
    95–96, 98–99, 112–13, 137, 174, 177
Manser, Flying Officer, Leslie, VC, 57
Martin, Flight Lieutenant, H.B., 82, 83,
    85, 93, 95–96, 98–99, 120, 125, 137, 151,
    173, 177
Maudslay, Squadron Leader, H.E., 85, 93,
    99–100, 137, 174
McCarthy, Flight Lieutenant, J.C., 86, 95,
    102–3, 150, 176, 177
McCormack, Sergeant, Bernard, 23, 27,
    132–33
Milan, 66, 72, 74, 181, 183
Möhne Dam, 77–79, 88, 93–94, 96–98,
    101–6, 142–45, 150, 155, 179, 183
Munro, Flight Lieutenant, J.L., 85, 101–2,
    109, 175

Nant-y-Gro Dam, 79
Newall, Marshal of the Royal Air Force,
    Cyril Louis Norton, 18
Nigger, (Gibson's dog), 51, 82, 93, 98, 105,
    155
Nuremberg, 72, 183

Operation Chastise, x, 78, 83, 89–92, 101,
    106, 108–9, 113–14, 116, 119, 130, 140,
    150, 154, 182
Operation Market Garden, 126, 128
Operation Overlord, 124
Operation Torch, 67
Ottley, Pilot Officer, W.H.T., 85, 102–3, 106,
    176
Oxford, 5–6, 9, 16, 79, 85–86, 159, 160

Paris, 54, 126
Peirse, Air Chief Marshal, Richard Edmund
    Charles, 52
Pitcairn-Hill, Squadron Leader, James
    Anderson, 28–29
Poland, 17–18, 119
Portal, Marshal of the Royal Air Force,
    Charles Frederick Algernon, 22, 55, 60,
    78, 81, 100, 115–16
Probert, Air Commodore, Henry, 60, 154

Reculver, 91
Rheydt, 129
Rice, Pilot Officer, G., 85, 102, 109, 175
Roosevelt, Franklin D, US President, 17, 116
Rowe, Group Captain, 54
Royal Air Force (RAF)
No 1 Group, 125
No 3 Group, 125
No 4 Group, 69
No 5 Group, 22, 37, 51, 53, 59, 66, 68, 72, 75, 84, 86, 88, 98, 113, 120, 126, 128, 152, 154, 162
No 6 Group (Canadian), 118
No 8 Group, 125
Bases
Abingdon, 26, 29, 163
Acklington, 21
Coningsby, 54, 57–59, 61–63, 69, 120, 124–25, 128, 140, 162–64, 172
Cottesmore, 36
Cranfield, 51, 53
Cranwell, 9, 38, 158
Duxford, 163
East Kirkby, 124–25
Fiskerton, 110
Grantham, 98, 100, 151, 163
High Wycombe, 53, 56, 66, 74
Lossiemouth, 21, 23–24, 165, 170–71
Manby, 42, 69
Manston, 24, 27, 61
Marston Moor, 120
Middle Wallop, 67
Mildenhall, 26
Montrose, 162
Netheravon, 10, 12–13, 169
Ringway, 20, 26
Scampton, 15–21, 23–26, 29, 33, 82, 87–89, 93, 99–102, 104–5, 120, 135–36, 155, 164, 170
Sutton Bridge, 11, 12, 169
Syerston, 64, 66–68, 73–74, 163
Tangmere, 50, 163
Turnhouse, 13, 14, 28, 162, 170
Upper Heyford, 36, 42
Uxbridge, 10
Wattisham, 18
Wellingore, 38–39, 43, 48, 140
West Malling, 38, 48–50, 52, 140, 163, 171–72

Woodhall Spa, 96, 128, 133, 134, 164, 172
Wyton, 18, 162
Yatesbury, 10, 168
14 Operational Training Unit, 36
16 Operational Training Unit, 36
51 Operational Training Unit, 51
Squadrons
Pathfinders Force, 62, 72, 123, 162
29 Squadron, xi, 38, 42–43, 48–51, 139, 160, 162–63
42 Squadron, 12
44 Squadron, 21, 54–55, 167
49 Squadron, 19, 21, 28–29, 66, 110
50 Squadron, 57, 64, 83
57 Squadron, 82, 83, 87, 88
61 Squadron, 66, 68, 132, 172
77 Squadron, 34
83 Squadron, x, 13, 14–15, 18–21, 23–25, 27–29, 34, 68, 83, 152, 162–63, 183
207 Squadron, 153, 167
219 Squadron, 50
256 Squadron, 49
264 Squadron, 49
106 Squadron, 55, 57–59, 62, 64, 67–68, 70, 72, 74–75, 83, 98, 150, 153, 163–64, 172
107 Squadron, 18
109 Squadron, 69
111 Squadron, 28
112 Squadron, 5
311 Squadron, 34
602 Squadron, 21
604 Squadron, 49
607 Squadron, 4
617 Squadron, xii, xiii, 58, 75, 77, 82, 83–84, 86–89, 94, 100, 103–6, 108–9, 112–13, 120, 123, 125–26, 135, 137, 150, 152–55, 164–65, 170–72, 179
630 Squadron, 125
Ruhr, Germany, ix, x, xii, 18, 60, 73, 88, 95, 98, 126, 142–44, 146

Saundby, Air Vice Marshal, Robert Henry Magnus Spencer, 56
Scharnhorst, x, 28, 61, 78
Schweinfurt, 55, 164
Shannon, Flight Lieutenant, D.J., 58–59, 61, 85, 94, 95

Sisson, Wing Commander, J.C., 27–28
Slee, Wing Commander, L.C., 66
Slessor, Air Vice Marshal, J.C., 52, 152–53
Snaith, Wing Commander, 18, 27–28
Sorpe Dam, 77, 88, 94, 100–4, 109, 142–45
Steenbergen, 129
Stuttgart, 69, 73, 182–83
Summers, Captain, Joseph, 8, 9, 80, 87, 137, 160
Sweden, 27

Threapleton, Squadron Leader, Sam, 21–22
Tiger Moth, 5, 10, 165–66
Tirpitz, 28, 88, 164–65, 170, 183
Townsend, Flight Sergeant, W.C., 85, 104, 177
Trenchard, Marshal of the Royal Air Force, Hugh Montague, 9, 76
Turin, 66–67, 68

Upkeep Bomb, 81, 87–88, 91, 97–101, 104, 109–11
Uppingham, 93
United States of America, 51, 66, 86, 100, 116–17, 119, 122, 125, 138

Victoria Cross, ix, 29, 33, 55, 57, 61, 74, 97, 105, 108, 116, 117, 121, 126, 130, 149, 163, 167, 182–83, 184

Walker, Air Chief Marshal, George Augustus, 64, 68–69, 140
Wallis, Sir Barnes Neville, 77, 78–81, 87–88, 91, 93–94, 98–99, 101, 117, 136, 137, 160–61, 179
Warburton, Wing Commander, Adrian, 5
Warwick, Squadron Leader, James, 128–29, 132–34
Watson, Pilot Officer, 'Watty', 23, 34, 40, 42
Weir, Sergeant, R, 4
Weser Dam, 95
Whitworth, Group Captain, John N.H., 93, 94, 102, 136, 138
Widdows, Wing Commander, Stanley Charles, 38–40, 43, 45–47, 48–50, 139
Wilhelmshaven, 17–18, 58–59, 183
Williams, Flying Officer, Charles, 90, 175
Withers, Pilot Officer, Jack, 23–24, 26

Young, Squadron Leader, H.M., 85, 86–88, 90, 93, 95–96, 98–100, 137, 138, 173

Tracing Your
Family History?

Read
YourFamily HISTORY
ESSENTIAL ADVICE FROM THE EXPERTS

FREE COPY

Your Family History is the only magazine that is put together by exper[t] genealogists. Our editorial team, led by Dr Nick Barratt, is passionate about family history, and our networks of specialists are here to give essential advice, helping readers to find their ancestors and solve thos[e] difficult questions.

In each issue we feature a **Beginner's Guide** covering the basics for those just getting started, a **How To** … section to help you to dig deeper into your family tree and the opportunity to **Ask The Experts** about your tricky research problems. We also include a **Spotlight** on [a] different county each month and a **What's On** guide to the best fam[ily] history courses and events, plus much more.

Receive a free copy of *Your Family History* magazine and gain essential advice and all the latest news. To request a free copy of a recent back issue, simply e-mail your name and address to marketing@your-familyhistory.com or call 01226 734302*.

Your Family History is in all good newsagents and also available on subscription for six or twelve issues. Fo[r] more details on how to take out a subscription, call 01778 392013 or visit **www.your-familyhistory.co.uk**.

Alternatively read issue 31 online completely free using this QR code

*Free copy is restricted to one per household and available while stocks last.

www.your-familyhistory.com